THE SCHOOL

IN THE

LEGAL STRUCTURE

SECOND EDITION

BY

EDWARD C. BOLMEIER

Emeritus Professor of Education
Duke University

AMERICAN SCHOOL LAW SERIES

CINCINNATI
THE W. H. ANDERSON COMPANY

FOREWORD

School law is not static. Constitutional, statutory, and administrative provisions governing the schools are constantly being added, amended or repealed. Moreover, judicial opinions regarding them change in accordance with changing social and political attitudes and conditions. Therefore, a revision of the first edition (1968) of "School in the Legal Structure" seems to be in order.

In this revision, some attention is given to recent developments in the legislative and executive branches of government concerning the schools. The main emphasis, however, is placed upon the most recent court decisions pertaining to issues treated in the book. A total of 105 new cases, 49 of which were adjudicated in federal courts, are cited.

A large proportion of recent cases referred to in this edition stem from social turbulence in which dissident students and teachers challenge the constitutionality of school board regulations designed to govern them. Consequently an avalanche of court cases has descended upon the federal courts dealing with "symbolic expressions" of rebellion against "the establishment," which is a right guaranteed to students and others by virtue of the Free Speech Clause of the First Amendment.

Impetus was given to federal court cases, involving the rights of students, following *Gault*, when the United States Supreme Court indicated applicability of the Fourteenth Amendment and Bill of Rights to minors, as well as adults. Then, the ruling in *Tinker* set the stage for an acceleration of litigation involving "symbolic expression" of rebellion and "due process rights."

Selected recent court cases, also cited in this edition, refer to curriculum issues—particularly where state-church entanglements are involved. Despite the Supreme Court rulings concerning *religious activities* in the public schools, the practice still persists—frequently with subsequent litigation.

iii

Sex education is a relatively new area of the curriculum for litigation. Several applicable cases have been reported in courts of record in the early 1970's, and more may be anticipated. Closely associated with the issues of sex education is that regarding "taboo" or alleged obscene expressions in teaching classes.

Some reviewers of *School in the Legal Structure* state that a valuable feature is the listing and annotations of "resource publications." The second edition brings this feature of the book up-to-date by adding annotations of fifty recent books pertaining to school law. Moreover, reference is made to other types of publications—particularly to the growing number of those now being sponsored by the National Organization on Legal Problems of Education (NOLPE).

EDWARD C. BOLMEIER
Duke University

AMERICAN SCHOOL LAW SERIES

ADVISORY EDITORS

ROBERT T. BAKER, LL.B.

of the Columbus Bar

LEGAL COUNSEL FOR THE OHIO SCHOOL BOARDS ASSOCIATION
and
BUCKEYE ASSOCIATION OF SCHOOL ADMINISTRATORS

EDWARD C. BOLMEIER

EMERITUS PROFESSOR OF EDUCATION, DUKE UNIVERSITY

WALTER L. HETZEL, LL.B.

SUPERINTENDENT OF PUBLIC SCHOOLS

Ames, Iowa

v

CONTENTS

Part II

THE SCHOOL IN THE STATE SPHERE

Chapter 5:   STATE CONSTITUTIONAL PROVISIONS FOR SCHOOLS

Chapter 6:   STATE LEGISLATURES AND THE SCHOOLS

Chapter 7:   STATE JUDICIARIES AND THE SCHOOLS

Chapter 8:   STATE BOARDS OF EDUCATION

Chapter 9:   CHIEF STATE SCHOOL OFFICERS

Part III

THE SCHOOL IN THE LOCAL SPHERE

Chapter 10: THE SCHOOL DISTRICT

Chapter 11: SCHOOL DISTRICT TORT LIABILITY

Chapter 12: THE SCHOOL BOARD

Chapter 13: DISCRETIONARY AUTHORITY OF SCHOOL BOARDS OVER SCHOOL PROPERTY

Chapter 17: DISCRETIONARY AUTHORITY OF SCHOOL BOARDS OVER THE CURRICULUM

Part I

THE SCHOOL IN THE FEDERAL SPHERE

Chapter 1

FEDERAL CONSTITUTION AND THE SCHOOL

Until recently the general public has been unaware of the extensive role the federal government may and does assume in public education. The trite expression, "education is a function of the state," was so generally accepted that many did not realize the potential authority of the federal government in promoting and controlling education.

Actually, from the very beginning of our educational development the federal government has assisted the local and state school systems by providing for educational opportunities. At first the assistance was provided conservatively and without noticeable control. The degree of federal participation increased slowly and gradually until about the middle of the present century, at which time the tempo accelerated markedly. By 1965 the growing federalization of education had become so pronounced as to cause public attention and concern throughout the nation.

In reference to the increasing role which the federal government is assuming in education, a publication of the American Association of School Administrators pinpoints reasons for the acceleration of the national trend.

During the past decade federal programs affecting public schools have increased in number and scope. At no other period in our history, except perhaps the decade 1860-1870, when the land grant colleges and the United States Office of Education were established, has education occupied such a prominent place on the agenda of the United States

1

Congress. This trend reflects a changed national posture toward the importance of education at the national level.

(1) When the nation fights poverty and unemployment, the public schools are one of its principal weapons.

(2) When the nation promotes economic growth, its investment in education brings unique dividends.

(3) When the nation provides for the common defense, it calls upon the schools to play a crucial role.

(4) When the nation builds unity out of diversity by delicately blending the cultures of people from many lands, it looks first and foremost to its schools.

(5) When the nation refers its complex problems to the people for final decision, it needs more than ever an informed electorate.[1]

In virtually all congressional acts supporting public education, assuring statements are made that the control will remain with the state and local school systems. Realistically, however, local autonomy over all aspects of educational programs financed by the federal government will never result. Complete divorcement of federal support and control is neither feasible nor desirable. Consequently the power of decision over public education is shifting rapidly from the local to the federal level.

A survey of a typical school system will reveal the effects of the federal government's involvements, not only in supporting education, but also in controlling it—at least indirectly. In fact all three branches of the federal government are making their imprints on the shaping of educational policy and decisions to which the local school system must conform.

The influence of the *legislative branch* of the federal government is evidenced by the special services and programs which are being conducted by local school systems but financed by federal funds in accordance with various acts of Congress. It is also becoming increasingly apparent that the *executive branch* of the federal government is exercising

---

[1] *The Federal Government and Public Schools.* American Association of School Administrators, Washington, D. C.: 1965, p. 3.

more authority over educational matters, especially through the United States Office of Education by the establishment and implementation of the much debated "guidelines." Influence of the *judicial branch* of the federal government may be noted by integration of the races in school groups which had been segregated prior to the United States Supreme Court decision of 1954; and also by the discontinuance of certain religious exercises conducted in the public schools before the prayer and Bible-reading decisions of the 1960's.

In view of the fact that the trend for federal participation in education is increasing steadily and rapidly it is important to know why this is legally permissible. A first step in gaining an understanding of the federal government's legal relationship to the public schools would be to examine our basic law—namely the United States Constitution.

1.1 Absence of specific provisions pertaining to education

The Constitution of the United States is conspicuous by its omission of any direct provisions or specific references concerning education. Moreover, the Tenth Amendment to the federal Constitution, ratified in 1791, stipulates that "the powers not delegated to the United States by the Constitution, nor prohibited by it to the States, are reserved to the States respectively, or to the people." It is no wonder then why it is frequently assumed that the federal government possesses no constitutional authority to promote and to control education in the states, and that such authority resides exclusively with the states and the people thereof.

Writers on the history of education in America have expressed various opinions as to why the federal Constitution was silent on the matters of education. Some contend that it was such a potentially-explosive issue that it was omitted from the Constitution because its inclusion might have jeopardized the acceptance of the entire document. Others have conjectured that, since so many of those who helped draft the Constitution represented the old aristocracy, education was to be considered a private rather than a public matter. Still others have suggested that even the theory of education had not been thought out and formulated adequately enough at the time the Constitution was framed to warrant provisions dealing with education.

Cubberley stated:

It is not surprising, however, when we consider the time, the men, and the existing conditions, that the founders of our Republic did not deem the subject of public education important enough to warrant consideration in the Constitution or inclusion in the document. . . . Were the Constitution to be reframed today there is little doubt but that education would occupy a prominent place in it.[2]

Shortly after our Republic came into being there were those who manifested concern about the omission of education in the Constitution. The fact that there were no direct provisions nor specific references in the Constitution concerning education, caused at least two presidents, Jefferson in 1806 and Madison in 1817, to recommend a constitutional amendment which would specifically grant power over education to the federal government.

1.2   Implied provisions applicable to education

More recently the tendency has been not to attempt amending the Constitution, but rather to read into it certain implied powers of the federal government over education. Students of school law are constantly seeking constitutional implications which empower the federal government to deal in educational matters.

One need not read beyond the Preamble (We, the people of the United States, in order to form a more perfect union, establish justice, insure domestic tranquillity, provide for the common defense, promote the general welfare, and secure the blessings of liberty to ourselves and our posterity, do ordain and establish this constitution for the United States of America) to get the hint that the framers of the Constitution intended that the federal government would have the

---

[2] Ellwood P. Cubberley, *Public Education in the United States*. Chicago: Houghton Mifflin Co., 1934, pp. 84-85.

power necessary to provide for the "general welfare" by educational measures or any other means.

It should be pointed out, however, that strictly speaking the Preamble is not part of the Constitution, but merely "walks before" it. By itself alone it can afford no basis for a claim of governmental power.[3] Nevertheless, as Corwin explains, it serves two important ends: "first, it indicates the source from which the Constitution comes, from which it derives its claim to obedience, namely, the people of the United States; secondly, it states the great objects which the Constitution and the Government established by it are expected to promote . . . the general welfare."[4]

The actual document does contain a number of provisions which may be, and have been, interpreted as authorizing the federal government to participate in promoting and controlling education. For example, it is stated in Article IV, Section 3:2 that "The Congress shall have power to dispose of and make all needful rules and regulations respecting the territory or other property belonging to the United States." The fact that the courts have already interpreted "money" to be "property" suggests the great potential the federal government possesses in collecting, expending, and regulating funds for educational purposes.

A provision of the original document which is frequently referred to as "the welfare clause" authorizing the federal government to participate in educational affairs is found in Article I, Section 8: "The Congress shall have power to lay and collect taxes, duties, imposts and excises, to pay the debts and provide for the common defense and general welfare of the United States. . . ."

Numerous other references to education may be found in the Constitution, which empower the federal government to participate in the promotion of education. The National Advisory Committee on Education listed fourteen different excerpts from the Constitution which have in one way or

---

[3] *Jacobson v. Massachusetts*, 197 US 11, 25 SCt 358, 49 LEd 643 (1905).

[4] Edward S. Corwin, *The Constitution and What it Means Today*. New York: Antheneum, 1963, p. 1.

another affected educational development in the United States.[5]

1.3 Power to tax for education

Apparently there has been no court case involving the power of Congress to tax and spend in support of education. Nevertheless there have been cases where the courts have ruled upon the constitutional authority of Congress to expend money for the "general welfare" in areas other than education but which would likely be equally applicable. For example, in *Helvering* v. *Davis*,[6] the court upheld the Social Security Act and thereby validated the expenditure of federal funds as an exercise of authority under the general welfare clause.

A greater future application of the legal principle that the federal government may tax and expend funds for the general welfare is suggested in the words of the court: "Nor is the concept of general welfare static. Needs that were narrow and parochial a century ago may be interwoven in our day with the well-being of the nation. What is critical or urgent changes with the times."[7] The tremendous increase of federal expenditure for educational purposes is ample evidence that times are changing and that the federal government is exercising its prerogative accordingly.

It is generally agreed that tax limits within which the federal government may tax and spend for the general welfare are extremely broad. In all probability they are broad enough to win judicial sanction of reasonable appropriations for the support of education.

There is more concern and difference of opinion as to how far the federal government may exercise control over the matter for which grants and appropriations are made. It has been assumed in some quarters that the Constitution permits the federal government to make grants and expend funds for educational purposes but that the authority for

---

[5] *Federal Relations to Education*, Part II: Basic Facts, Report of the National Advisory Committee on Education, Washington, D. C.: National Advisory Committee on Education, 1931, pp. 4 to 9.

[6] (Mass.) 301 US 619, 81 LEd 1307, 57 SCt 904 (1937).

[7] *Ibid.*

control of all operations is vested only in the states. A contrary view is expressed in a decision of the Supreme Court of the United States where the court sustained the power of the federal government to enforce restrictions and stipulations in land grants to states. The court said in part "The United States, being the grantor of lands, could impose conditions upon their use, and have the right to exact the performance of the conditions."[8]

It is not likely, however, that Congress could use its taxing and spending power for the *primary* purpose of regulating educational policies of the states. *United States* v. *Butler* is a case in point, even though it does not deal with a school matter. Here the Court held the Agricultural Act unconstitutional because it was obviously a "plan to regulate and control agricultural production, a matter beyond the power of the federal government."[9] The court emphasized that the federal government could not use its taxing power as a means to "enforce a regulation of matters of state concern with respect to which Congress has no authority to interfere."[10] In view of the fact that education is also considered a matter of state concern, it may reasonably be assumed that a congressional act primarily designated to regulate the educational policies of the states would not win judicial sanction.

This does not mean that the Congress would be denied the authority to impose any regulations over expenditures in behalf of the general welfare. The regulation should be the means rather than the end. Edwards asserts that "While Congress cannot use its taxing and spending power to purchase control of some matters reserved to the states, it may use this power to induce the states to cooperate with the national government in meeting some social needs nationwide in scope."[11] He adds: "Certainly education is a matter of national concern. It would seem, therefore, that the

---

[8] *Ervien, Commissioner of Public Lands of the State of New Mexico v. United States*, 251 US 41, 64 LEd 128, 40 SCt 75 (1919).

[9] 297 US 1, 80 LEd 477, 56 SCt 312 (1936).

[10] *Ibid.*

[11] Newton Edwards, "Federal Authority over Education," *The Yearbook of School Law* (ed. Lee O. Garber), 1955, p. 83.

national government would not be invading the reserved powers of the states by employing its taxing and spending power to collaborate with the states in the promotion of education."[12]

1.4   Human-rights provisions pertaining to education

In recent years there has been more concern manifested over "human rights" provisions of the Constitution than over those pertaining to the general welfare.

When one thinks of constitutional provisions regarding human rights his first impulse may be to think only of the Bill of Rights—the ten amendments adopted in 1791. One may not realize that human rights were considered in framing the original Constitution. It has been pointed out that "the original Constitution contained a considerable number of safeguards for human rights and was consequently equivalent to a bill of rights even though it did not carry the name."[13]

Of course human rights are spelled out more specifically in the amendments. This has been evidenced in the recent court cases. The First Amendment and the Fourteenth Amendment have especially been involved in cases dealing with racial discrimination and religion in the schools. Less frequently the Fifth Amendment, dealing with self-incrimination, has been referred to in cases involving alleged subversive affiliations.

Amendments I to VIII in the Bill of Rights restrained only the federal government in dealing with human rights. This left the states almost completely free to infringe the most basic human rights in any way their governments might wish. Not until the Fourteenth Amendment was adopted in 1868 did it become possible for the federal courts and Congress to "put the brakes" on state action governing human life.

---

[12] *Ibid.*

[13] Zechariah Chafee, Jr., *Documents of Fundamental Human Rights.* New York: Antheneum, 1963, Vol. 1, p. 4.

The court cases concerning religious instruction in the public schools aptly illustrate the necessary concomitance of the Fourteenth Amendment to restrain the states in matters of human rights.

The First Amendment (1791) stipulates that "Congress shall make no law respecting an establishment of religion, or prohibiting the free exercise thereof. . . ." It should be noted here that the First Amendment applied only to Congress. It did not prohibit state legislatures from enacting laws "respecting an establishment of religion or prohibiting the free exercise thereof."

With the adoption of the Fourteenth Amendment (1868) "states rights" were dealt a severe blow. Because of its significant application to school law cases, Section 1 of the Fourteenth Amendment is cited in its entirety:

All persons born or naturalized in the United States, and subject to the jurisdiction thereof, are citizens of the United States and of the State wherein they reside. No State shall make or enforce any law which shall abridge the privileges or immunities of citizens of the United States; nor shall any State deprive any person of life, liberty or property, without due process of law; nor deny to any person within its jurisdiction the equal protection of the laws.

In commenting on Section 1 of the Fourteenth Amendment, Corwin states that "The opening clause of this section makes national citizenship primary and state citizenship derivative therefrom."[14]

As the Fourteenth Amendment has been interpreted neither a state nor the federal government has the authority to enact laws "respecting an establishment of religion or prohibiting the free exercise thereof."

In ruling on the case of *Cantwell* v. *Connecticut*, Justice Roberts emphasized this point:

The fundamental concept of liberty embodied in the Fourteenth Amendment embraces the liberties guaranteed

---

[14] Corwin, *op. cit.*, p. 248.

by the First Amendment. . . . The First Amendment
declares that Congress shall make no law respecting the
establishment of a religion or prohibiting the free exercise thereof. The Fourteenth Amendment has rendered
the states as incompetent as Congress to enact such laws.[15]

1.5   Provisions establishing branches of government

In addition to the aforementioned provisions of the federal
Constitution having educational implications, the Constitution also provides for the establishment and functions of the
three main branches of the federal government. Article I
provides for the legislative branch (Congress); Article II
refers to the executive branch; and Article III deals with
the judicial branch. As will be noted in the following sections of this chapter, each of these three branches assumes
authority and performs functions which have significant
bearing on the school.

The idea for three separate branches of the federal government was for a "separation of powers." In a voluminous
publication of the federal government dealing with the
Constitution of the United States it is stated:

The second great structural principle of American Constitutional Law is supplied by the doctrine of the Separation of Powers. The notion of three distinct functions of
government, approximating what we today term the legislative, the executive and the judicial is set forth in
Aristotle's Politics, but. . . . It was Montesquieu's fundamental contention that "men entrusted with power tend
to abuse it." Hence it was desirable to divide the powers
of government, first, in order to keep to a minimum the
powers lodged in any single organ of government; secondly,
in order to be able to oppose organ to organ.[16]

Consequently no one branch of the federal government
has exclusive control over a school matter. The legislative
branch (Congress) may enact a law authorizing the expendi-

---

[15] 310 US 296, 84 LEd 1213, 60 SCt 900 (1940).
[16] *The Constitution of the United States: Analysis and Interpretation.*
U. S. Government Printing Office, Washington: 1964, p. 9.

ture of federal funds for school purposes; the executive branch (Department of Health, Education and Welfare) may impose regulations by which the funds are to be allocated; and the judicial branch (federal courts) may interpret the constitutionality of the act itself, and the manner of its executive implementation.

Chapter 2

LEGISLATIVE BRANCH (CONGRESS) AND THE SCHOOL

Since implied provisions of the Constitution authorize the federal government to expend funds in support of public education, numerous acts have been passed by the Congress to provide support in various situations.

Although many of the federal acts in support of education have been for the higher institutions, those referred to here will be those applying only to the elementary and secondary levels.

A precise classification of the many federal acts in support of public education is difficult, because many of them have similar and overlapping purposes. Moreover, some of the acts have been enacted merely to augment or alter in some manner the provisions contained in earlier acts.

Rather than enumerating all the acts promiscuously in their chronological order, they will be presented here in the somewhat discriminating categories: (1) Land and money grants; (2) Grants for vocational education; (3) Emergency relief grants; (4) Aids for school-lunch program; (5) Grants to federally impacted areas; (6) Donations of surplus property; (7) Programs to aid various school subjects; (8) Civil Rights Act of 1964; and (9) Elementary and Secondary Education Act of 1965.

12

2.1   Land and money grants—beginning 1785

(a) *The Ordinance of 1785.*   This congressional act prescribed that lands should be surveyed into townships of 36 square miles each, and specified that the sixteenth section (one square mile) of each township should be reserved for schools within the township.[1] This ordinance merely prescribed the method of surveying and set aside the sixteenth section for schools. It was many years later before the territories were actually surveyed, sold, and occupied by settlers interested in the establishment and maintenance of schools.

(b) *The Ohio Enabling Act of 1802.*   Ohio became the first state to receive the school lands reserved by the Ordinance of 1785. As other states were admitted to the Union the policy was extended, with some of the newer states receiving as many as four sections for the support of public schools. Altogether, thirty states received grants of land under enabling acts similar to that of Ohio.[2]

(c) *Salt Land Grants.*   Upon its admission in 1802 Ohio was granted 24,216 acres of salt lands, the proceeds of which were to be used at the discretion of the state. This established a policy of grants which continued until 1875, with only five of the states admitted during this period failing to receive such grants. Fourteen states benefited from gifts of salt lands and a number of these applied the proceeds to their permanent school funds.[3]

(d) *The United States Deposit Fund of 1833.*   In this year ten million dollars of federal funds were withdrawn from the Bank of the United States and distributed among the banks of the various states. Although not specified for this purpose a number of the states used the income from these funds for the common schools.[4]

(e) *Act to Regulate the Deposit of Public Money.*   Unlike the times of today, in 1836, the federal government was

---

[1] Fletcher Harper Swift, *Federal and State Policies in Public School Finance.* Boston: Ginn and Co., 1931, p. 12.

[2] W. Monfort Barr, *American Public School Finance.* New York: The American Book Co., 1960, p. 184.

[3] Swift, *op. cit.*, p. 21.

[4] *Id.*, p. 34.

faced with a problem of surplus revenues. A solution was found by returning the excess funds to the states under the guise of "loans." Altogether, more than $28 million was distributed through this act prior to the panic of 1837, after which no further payments were made. Many of the twenty-six states receiving funds through the provision of this act used the proceeds for the support of schools.[5]

(f) *Internal Improvement Act of 1841.* This act provided a grant of 500,000 acres of land to each of the public land states for internal improvements. Nineteen states received such grants and nine of these placed all or part of the proceeds from the sale of these lands in the permanent common school fund.[6]

(g) *Swamp Land Grant Act of 1850.* Under terms of this act fifteen states received more than sixty million acres of swamp and over-flowed lands which were considered unfit for cultivation. Twelve of the fifteen states devoted all or part of the revenues from these lands to the support of the common schools.[7]

(h) *Federal Forest Reserve Act (1908).* In this year Congress authorized that 25 percent of the income from the National Forest Reserve be paid to those states in which such income originated, for the benefit of public roads and public schools. The forty states and two territories receiving funds from this source have used a considerable part for the support of schools.[8]

(i) *Oil and Mineral Leasing Act of 1920.* By this congressional act states were to receive a percentage of the income from the extraction of nonmetallic minerals from public lands within their boundaries. More than twenty states receiving revenues through the terms of this act have devoted a large portion to the support of the schools.[9]

---

[5] Hollis P. Allen, *The Federal Government and Education.* New York: McGraw-Hill Book Co., 1950, p. 65.

[6] Swift, *op. cit.*, pp. 22 to 23.

[7] *Id.*, p. 24.

[8] Allen, *op. cit.*, p. 65.

[9] *Id.*, pp. 65, 66.

(j) *Public Domain Grazing Lands (1934)*. Legislation was enacted in 1934 which provided that 50 percent of the money received from grazing districts should be paid to the respective states and expended in accordance with prescriptions of the state legislatures. A number of the states receiving such funds applied a portion of them to the public schools.

2.2 Grants for vocational education—beginning 1917

(a) *The Smith-Hughes Act (1917)*. This act marked the beginning of direct federal grants of cash funds to schools below the college level. It provided for annual appropriations of $7,000,000 allotted on the basis of rural population. Since its inception this act has been the subject of considerable controversy because of the federal control it provides over the public-school offering. The Smith-Hughes Act requires the approval by federal authorities of state plans for courses of study, the preparation of teachers, and even the allocation of the time of the pupils. The most disputed feature of the act is that which requires the state to provide at least 50 percent of the cost of the program. The objections raised by members of the teaching profession in opposition to the original provisions of the Smith-Hughes Act are partially responsible for the provisions regarding matching of funds contained in the following three acts enumerated here.

(b) *The George-Reed Act (1929)*. This act authorized a supplemental appropriation to be distributed to the states of $500,000 a year to $2,500,000 by 1934, after which there were to be no further appropriations under the provisions of the act. The funds were to be equally divided between vocational education in home economics and agriculture.[10]

(c) *The George-Ellzey Act (1934)*. This act varied only in slight degree from its predecessor, which expired in 1934. It provided for supplemental funds for vocational education, with an extension of activities over the previous act to include training in trades and industry. Under the term of

---

[10] Allen, *op. cit.*, p. 74.

this act an annual appropriation of $3,000,000 was authorized for a period of three years only.[11]

(d) *The George-Deen Act (1936).* Whereas the two previously mentioned acts merely supplemented slightly the amounts available through the Smith-Hughes Act, this act authorized an increase of funds which virtually doubled those provided for in the original act. Another significant feature of this act is that which added distributive occupations to vocational curriculum.[12]

(e) *The George-Barden Act (1946).* This act which superseded the George-Deen Act provided for an additional appropriation of $28,850,000 beyond that provided for in the original Smith-Hughes Act. The supplemental appropriations allocated $10,000,000 for agriculture; $8,000,000 for home economics; $2,500,000 for distributive occupations; and $350,000 for administration by the United States Office of Education.[13]

In 1956 Public Law 84-1027 authorized an additional $375,000 for vocational education in the fishery trades and industries and in distributive occupations.[14] In the same year Public Law 911 added Title II to the George-Barden Act, authorizing an appropriation of $5,000,000 per year over a five-year period for practical nurse training. This title has now been made permanent.

The George-Barden Act was again amended in 1958, this time by the National Defense Education Act which added Title III, authorizing $15,000,000 annually for the training of skilled technicians. Whereas the provision was originally for only four years, it has since been made permanent.[15]

At present the George-Barden Act authorizes approximately $50,000,000 a year for the promotion of vocational education in trades and industries, agriculture, home eco-

---

[11] *Ibid.*
[12] *Id.*, p. 75.
[13] Allen, *op. cit.*, pp. 75 to 77.
[14] 70 Stat. 1126.
[15] *Education '65: A Report to the Profession* OE-11006. U. S. Government Printing Office, Washington, D. C.: 1966, p. 1.

nomics, distributive occupations, practical nursing, the fishery trades, and skilled technical education. Not all of these funds are allocated to the secondary schools, since some of them go to special technical education and community college centers.[16]

(f) *The Vocational Education Act of 1963.* This act was designed to move beyond the rigid and limited provisions of the Smith-Hughes and George-Barden Acts. The act makes provisions for four categories of eligible individuals: (1) those attending high school, (2) those who have completed high school or who have dropped out and are free to study full time, (3) those who are employed but who need training or retraining, and (4) those who have handicaps which prevent their effective participation in regular vocational education programs. Funds for the permanent program authorize $60,000,000 for 1963-1964, $118.5 million for 1964-1965, $177.5 million for 1965-1966, and $225,000,-000 for 1966-1967 and each fiscal year thereafter. The act also amends the Smith-Hughes and George-Barden Acts, making them more flexible within the established categories, but does not affect the previously authorized annual appropriations.[17]

Today, Congress is aware that training and research in many areas of vocational education are required to keep pace with technological and occupational changes. To meet these changes, "more than $375 million in Federal funds was available for fiscal year 1970 for a variety of vocational education programs authorized under the Vocational Education Amendments of 1968."

Under this legislation, Federal grants are made to the states to promote vocational education for all persons wishing to enter occupational fields and to assist secondary and post-secondary students, dropouts, high school graduates and those with educational, socio-economic, and physical and mental handicaps. State allocations are determined by a

[16] *Education '65: A Report to the Profession*, pp. 1-2.
[17] *Id.*, p. 5.

Congressional formula based on the number of persons in various age groups needing vocational education and on the state per capita income. "States are generally required to match Federal allocations, but the Federal share may range up to 100 percent for certain parts of the program."[18]

According to a report of the Chief of the Planning and Evaluation Branch, OE's Division of Vocational and Technical Education, the enrollment in the program has increased markedly since its inception and will continue to do so in the years ahead: "Since the passage of the 1963 vocational education legislation, there has been a steady increase in vocational education enrollments from 349,000 in 1964 to an estimated 8.1 million in 1968. Projections indicate an enrollment of 14 million by 1975."[19]

2.3 Emergency relief grants—beginning 1933

During the relatively brief period from 1933 to 1935 numerous "educational projects were undertaken, including federal aid totaling about $22,000,000 to provide funds to keep schools open in many rural areas." [20]

(a) In 1933 the *Federal Relief Administration* (FRA) authorized the expenditure of relief funds in the employment of certain needy unemployed teachers, who previously had been assigned to public schools in rural areas where many schools were closed or programs were curtailed because of lack of funds. Although the undertaking was to be financed by federal funds, the supervision of the program was delegated to state educational authorities. [21]

(b) The *Works Progress Administration* (WPA) was established in 1935 as an independent agency of the govern-

---

[18] "Federal Funds Support for Vocational-Technical Education." *American Education*, July 1970, pp. 31-32.

[19] Russo, Michael, "14 Million Vocational Students by 1975." *American Education*, March, 1969, p. 10.

[20] Allen, *op. cit.*, p. 98.

[21] Education Policies Commission, *Federal Activities in Education*. Washington, D. C.: Education Policies Commission of the NEA, 1939, p. 88.

ment. In 1939 it was transferred to the Federal Works Agency and its name was changed to Works Projects Administration. Among the various activities of this agency were (1) general adult education, (2) literary and naturalization classes, (3) avocational and leisure-time activities, (4) vocational education, (5) nursery schools, (6) homemaking education, and (7) correspondence instruction.

(c) When the *Civilian Conservation Corps* (CCC) was created in 1933, its primary objectives were (1) to provide employment to idle young men and (2) to conserve natural resources—particularly the forests, parks, roads, and fields. At first the education of the young men was a secondary objective, but later developed into one of the most promising phases of the program. [22]

(d) The *National Youth Administration* (NYA) was organized as an emergency measure with the chief purpose of assisting young persons not employed and unable to continue their education because of insufficient financial support. [23]

(e) *Manpower Development and Training Act.* This act is an important extension of the nation's commitment to the fullest possible creative use of its human resources. Enacted in 1962 and amended in 1963 and 1965, it authorized skill training for the unemployed and underemployed. Congress appropriated $438,900,000 to continue this program in fiscal 1966. [24]

Since its inception the program made available by the MDTA has enrolled some 848,000 trainees in institutional projects alone. Over 177,000 were enrolled for fiscal year 1969.

Originally designed to reduce high unemployment and fill skill-shortage occupations, the MDTA has been amended several times to open up more training opportunities for young people. It is directed specifically toward the disadvantaged.

---

[22] *Id.*, p. 94.
[23] Aubrey Williams, "National Youth Administration," *School Life*, XXV (April, 1940), 200.
[24] *Education '65: A Report to the Profession*, p. 11.

A disadvantaged person is characterized by the Department of Health, Education and Welfare (DHEW) as: (1) a school dropout, (2) a minority member, (3) under 22 years of age, (4) over 44 years of age, or (5) handicapped.[25]

(f) *Education Professions Development Act (EPDA).* Federal efforts to meet educational manpower needs, previously administered under six separate programs were combined in 1967 under EPDA, thus "fiscal year 1970 marked the first year of full-fledged EPDA activity. More than 115,-000 persons, from teachers and aides to school administrators and teacher trainees, were trained or retrained through 1,200 projects funded under 14 EPDA programs. These projects were conducted during the 1970-71 school year at a total cost of $116 million."[26]

2.4 Aids for school-lunch programs—beginning 1935

(a) *Public Law 320 (1935).* This law authorized the Secretary of Agriculture to encourage the consumption of surplus agricultural commodities, thereby diverting them from the normal channels of trade.[27] During the first year this program was in operation approximately $250,000 worth of commodities were donated to schools.[28]

(b) *Public Law 461 (1936).* This law clarified the term "diversion" as authorized under Public Law 320. This program of donation to schools was continued under the direction of the Federal Surplus Commodities Corporation.[29]

(c) *The School Milk Program (1940).* Under this program, made possible under Public Law 320, the federal government reimbursed schools for a portion of the cost of milk served to children.[30]

---

[25] "OE's Role in Manpower Development and Training." *American Education*, March, 1970, pp. 34-35.

[26] "Meeting Education Manpower Needs." *American Education*, May, 1971, p. 32.

[27] Allen, *op. cit.*, p. 83.

[28] Clayton D. Hutchins and others, *Federal Funds for Education.* Washington, D. C.: United States Government Printing Office, 1954, p. 47.

[29] Allen, *op. cit.*, p. 83.

[30] Hutchins and others, *op. cit.*, p. 73.

(d) *The Indemnity Plan (1943).* Due to the increased demands for food during World War II, surplus foods rapidly declined and donations to schools dwindled. To compensate for this decrease in commodity assistance the Department of Agriculture was authorized to provide cash assistance to the schools in the form of partial reimbursements for lunches served.[31]

(e) *The National School Lunch Act (1946).*[32] This act brought all previous school lunch efforts together under one federal program. It authorized (1) the donation of surplus agricultural commodities, (2) the purchase and distribution of goods specifically for the school lunch program, and (3) the partial reimbursement of schools for the purchase of foods and cost of equipment for food storage and preparation.[33]

The act was amended in 1962 by Public Law 87-823 which, in addition to other minor provisions, authorized $10,000,000 for fiscal 1963, ". . . and such sums as may be necessary for each succeeding fiscal year . . ."[34] to aid schools in poor economic areas in the provision of lunches for pupils unable to pay. In fiscal 1963 schools received more than $288,000,000 in assistance through the terms of the National School Lunch Act.[35]

(f) *Special Milk Program (1954), Public Law 690.* This program supplemented the National School Lunch Act through the authorization of $50,000,000 per year. Succeeding acts have periodically extended the program with increased expenditure. Fiscal 1963 expenditures under the special milk program were $93,893,000.[36]

2.5   Grants to federally-impacted areas—beginning 1941

---

[31] *Ibid.*
[32] Public Law 396.
[33] Hutchins and others, *op. cit.,* p. 74.
[34] *Ibid.*
[35] *The Budget of the United States Government.* Washington, D. C.: United States Government Printing Office, 1964, p. 112.
[36] *Id.,* p. 110.

(a) *The Lanham Act (1941)*. This was a temporary emergency act providing aid to communities where war-incurred federal activity had caused an influx of civilian or military personnel, thereby creating a financial burden to the community. From 1941 to 1947, more than $187,000,000 was spent on programs of: (1) school construction and equipment; (2) school maintenance and operation assistance; and (3) child care.[37] With the end of the war the program rapidly diminished and was eventually discontinued.

(b) *Public Law 815 (1950)*. Originally this law was a temporary measure but since has been extended through 1965.[38] A 1963 report states that, since the enactment of Public Law 815 in 1950, about $1.07 billion in federal funds has been provided for school construction, providing classrooms for over 1.5 million children.[39]

(c) *Public Law 874 (1950)*. As a companion to Public Law 815, this act also authorized federal assistance to local education agencies for schools within federally affected school districts. Eligibility of school districts to receive aid is based upon percentage of federally connected pupils enrolled. As of 1963 there were 4,182 eligible school districts with 1.8 million federally connected pupils included within a total enrollment of over 12,000,000.[40]

2.6 Donations of surplus property—beginning 1944

(a) *The Surplus Property Act (1944)*.[41] Although the federal government had made provisions for limited donations of surplus property to schools as early as 1919,[42] it was not until 1944 that legislation establishing an orderly procedure for the disposal of such was passed. This act provided for the donation of government real and personal

37 Allen, *op. cit.*, p. 105.

38 Public Laws 85-620, 87-344, and 88-210.

39 *The Federal Government and Education*, a report prepared for the Committee on Education and Labor, Washington, D.C.: United States Government Printing Office, 1963.

40 *Administration of Public Laws 874 and 815*, Thirteenth Annual Report of the Commissioner of Education, Washington, D. C.: United States Government Printing Office, 1963, p. 1.

41 Public Law 457.

42 Public Law 155.

property no longer needed for defense purposes to tax-supported and tax-exempt nonprofit educational institutions.

(b) *Federal Property and Administrative Services Act (1949).*[43] The law augmented the previous act by making available for donations such items as surplus office machines, furniture, and related items normally used in housekeeping functions of the various departments and agencies of government.

2.7 Programs to aid various school subjects—beginning 1950

(a) *The National Science Foundation.*[44] This federal agency was established in 1950 "to promote the progress of science; to advance the national health, prosperity, and welfare; to secure the national defense; and for other purposes." [45] The public schools receive indirect aid from the act through a number of programs conducted by the National Science Foundation. Although these programs put no actual cash funds into the schools at this level, they do make a valuable contribution through their work in course improvement and in training of teachers at the elementary and secondary levels. [46]

(b) *National Defense Education Act (1958).* [47] This act was originally enacted for only four years but was extended for two years in 1961, two years again in 1963, and again in 1965. The provisions of this act authorize the expenditure of federal funds for the expansion and improvement of educational programs at all levels from the elementary school through graduate training. Its purpose, to meet the needs of the times in a critical era, cannot be disputed. Specifically it provides for the appropriation of funds for student loans; improvement of teaching science, mathematics, and foreign languages; increased guidance and testing services; and research. Detailed provisions of the entire program are de-

---

43 Public Law 152.
44 Public Law 507.
45 *Ibid.*
46 *The Federal Government and Education,* p. 121.
47 Public Law 85-864.

scribed in ten titles, a number of which provide either direct or indirect aid to the public schools. [48]

A decade after the passage of the 1958 National Defense Education Act, former Secretary of HEW, Wilbur J. Cohen, made a progress report in which he indicated that the scores of other bills introduced since the 1880's, designed to strengthen education, were doomed for various reasons. He stated: "Some failed because of the church-state issues and, in some cases, the fear of Federal control. Others were cut down in the quarrel about how to distribute funds among big and small and rich and poor states. Still others lost out because of the integration issue."[49]

In addition to pointing out the beneficial effects of the original and amended titles of the Act, Cohen stated:

Beyond its impact on education the NDEA is also important historically as a trail blazer. For example, its passage unified disparate interests in the critical church-state issue, an experience that has proved important in developing subsequent legislation. The NDEA has special significance in being developed cooperatively by a Democratic Congress in a Republican administration and later expanded in two Democratic administrations on a bipartisan basis; so that it became truly a bipartisan measure.[50]

In addition to those referred to above, Congress has enacted numerous other acts which provide financial support to schools in one way or another. For example, beginning in 1958, several laws were passed for the purpose of aiding the handicapped: (1) *Public Law 85-926 (1958)* authorized grants for the training of teachers of the mentally retarded; (2) *Public Law 85-905 (1958)* authorized funds for the

---

[48] United States Department of Health, Education, and Welfare, *Report on the National Defense Education Act Fiscal Years 1961 and 1962.* Washington, D. C.: United States Government Printing Office, 1963.

[49] Wilbur J. Cohen, "An Idea that Grew on NDEA's 10th Anniversary." *American Education,* September, 1968, pp. 2-3.

[50] *Id.,* p. 3.

acquisition and distribution of films and related materials for the education of the deaf; (3) *Public Law 87-276 (1961)* authorized funds for training teachers of the deaf; and (4) *Mental Health Center Construction Act (1963)* augmented the provisions of the previous laws in this category by extending aid to the hard of hearing, deaf, speech impaired, visually handicapped, emotionally disturbed, crippled, and the otherwise impaired, as well as the mentally retarded. [51]

2.8   Civil Rights Act of 1964

Although not strictly an education law, the Civil Rights Act has definite educational implications. Several titles of the act have to do with implementation of desegregation of races in the public schools. For example, Title IV empowers the Attorney General to initiate civil action against local school boards which deny equal rights to any young people. Section 601 of Title VI provides that "No person in the United States shall, on the grounds of race, color, or national origin, be excluded from participation in, be denied the benefits of, or be subjected to discrimination under any program or activity receiving Federal financial assistance."

Accordingly the specific discriminatory practices which are prohibited include:

(1) Any difference in quality, quantity, or the manner in which the benefit is provided.

(2) Segregation or separate treatment in any part of the program.

(3) Restriction in the enjoyment of any advantages, privileges, or other benefits provided to others.

(4) Different standards or requirements for participation.

(5) Methods of administration which would defeat or substantially impair the accomplishment of the program objectives.

(6) Discrimination in any activity conducted in a facility

---

[51] "Notes on the Notable Federal Programs and Activities," *School Life* (December, 1963), p. 5.

built in whole or in part with federal funds.

(7) Discrimination in any employment resulting from a program established primarily to provide employment.

It may be observed that the Civil Rights Act, like the Economic Opportunity Act, utilizes education as a means to achieve its objectives. In the Economic Opportunities Act education is a weapon against poverty; in the Civil Rights Act it is a means of ensuring freedom and equal opportunity in our society.

The Civil Rights Act of 1964, as applied to the Elementary and Secondary Education Act of 1965, presents a frustrating problem for school boards who seek to reap the benefits of the latter act, but are reluctant to comply with the provisions of the former act. It is cause for confusion, dispute, and litigation.

When the Civil Rights Act was enacted on July 2, 1964, the Office of Education published no guidelines for implementation or interpretation. Consequently school officials found it necessary to make their own interpretations and decisions.

Due to the many demands for clarification of Title VI, the first set of guidelines for school desegregation was issued in April 1965. Then in March 1966, the Office of Education issued—with very little modification—its second set of guidelines for the 1966-1967 school year.

In commenting on the adequacy of the desegregation guidelines, Assistant Commissioner for Equal Educational Opportunities, Seely stated:

> . . . the guidelines apply only to school districts in the 17 Southern and border States. The reason is that these States —in contrast to the Northern and Western States—have maintained dual school systems (one for white students, another for Negroes) as a matter of formal and obvious public policy. School segregation exists in the North just as surely as it does in the South, but in the Northern cities, segregated schools result mostly from segregated housing patterns rather than from law and school policy. [52]

---

[52] David S. Seeley, "Desegregation Guidelines," *American Education*, February 1967, p. 21.

2.9 Elementary and Secondary Education Act of 1965

This act constituted the first major legislation of national significance to be enacted by the 89th Congress. Keyed to "poverty" the Elementary and Secondary Education Act virtually doubled the amount of federal aid available to public schools. The major provisions of the original act, with the main 1967 amendments, are as follows:

Title I provides for payment of one-half the average per pupil expenditure for children from families with an income below $2,000 per year.

An amendment of Title I "has changed the formula for distribution of funds among the States so that poorer regions of the country will receive more adequate grants."[53]

The latest in a long series of "comparability" regulations for distribution of Title I funds was signed in 1971, by HEW Secretary Elliot L. Richardson. The new rules—supposedly affecting how nearly $1.5 billion is passed among 16,000 school districts—are aimed at assuring that federal aid to schools in poor neighborhoods will not be used simply to make up the difference between what school districts spend on those schools and what the districts spend on schools in more affluent neighborhoods.

Henceforth:
each school district will have to report on how its middle class and poor schools compare when applying the funds for the 1971-72 school year, and evidence that the schools are comparable—within a five percent tolerance—will be required in order to get Title I money for the 1972-73 year.[54]

Title II authorizes distribution of $100,000,000 to states for

---

[53] "What's New in the ESEA Amendments," *American Education,* February 1967, p. 18.

[54] "New Title I Rules Require Comparability." *Nation's Schools,* June, 1971, p. 26.

acquisition of library resources, including textbooks and audio-visual materials. The ability of local school officials to budget these funds will depend on the state plan, approved by the United States Commissioner of Education.

An amendment of Title II broadened the coverage of beneficiaries to include "children in schools operated by the Bureau of Indian Affairs and children of Armed Forces personnel in schools operated by the Department of Defense."[55]

Title III provides $100,000,000 for grants to local school districts for establishment of supplementary education centers. An extremely wide range of activities may be authorized under this title. Under its terms, school authorities are required to cooperate with other educational and cultural interests in the community.

An amendment of Title III increased allowances of funds "toward such critical educational needs as preschool education and replacing inadequate facilities."[56]

Title IV makes another $100,000,000 available over a five-year period, for regional educational research and training facilities. Grants will be awarded to institutions of higher education and other nonprofit organizations to undertake programs which will benefit public schools.

By amendment to Title IV it was provided that "research training contracts may be made with private organizations other than nonprofit agencies."[57]

Title V appropriates $25,000,000 to strengthen state departments of education. Grants will be made available to undertake special projects which will improve services rendered to local school districts.

---

[55] "What's New in the ESEA Amendments," *American Education*, February 1967, p. 9.

[56] *Ibid.*

[57] "What's New in the ESEA Amendments," *American Education*, February 1967, p. 20.

The main amendment to Title V was "to eliminate the 'matching funds' requirement in the original act." [58]

An amendment to the new Title VI requires the establishment, by July 1967, of a bureau in the Office of Education, for the education and training of handicapped children, "dealing with education, training, and research affecting handicapped children — including the mentally retarded, hard of hearing, deaf, speech impaired, visually handicapped, and other children who, because of their impairments, require special educational services." [59]

The amendment to Title VII — general provisions — authorizes additional funds in 1968 for the "dissemination of information—advice, counsel, technical assistance, demonstrations—to States or local educational agencies requesting it." [60]

"As another general provision, Congress stipulated that nothing in the act may be construed to require the assignment or transportation of teachers or students to overcome racial imbalance." [61]

The official publication *American Education* of the United States Office of Education has inserted in its November, 1970 issue a six-page (26-32) federal chart which presents most succinctly but authentically: (1) types of financial assistance available, (2) the title of the act authorizing the assistance, (3) the purpose for which the assistance is given, (4) the amount of the appropriations, (5) who is eligible to apply for the assistance, and (6) to whom the application should be made.

The numerous acts of the federal government authorizing several billions of dollars to be expended annually for educational purposes is ample proof that the legislative branch of the federal government is assuming a significant role in public education. With the ever-broadening concept of the

---

[58] *Ibid.*
[59] *Ibid.*
[60] *Ibid.*
[61] *Ibid.*

"welfare clause" as contained 'in the federal constitution, a greatly accelerated trend for federal support of the public schools may be anticipated.

2.10   Uncertain trend in federal-aid reform

Many of the major acts for federal aid to education were passed during the Johnson Administration. During the early years of the Nixon Administration there was a slow-down in federal aid legislation. Most of the legislation had to do with the amendments of prior acts.

Among the more significant acts enacted during the 1967-1970 period were:

(a) *1967 Education Professions Development Act* which extended Teacher Corps for three years, providing $1.1 billion for broadened training programs for educational personnel.

(b) *1968 Handicapped Children's Early Education Assistance Act* which authorized establishment of model education centers for handicapped preschool children, providing for experimentation that would produce successful teaching approaches and prototype programs for the handicapped child of preschool age.

(c) *1970 Environment Quality Education Act. HR 14252* which provided $29 million over three years for curriculum development, teacher training, and community programs in environmental education, and contained a "small grants" provision allowing civic and volunteer organizations to apply for funds.

(d) *1971 Education Appropriation Act* which indicated the relative authority of the executive and legislative branches of the federal government in appropriating funds for education. On July 11, 1971, President Nixon signed into law the largest appropriation bill in the history of the Office of Education, $5.15 billion, which exceeded by $375 million the budget request of the President. The big increases over the President's budget requests were as follows: (1) $173 million above the $440 million requested by the President for assistance to school districts having heavy concentration of federal employes; (2) $138 million above the $1.85 billion requested by the President for general assistance to elementary and secondary education; and (3) $100 million above the $469 million requested by the President for vocational and adult education.

If Congress moves further toward the appropriation of public funds, in which parochial and other private schools would share, the constitutionality of the legislation could conceivably be challenged. The United States Supreme Court's 1971 invalidation of state statutes which provided for the allocation of public funds to parochial elementary and secondary schools is indicative.

Proposed legislation which is highly controversial, and which could lead to litigation, concerns the so-called *voucher system*, whereby pupils or parents would be issued vouchers to defray educational costs at schools of their choice—parochial, private or public. Obviously to be fiscally effective the voucher system would necessitate huge federal appropriations.

It is reported that despite bitter opposition from virtually all organizations in the educational "establishment," the Nixon Administration appears determined to push ahead with its proposed education voucher experiment. That it would meet with strong opposition and probable litigation is reflected by the resolution of the American Association of School Administrators at its 1971 annual convention in Atlantic City. The resolution condemned the voucher plan on the grounds that it would:

(1) transfer control of schools from public to private hands; (2) permit "non-educational issues," such as race or ideology to determine a school's income and hence "its survival"; (3) generate "a massive bureaucracy"; (4) "foster further segregation within our society"; (5) pro-

vide support for church-affiliated schools.[62]

Even though the total of federal support for public education is likely to increase, the unaltered continuation of certain grants is unlikely. Many of the early grants are no longer justified; others need to be provided to meet changing needs of the times. Public officials, educators and others are advocating an evaluation of the present grant program to determine proper future emphases. Despite the reluctance to repeal outmoded acts of the Congress, the necessity to do so is becoming more apparent as is indicated in a Washington Report:

> . . . with each passing year it becomes more apparent that mass public education in the United States is in trouble, and Congress is becoming more receptive to the idea that new approaches may be necessary. The biggest problem here is that the programs now being widely branded as failures were the proud achievements of Congress only a few years ago, and among Congressmen, as among human beings generally, the willingness to admit failure is not universal.[63]

Despite general acceptance of the various federal grants for education there is a growing concern over the procedures and priorities for allocating the funds. No one is more aware of the needs for evaluation and reform than are the governmental officials themselves. Comments in the President's Message on Education Reform (April, 1970) are indicative:

> We must stop imagining that the Federal Government had a cohesive education policy during a period of explosive expansion—when our Federal education programs are largely fragmented and disjointed, and too often administered in a way that frustrates local and private efforts.

---

[62] "OEO Releases Voucher Timetable." *The Nation's Schools*, April, 1971, p. 29.

[63] "The Proposed National Institute of Education." *School Management*, April, 1971, p. 4.

We must stop congratulating ourselves for spending
nearly as much money on education as does the entire
rest of the world—$65 billion a year on all levels—when
we are not getting as much as we should out of the dollars we spend.[64]

In a message to Congress in April 1971, the President
proposed a $213 million increase the next year for all ele-
mentary and secondary school aid. It was pointed out in
the message that automatic allocations from the education
fund would enhance innovation and improvement in the
schools by freeing state and local governments from the
overlap, red tape and conflicting guidelines of the thirty-
three federal programs that would be consolidated.

The President said: "Because federal programs are re-
sistant to change, we see money being spent on programs
which might have outlived their usefulness or that simply are ineffective, while funds for new ideas cannot be
obtained."[65]

The necessity for reform was also enunciated by James
Gallagher who, before his resignation, was the Deputy Assistant Secretary of DHEW and Deputy U. S. Commissioner
for Planning Research and Evaluation. He stated:

Unless we can organize ourselves at the federal level
to keep our educational promises, to identify one clear
spokesman for federal educational policy, to support and
give leadership to special programs directly related to educational improvement then the federal government may
well be crying out for educational reform on the outside,
when the needs for reform may be greatest on the inside
of the federal establishment.

Gallagher offered three suggestions for reform: (1) establishment of a separate, cabinet-level department of education; (2) acceptance of the idea that the federal government has a special responsibility for research in

---

[64] Richard M. Nixon, "Message on Education Reform." *American Education,* April, 1970, pp. 30-34.
[65] *Durham Herald,* April 7, 1971.

education; and (3) setting aside about 20 percent of the educational budget for long-range goals.[66]

Elliot L. Richardson, Secretary of the U. S. Department of Health, Education and Welfare, frequently raises his voice for reform. For example, in a guest editorial for *The School Administrator*, September 1970, p. 2, Richardson says:

> If progress is to continue, we must retain the strong sense of the need for reform that has prompted the recent innovations in our grant management techniques. With the continuing assistance and encouragement of school administrators, I am confident that the next few years can bring thorough improvements in the mechanisms which channel federal funds into America's schools.

At a Miami Beach meeting of the Council of Chief State School Officers, HEW Secretary Richardson again expressed proposals for a top-to-bottom overhaul of all federal legislation dealing with education programs. His expressed goal was to give the states considerable leeway to spend federal funds, programs, and regulations.

Richardson would consolidate the present tangle of laws and programs into a proposed Education Assistance Act of 1972. Into the Assistance Act would go all education programs aiding elementary and secondary schools. He would require comprehensive state plans, and the money would flow through each state to its local school districts. In effect, "block grants" would be assured to states in the following major areas: vocational education, impact aid, education for children from poor families and for children of the disadvantaged and handicapped, and supporting service for state education agencies, libraries, and educational technology.[67]

Of course attempts for reform in granting federal funds for education—even though well conceived—are difficult to bring to fruition. Proposals made by the higher echelon of

---

[66] "A Statement of Personal Conviction." *Hot Line,* July, 1970, p. 4.
[67] "Report from Washington." *Nation's Schools,* January, 1971, p. 19.

the executive branch must be converted into legislative acts before becoming law. Moreover, Congressional support is frequently subject to the wishes of the constituencies of the school districts. A Washington note in *School Management* (May 1970, p. 10) is illustrative:

> Just how rare and difficult it is the administration will learn as it pursues its effort to make drastic revisions in the impacted areas program. Like Presidents Eisenhower, Kennedy and Johnson before him, President Nixon would like to cut back on this hardy perennial, which is now deeply rooted in Congress and has grown so through the years that if it were fully funded it would cost more than $1 billion. Even those in Congress who would like to see changes made concede it is all but impossible if those changes would result in taking money away from districts now receiving it. It is likely to come to an end only when a program of general aid to education is adopted. That may not be far off.

Chapter 3

EXECUTIVE BRANCH (U. S. OFFICE OF EDUCATION) AND THE SCHOOL

At first it might seem difficult to see any relationship of the executive branch of the federal government to education. However, when one considers that the President's cabinet, representing the eleven executive departments, falls within the framework of the executive branch, it becomes apparent that the school is affected in many ways by the organization and functions of this branch of the federal government.

Ever since its creation, the Office of Education has been an agency in one of the departments of the executive branch of the federal government. Despite considerable demands from schoolmen and others the office has never had independent departmental status.

3.1 Historical development of the Office of Education

Federal interest in education was given considerable impetus about 1840 when the federal census gathered its first data on illiteracy in the United States. At about the same time, Henry Barnard came to Washington in search of reliable data about the nation's schools. Since he could not find any he immediately initiated a movement for the establishment of a department of education in the federal government to improve the deplorable condition revealed in his investigation.

Finally, in 1867, a federal agency which was first referred to as a "Department of Education" was created by an act of Congress,[1] with Henry Barnard as the first commissioner.

---

[1] 14 Stat 434, 20 USC 1.

36

The functions to be performed by the new office were defined as follows: "to collect such statistics and facts as shall show the condition and progress of education, and to diffuse such information as shall aid the people of the United States in establishing and maintaining efficient school systems, and otherwise promote the cause of education."[2]

For some time after the establishment, this federal educational agency was not held in high esteem by schoolmen and congressmen. It was treated somewhat like an unwanted child without even a permanent name or home. After a little more than one year from the time of its creation it ceased to exist as a "Department of Education" and became an "Office of Education" in the Department of Interior. In 1870, the agency was named the "Bureau of Education," by which name it was known until 1929, when the title of "Office of Education" was restored.

Although the agency is still known as the "Office of Education" it has continued to undergo further changes. In 1939, the Office was transferred from the Department of Interior to the Federal Security Agency,[3] in accordance with the President's Reorganization Plan No. 1. Even though this transfer did not give the Office of Education a more independent status, it did provide it with much better housing accommodations in the Interior Building which was new at that time.

On April 11, 1953, the Department of Health, Education, and Welfare replaced the Federal Security Agency, and the Office of Education became one of the units of the new department.[4] Despite the gradual improvement of the status of the Office of Education in the structure of the federal government there are many who believe it is not yet satisfactory. Some schoolmen and others have at times advocated the creation of a federal department of education, with the head being a member of the President's cabinet. In more recent years that idea has been somewhat discarded because

---

[2] *Handbook Office of Education.* Washington, D. C.: United States Government Printing Office, OE-11002A, 1963, p. 27.

[3] 53 Stat 1424, 20 USC § 1.

[4] 67 Stat 631, 20 USC § 1.

of the fear that it would put education into partisan politics and probably would lead to a larger federal educational establishment than would be desirable. A strongly supported alternative has been to set up the United States Office of Education as an independent agency of the federal government with a national board of education composed of outstanding citizens. It is generally recommended by school administrators that (1) the Office should be an independent agency of the federal government under the general control of a policy-making board of laymen broadly representative of the general public; (2) the board members should be appointed by the President, with the consent of the Senate, to long overlapping terms; (3) a professionally qualified and competent United States commissioner of education should be appointed by the board to serve as its executive officer; and (4) sufficient funds should be provided to perform adequately the functions ascribed to the office. Although bills with these provisions have been introduced they have not as yet received sufficient congressional support to make them law.

3.2   Functions of the Office of Education

The functions of the Office are redefined from time to time. The statutory functions of the Office at the time of its inception were to "collect such statistics and facts as shall show the condition and progress of education, to diffuse such information as shall aid the people of the United States in the establishment and maintenance of efficient school systems, and otherwise to promote the cause of education." Subsequent acts and executive orders have added related functions, including responsibilities for federal assistance to education and special studies and programs.[5]

The broad functions of the Office as they were more elaborately spelled out in 1948 included:

1. The collection of information with respect to education in the States and in other countries so as to make

[5] *United States Government Organization Manual 1970-71.* Washington, D. C.: United States Government Printing Office, 1970, p. 347.

possible intelligent comparisons and conclusions regarding the efficiency of educational programs.

2. The formulation and recommendation of minimum educational standards which ought to be made to prevail in the schools and colleges of all the States and the preparation of suggested proposals and plans for improving various educational practices, arrived at by cooperative planning among private and public educational organizations and lay groups, such recommendations and proposals to be influential only if their merit and appropriateness warrant voluntary acceptance by the States and institutions.

3. The provision of services of a national character that cannot well be undertaken by single States acting alone, e. g., the collection, interpretation, and dissemination of national statistics, the conduct of national and other important surveys, the convening of conferences of national significance.

4. Pointing out desirable educational ends and procedures, evaluating educational trends and giving educational advice and discriminating praise.

5. The offering of consultative services to States, school systems, and higher educational institutions on problems of reorganization, finance, administration, and curriculum.

6. The coordination of government activities relating to education through schools and colleges.

In all such functions it is apparent that encouragement and stimulation rather than control are envisaged as the objectives of the Office of Education with respect to education in the States.[6]

A more recent and succinct list of functions of the Office include: (a) "making studies and collecting and disseminating information and statistics dealing with education; (b) administering grants which are distributed to the States on formula basis; (c) providing consultative services to educational and cultural agencies; (d) contracting with colleges,

---

[6] Andrew H. Gibbs, "The Office of Education," *The Phi Delta Kappan* (October, 1948), p. 36.

universities, State and private agencies for studies and research on educational problems; and (e) operating programs under agreement with other federal agencies."[7]

As the only federal agency which has as its concern education at all levels and in all areas, it collaborates with other federal agencies in reviewing and assessing the impact of federal programs on education. Accordingly the Office proposes federal policies to assist educational progress and growth through programs that are selective, stimulative, and where possible, transitional.

Until recent years the functions performed by the United States Office of Education were not spectacular in the eyes of the public. Following the enactment of the Civil Rights law in 1964, however, the Office appeared in the limelight, by being authorized and required by Congress to implement the law by the formulation of guidelines in determining school-district eligibility for receiving federal funds for educational purposes.

The guidelines which were set forth were controversial, to say the least. All news media have indicated reactions of politicians, educators, and others as to the propriety and legality of the guidelines.

Early reaction to the guidelines was manifested by the governor of Alabama who directed the "Anti-Guidelines Bill" (number 446) through the 1966 Alabama legislature. The opposition to the guidelines is indicated in the introduction of the bill which states that the purpose is:

> . . . To preserve the integrity of the local public school systems against unlawful encroachment in the administration and control of local schools, to provide for the determination by the courts of the justices of the Supreme Court of Alabama of the legality of requirements for federal financial assistance to local school systems, to provide financial assistance in the operation and administration of the public schools when federal assistance is withdrawn by reason of the failure or refusal to make an agreement,

---

[7] *Handbook Office of Education*, p. 5.

adopt a plan or perform some act not required by law, and to appropriate state funds for such purpose; and to provide for the method of making payments from such appropriations; to provide for a Commission, which with the Governor, is authorized to assist but not interfere with local, City and County Boards of Education.

Opposition to the guidelines is by no means limited to local and state officials. Senator Robert Byrd of West Virginia made the following statement on the floor of the Senate, September 28, 1966:

> ... (A review of events) shows us that the executive branch of the Government—led and spurred on by bureaucrats in the Office of Education—is moving to effect a monolithic, federally controlled system of education by a reasoned misuse of the Federal purse powers. It shows us that, in the eyes of Federal educational officials, the schools are seen less as instruments of education and more as the readiest means of achieving the social and political goals of a small minority. And it shows us that this minority, to achieve its ends, will attempt to overcome any obstacle even if such obstacle is posed by such basic components of the American way of our tradition of State-local control of education or our long-held concept of the neighborhood school. These are the things which basically concern me with regard to the revised guidelines.[8]

A contrasting view to these two statements quoted above was made by former HEW Secretary Gardner:

> ... The Federal Government, far from trying to dominate, is trying increasingly to preserve the pluralism of our society. We are heading toward a new kind of creative federalism, toward the establishment of new relationships that will see us through not only the complexity of today but the increasing complexity of the decades to come.[9]

---

[8] United States, *Congressional Record*, 89th Congress, 2d Session, 1966 (September 28), p. 23318.

[9] *HEW, 1965: Year of Legislative Achievements in Health, Education, and Welfare.* Washington, D. C.: United States Government Printing Office, 1966, pp. iii-iv.

With the consistent allegation of unconstitutionality it was to be expected that the legality of the guidelines would be challenged in the courts. Consequently on December 29, 1966, the Fifth United States Circuit Court of Appeals which embraces the states of Alabama, Florida, Georgia, Louisiana, Mississippi, and Texas rendered a decision regarding the legality of the controversial federal school desegregation guidelines and declared that "tokenism" must end in the South.

In its decision the court made the following key points:

(1) It said that the seven districts involved—and by implication all those in the South—must desegregate all grades by next fall (1967) and achieve substantial faculty desegregation by the following year.

(2) It upheld the validity of stiffened school racial guidelines to determine eligibility of school districts for federal school aid.

(3) It directed lower courts to use standards set forth in the revised guidelines to determine the pace of school desegregation apart from the question of qualifying for federal aid.

Obviously the court decision was a major victory for the Justice Department which filed suit in the spring of 1966 in order to speed desegregation. It also strengthened the hand of the Department of Health, Education, and Welfare, and especially the United States Office of Education, which faced strong southern criticism since it issued the guidelines.

With judicial support of the 1966 guidelines, the United States Office of Education released those for 1967 which are substantially the same as those of the previous year, except that freedom of choice should be conducted earlier.

Since the issuance of guidelines for 1967, there have been many federal court cases in which the slow pace of school desegregation was contested. Ultimately the United States Supreme Court rendered a decision in 1969 which held that "the obligation of every school district is to terminate dual school systems at once."[10] Two years later, in 1971, the

---

[10] Alexander v. Holmes County Board of Education (Miss), 396 US 802, 24 LEd(2d) 59, 90 SCt 29 (1969).

Supreme Court[11] upheld the constitutionality of busing as a means of effecting the "unitary school system."

Obviously these two landmark decisions caused school districts to seek up-to-date guidelines and directives to comply with the law. But, under the present administration, the authority of the Office of Education and other federal agencies to set guidelines for the busing of pupils is restricted by threats from the President, who has repeatedly voiced his opposition to the technique as a means of desegregation.

3.3 Organization of the Office of Education

The Office of Education is reorganized from time to time to meet the demands of the times. The structural framework of the Office, which was the result of the reorganization plan of 1962, included three operating bureaus and four staff offices.

The three bureaus were (1) Bureau of Educational Research and Development; (2) Bureau of International Education; and (3) Bureau of Educational Assistance Program.

The Office of Program Legislative Planning (1) identified and studied emerging trends and problem areas in education; (2) conducted conferences on educational problems; (3) maintained liaison with other federal agencies; (4) developed professional publications; and (5) provided advisory services on proposed legislation relating to education.

The Office of Administration (1) provided leadership and management services to the operating bureaus, (2) provided audit, fiscal, budget, personnel, and administrative services for the Office; and (3) represented the Office in its relationship with various Departments and committees of the Congress.

The Office of Information was the central channel by which educational news and information of the Office was disseminated. It was responsible for the production of the official organ of the Office, *American Education*.

---

[11] Swann v. Charlotte-Mecklenburg Board of Education (NC), 91 SCt 1267 (1971).

The Office of Field Services (1) provided consultative services; (2) developed materials for teaching of civil defense skills in emergency situations; and (3) developed and maintained liaison with other offices and departments responsible for civil defense.

The organization of the Office as described above appeared to be fairly well stabilized for a few years. But the Office was reorganized again in 1966, following the recommendation of a special task force established by President Johnson, and including persons from the Bureau of the Budget, the Civil Service Commission, and the Atomic Energy Commission, all of whom were specialists in problems of large organization. Their task force recommended to the White House the organization along lines that were "more closely related to the total thrust of legislation" then existing and anticipated for the following few years. [12]

As designated in the United States Government Organization Manual for 1971:[13]

The Office of Education consists of the Office of the Comissioner; the Deputy Commissioner; four Deputy Commissioners for School Systems, Higher and International Education, Planning, Research, and Evaluation, and Instructional Resources; Associate Commissioners for Federal-State Relations and Regional Office Coordination; and Assistant Commissioners for Administration, Public Affairs, and Legislation which provide staff, administrative, and program support as indicated by their titles. The major program organizations are described below.

REGIONAL OFFICE COORDINATION. A regional office organization, composed of 10 field office locations, serves as an operating extension of the Office of Education for service to and close working relationships with States and other recipients of educational aid. As such, the field

[12] United States Congress, House, Special Subcommittee on Education, Committee on Education and Labor. *Statement of Harold Howe II*, 89th Congress, 2d Session, 1966, pp. 1-2.

[13] Pages 347-349.

organization performs review and approval of State plans, proposals and amendments under formula grant programs, related funds management, program reviews and recommendation, and other program responsibilities as may be assigned.

BUREAU OF ELEMENTARY AND SECONDARY EDUCATION. The Bureau is responsible for administration of a program of grants to State education agencies, grants to local school districts and institutions of higher education, and the monitoring of concomitant programs. The Bureau is composed of the following six Divisions: Plans and Supplementary Centers, State Agency Cooperation, School Assistance in Federally Affected Areas, Compensatory Education, and Equal Educational Opportunities.

BUREAU OF ADULT, VOCATIONAL AND TECHNICAL EDUCATION. The Bureau administers grants to States for programs of vocational and technical education, and for education programs for adults. It also contracts with States for the conduct of adult education programs in civil defense and radiological monitoring. The Bureau is composed of the following three Divisions: Vocational and Technical Education, Adult Eduction Programs, and Manpower Development and Training.

BUREAU OF EDUCATION FOR THE HANDICAPPED. The Bureau assists States, colleges and universities, and other institutions and agencies in meeting the educational needs of the Nation's 5 million handicapped children who require special services. It administers programs such as support of training for teachers and other professional personnel; grants for research; financial aid to help States initiate, expand, and improve their resources; and media services and captioned films for the deaf. It includes the following three Divisions: Educational Services, Training Programs, and Research.

BUREAU OF HIGHER EDUCATION. The Bureau administers support and assistance programs directed to higher education. It includes the following five Divisions: Student Financial Aid, University Programs, Academic Facilities, College Support, and Student Special Services.

INSTITUTE OF INTERNATIONAL STUDIES. The Institute assists in the improvement and expansion of American educational resources for international studies and services. To this end it establishes policies for and coordinates and administers the Office of Education international programs and activities which stimulate and support exchange, training, and research. It is composed of the Divisions of Foreign Studies, International Exchange and Training, and the International Services and Research Staff.

THE NATIONAL CENTER FOR EDUCATIONAL RESEARCH AND DEVELOPMENT. The Center is responsible for administration of the Office of Education's program to improve education through support for research and related activities conducted outside the Office. It includes the following four Divisions: Elementary and Secondary Education Research, Higher Education Research, Comprehensive and Vocational Education Research, and Educational Laboratories.

NATIONAL CENTER FOR EDUCATIONAL STATISTICS. The Center is responsible for developing the statistical program for the Office of Education, coordinating the information-gathering activities for all programs, and for performing special analyses of and disseminating the statistical data so gathered. It is composed of the following three Divisions: Survey Operations, Statistical Information and Studies, and Survey Planning and Analysis.

NATIONAL CENTER FOR EDUCATIONAL COMMUNICATION. The Center is responsible for developing an Office of Education Program for dissemination of new ideas and practices in education. It pursues this aim by publishing a wide range of information on new research and new practices in education. It also actively advocates and encourages innovation in educational institutions by providing information and technical assistance. It includes the following two Divisions: Practice Improvement and Information Resources.

THE OFFICE OF PROGRAM PLANNING AND EVALUATION. The Office has primary responsibility for the planning and evaluation of overall Office of Education programs. It also provides guidance and coordination for bureaus and staff offices in establishing their objectives and for their program planning and evaluation.

BUREAU OF EDUCATIONAL PERSONNEL DEVELOPMENT. The Bureau administers the Education Professions Development Act of 1967 (except Part E—Training Programs for Higher Education Personnel). Through programs of financial assistance and technical and professional advice to educational institutions and agencies, the Bureau endeavors to improve the quality of teaching and help meet critical shortages of adequately trained educational personnel. It consists of the following five Divisions: Assessment and Coordination, Program Resources, College Programs, the Teacher Corps, and School Programs.

BUREAU OF LIBRARIES AND EDUCATIONAL TECHNOLOGY. The Bureau administers grants to States for the development and construction of public library facilities, and for acquisition of library resources. It also administers grants for educational television broadcasting, facilities, and provides technical assistance in the area of educational technology. It includes the following two Divisions: Library Programs and Educational Technology.

3.4 Commissioners of education

Ever since its establishment in 1867, the Office of Education has been directed by a commissioner of education. Henry Barnard, who was the main pioneer in the establishment of the Office, was the first to serve as commissioner.

"The U. S. Commissioner of Education is the chief education officer of the Federal Government, responsible for formulating educational policy and coordinating educational activities at the national level."[14]

The commissioner is appointed by the President with the consent of the Senate. Apparently there has never been an instance in which the Senate has failed to confirm the President's appointment of commissioner of education. Even in 1971, when the President's appointment of Sidney P. Marland faced stiff opposition from AFL-CIO, AFT, and other labor groups, the appointment was promptly approved by the Senate.

The tenures of office for the commissioners have varied greatly. Some have held office for very brief periods, whereas others have served for relatively long periods. Nineteen different men have held the office of United States Commissioner of Education. This may indicate a rather rapid turnover during a period of slightly more than a century. It should be realized, however, that several of the changes in office have been due to the custom of the commissioner, as it is with the secretaries of the various departments, to tender his resignation with the incoming of a different party administration.

COMMISSIONERS OF EDUCATION

Commissioner	Tenure
Henry Barnard	1867 to 1870
John Eaton	1870 to 1886
N. H. R. Dawson	1886 to 1889
William T. Harris	1889 to 1906
Elmer E. Brown	1906 to 1911
Philander P. Claxton	1911 to 1921
John James Tigert	1921 to 1928
William John Cooper	1929 to 1933
George F. Zook	1933 to 1934
John W. Studebaker	1934 to 1948

14 *Handbook Office of Education,* p. 7.

Earl James McGrath	1949 to 1953
Lee M. Thurston	1953 to 1953
Samuel Miller Brownell	1953 to 1956
Lawrence G. Derthick	1956 to 1961
Sterling M. McMurrin	1961 to 1962
Francis Keppel	1962 to 1965
Harold Howe II	1965 to 1968
James E. Allen, Jr.	1969 to 1970
Sidney P. Marland	1971 to ——

3.5 Dissatisfaction with the "Establishment"

Frequently certain objectionable acts of the executive branch prompt educators and others to renew their demands for a "shakeup" in the establishment. A statement by Forrest E. Conner, former Executive Secretary of the American Association of School Administrators, is illustrative. Contending the firing of Commissioner Allen typifies the low priority assigned to public education by the White House, Conner issued the following proposal:

It seems high time that the priority which American people have placed upon education in this country be reflected in the upper echelons of federal Government. The AASA along with many other of the large education-related organizations of this country have long advocated the establishment of a cabinet post of Secretary of Education and Manpower Development in order to give education its proper priority among the domestic needs of this country. The events of the past few days have brought that need and these priorities into sharp focus to the point where every person whether concerned citizen or educator should insist on a separate cabinet post for education and the accompanying importance in the domestic scene which it would typify.[18]

---

[18] "A Statement." Forrest E. Connor, Executive Secretary, AASA. *Hot Line*, July, 1970, p. 2.

It is doubtful, however, that an independent Department of Education would assure permanence of personnel, as was evidenced in 1970 when several secretaries of departments were ousted from their cabinet posts.

Another authority in school administration, Calvin Grieder, poses these questions:

> Can the federal government best serve public education by *supplanting* the 50 state education departments—as it seems determined to do—or by *assisting* the states, and through them the community school districts which actually operate the schools? Is it too much to hope that USOE will return to the service for which it was created, and give up trying increasingly to shape and control education?

In elaborating on these queries, Grieder says:

> It looks as though there is no longer to be even a pretense of the federal government's being a "junior partner" in American education. This is a sad change, for the state education systems need the counsel, the financial help, and the research and statistical services that the federal government can furnish. And of course the nation must rely on the states to carry on the vast and far-flung American school system. The very thought of the government's controlling and then administering it is appalling.[16]

No person is in a more favorable position to elucidate on the shortcomings and potentialities of the Office of Education than is its Commissioner. Consequently the Commissioner of Education is called upon by Public Law 91-230 to discuss the "condition of education in the nation" in his Annual Report to the Congress. Some of Commissioner Marland's observations with respect to the federal role of the office were expressed in his 1971 Report as follows:

> I believe the Federal role in education should be one

---

[16] Calvin Grieder, "USOE Pushes for Federal Control of Public Schools." *Nation's Schools*, September, 1970, p. 14.

of increasing the effectiveness of the human and financial resources of our schools, colleges, and universities. The present overall level of Federal assistance to education is something less than seven percent of our total investment. I envision the Federal share rising eventually to three or four times that level.

Most of all, I ask that the OE provide national leadership. Services, yes; supporting funds, yes. But I hold that this Office, made up of nearly 3,000 people must have a larger and more effective role. If our situation changes over the next year or two, as I hope it will, and we are able to diminish substantially our preoccupation with administration and paperwork, hundreds of OE staff members will be freed to bring leadership, technical assistance and stimulation to the States and localities. The dedicated, creative, and talented people who staff this Office will be instantly available to help where the problem is, whether it be a question of racial discrimination, curriculum, improved ways to teach, introduction of new technology, evaluation, or whatever. This Office will then be what it has long desired to be, a respectful and willing companion to the States and communities in serving the educational needs of the Nation.[17]

On another occasion Commissioner Marland expressed more plans for improving efficiency and effectiveness of the Office. In an interview he said:

We have placed high emphasis on planning and management in the regrouping of our top staff. We will greatly simplify present administrative procedures through which program support and formula grant funds are distributed to states, communities and institutions. Some of this improvement will necessarily be contingent upon new legislation, such as the grants consolidation actions implicit in special revenue-sharing legislation.[18]

[17] S. P. Marland, Jr., "The Condition of Education in the Nation." *American Education*, April, 1971, p. 5.
[18] "USOE's Marland Asks Realignment of Federal Education Priorities." *Nation's Schools*, April, 1971, p. 37.

In 1970 President Nixon sent Congress a proposal for a National Institute of Education to serve as a focal point for research and experimentation in education. For a year the proposal lay dormant. With the appointment of a new leader in the OE, however, the proposal was revived and given congressional consideration because:

> . . . with each passing year it becomes more apparent that mass public education in the United States is in trouble, and Congress is becoming more receptive to the idea that new approaches may be necessary. The biggest problem here is that the programs now being widely branded as failures were the proud achievements of Congress only a few years ago, and among Congressmen, as among human beings generally, the willingness to admit failure is not universal.[19]

There are those who believe that much of the criticism launched against the federal government's participation in public education is caused by prejudice and misunderstanding. In an attempt to enlighten the public as to the federal government's true role in public education, the official organ of the U. S. Office of Education, *American Education*, plans to devote space in forthcoming issues to that purpose, as stated:

> So that those in the field can better know and understand the capabilities and limitations of the Federal partner, we propose to use this space in following issues to explain the structure and some of the more vital operation of the Office of Education. Many teachers and school administrators visualize the Office as a massive concrete pile, veined with hallways which are lined with doors promiscuously marked "Bureau," "Division," "Branch," or "Center" and behind which faceless people shuffle papers and push computer buttons. Actually, education in Washington was organization and real people. It is

---

[19] "The Proposed National Institute of Education." *School Management*, April, 1971, p. 4.

important to divulge this. Only partners who have a complete understanding of one another's strengths and weaknesses are able to move with confidence and direction toward this goal.[20]

---

[20] "From the Editor." *American Education*, January-February, 1971, inside front cover.

Chapter 4

JUDICIAL BRANCH (FEDERAL COURTS) AND THE SCHOOL

As far as schools are concerned, more public attention has been focused on the judicial branch of the federal government in recent decades than on either of the other two branches. Also more criticism has been launched against this branch of government because of the manner and degree in which it has assumed its constitutional obligations for the protection of rights and liberties in school situations. Before carrying the criticism of the federal judiciary to extremes it might be well to give some attention to (1) the system of federal courts as provided for in the Constitution, (2) the processes by which the courts carry out their constitutional mandate, and (3) the most pertinent decisions on cases involving school matters which have been carried to the highest court in the land.

4.1   System of federal courts

Article III, Section 1 of the Constitution of the United States provides that the "judicial Power of the United States, shall be vested in one supreme Court and in such inferior Courts as the Congress may from time to time ordain and establish."

This constitutional provision places the Supreme Court at the pinnacle in the judicial hierarchy as the ultimate repository of judicial power. As its title implies it is "supreme" as the judicial authority.

Immediately below the Supreme Court in authority are the courts of appeals (circuit courts). The United States is divided into 10 judicial circuits, plus the District of Columbia as an additional circuit. In each of these circuits is a United States court of appeals. Each of the states is assigned to one of the circuits.

The purpose of these courts is to relieve the Supreme Court of considering all appeals in cases originally decided by the federal trial courts. They are empowered to review all final decisions of district courts, except in very rare instances in which the law provides for the direct review by the Supreme Court.

Next in line of authority immediately below the appellate courts are the United States district courts. These courts are the trial courts with general federal jurisdiction. Each state has at least one district court, while some of the larger states have as many as four. Altogether there are 88 district courts serving the 50 states and the District of Columbia.

"Cases from the district courts are reviewed by the United States courts of appeals, except that injunction orders of special 3-judge district courts, certain decisions holding acts of Congress unconstitutional, and certain criminal decisions may be appealed directly to the Supreme Court."[1]

4.2   Jurisdiction of the Supreme Court

Since 1789, when the Constitution was ratified, Congress has made a variety of "exceptions" and "regulations" governing the appellate jurisdiction of the Supreme Court. This is an important congressional power for the reason that while Congress cannot expand or extend the jurisdiction of the Supreme Court beyond the limits set by the Constitution, it can impose restrictions and requirements within the limits set by the Constitution.

In broad terms, the Supreme Court is given jurisdiction by Congress to review: (1) all cases in lower federal courts, and (2) all cases in state courts in which there is involved

[1] *United States Government Organization Manual 1966-67*, p. 47.

a question of the meaning or effect of a federal statute or a constitutional provision.

Before reviewing school cases which have been decided by the Supreme Court, consideration should be given to the procedural methods by which the vast number of federal and state cases which are potentially appealable are sifted by the Supreme Court in order to reduce the number of cases actually brought before the Court. There are two methods: (1) the *writ of certiorari*; and (2) *appeal*.

The *writ of certiorari* is an order issued by a higher tribunal to an inferior body ordering it to certify up to it the record in a case before the inferior court. Certiorari is obtained in the case of the United States Supreme Court upon petition to the Court by the parties.

Appeal is the second method of obtaining review by the Supreme Court of a lower court case. This is handled by a party filing a jurisdictional statement which sets forth the reasons why the case qualifies for Supreme Court review and why it has sufficient merit to warrant further hearings by the Supreme Court.

By these procedural techniques the Supreme Court gives preliminary scrutiny to every case coming to it to determine whether further action by the Court is warranted. To illustrate how effective this system is, it is noted that approximately 87 percent of all cases submitted to the Supreme Court are disposed of without argument.

In the early stages of our educational development, state educational legislation and administrative policies did not often clash with provisions of the federal Constitution. However, with the greatly-increased enrollments, expanded and extended school programs, and the manifest concern for human rights, there has been considerable state legislation and local administrative practices which have come in conflict with the provisions of the federal Constitution—particularly the First Amendment and the Fourteenth Amendment.

Consequently the instances in which the United States Supreme Court has been called upon for rulings in school cases have become more frequent. Keesecker, in 1949, reported no Supreme Court decisions on education during the 20-year period 1789-1808; only *one* for the period 1809-28; *one* for 1829-48; *one* for 1849-68; *none* for 1869-88; *three* for 1889-1908; *five* for 1908-28; and *fourteen* for 1928-48.[2] At the rate the Court has been rendering decisions on school cases recently, and the growing controversy over human rights, it is quite likely that there will be more court decisions during the current 30-year span, ending in 1978, than during the entire 170-year period preceding.

The following Supreme Court cases selected for review are illustrative but not exhaustive. Many more cases could have been added had all those with educational implications been included. Moreover, a number of cases have been omitted because they deal only with situations in higher institutions which are not within the scope of this publication. The cases which are referred to here do provide substantial evidence that the United States Supreme Court is assuming an increasing role in shaping educational policy and practice throughout the nation.

4.3 U. S. Supreme Court and racial segregation

Plessy v. *Ferguson* (1896) (Louisiana).[3] This case does not deal directly with a school situation. The many school cases in which it is cited, however, give evidence of its applicability to school cases in which segregation of the races is involved. The case concerned the constitutionality of an act of the general assembly of the state of Louisiana, passed in 1890, providing for "equal but separate accommodations for the white and colored races, by providing two or more passenger coaches for each passenger train. . . ."

Plessy, a Negro, violated the act by refusing to leave a coach designated for whites. Upon his arrest he challenged the constitutionality of the act because it forbade admission solely because of color, which allegedly was violative of the Fourteenth Amendment. The Supreme Court upheld the

---

[2] Ward K. Keesecker, "Supreme Court Decisions Affecting Education," *School Life*, XXXVII (February, 1949), 4.

[3] 163 US 537, 41 LEd 256, 16 SCt 1138 (1896).

constitutionality of the state law with the claim that it was necessary to insure absolute equality for both races before the law.

Noteworthy in this case is the strong dissent by Justice Harlan in which he predicted "the judgment this day rendered will, in time, prove to be quite as pernicious as the decision made by this tribunal in the *Dred Scott* case." History has largely given some confirmation to Justice Harlan's prophesy.

The "separate but equal" concept prevailed for over a half century in school legislation and policy, after which it began to crumble. In 1954 it was completely abandoned by the Supreme Court as a legal principle.

Cumming v. *Board of Education* (1899) (Georgia).[4] In this case the complaint was made by plaintiffs that the Richmond County Board of Education, Georgia, used the funds in its hands to assist in maintaining a high school for white children, without providing a similar school for colored children. The state court did not deem the board's action in suspending the high school for colored children for economic reasons a sufficient reason for not permitting continuance of the white high school.

The Supreme Court upheld the ruling of the state court. In so doing it placed a somewhat different interpretation on the Fourteenth Amendment than those of today, as is indicated by its statement:

> While we admit that the benefits and burdens of public taxation must be shared by citizens without discrimination against any clan on account of their race, the education of the people in schools maintained by state taxation is a matter belonging to the respective States, and any interference on the part of Federal authority with the management of such schools cannot be justified except in case of a clear and unmistakable disregard of rights secured by the supreme law of the land.[5]

---

[4] 175 US 528, 44 LEd 262, 20 SCt 197 (1899).

[5] *Cumming* v. *County Board of Education* (Ga), 175 US 528, 44 LEd 262, 20 SCt 197 (1899).

Alston v. *School Board of Norfolk* (1940) (Virginia).[6] The issue in this case had to do with inequality between salary schedules for white and Negro teachers. Alston, a Negro teacher, contended that the inequality of the salary schedules violated the "due process" and "equal protection" clauses of the Fourteenth Amendment.

A United States district court dismissed the case with the contention that Alston waived his constitutional rights by having signed a contract for a specified amount of money. The circuit court of appeals, however, ruled that the discrimination against Alston was unconstitutional, that his rights were infringed upon, and that he had not waived his rights to sue by signing a contract to teach. The United States Supreme Court refused a petition for certiorari, thus affirming the circuit court of appeals.

Brown v. *Board of Education* (1954) (Kansas, South Carolina, Virginia, and Delaware).[7] On May 17, 1954, one of the most spectacular and significant judicial decisions of the century was handed down, without dissent, by the United States Supreme Court. In essence, the court held that segregation of white and Negro children in the public schools solely on the basis of race, denied to Negro children the equal protection of the laws guaranteed by the Fourteenth Amendment.

Following are several pertinent excerpts from the opinion of the court delivered by Chief Justice Warren:

(1) The history of the Fourteenth Amendment is inconclusive as to its intended effect on public education.

(2) The question presented in these cases must be determined, not on the basis of conditions existing when the Fourteenth Amendment was adopted, but in the light of the full development of public education and its present place in American life throughout the Nation.

(3) Where a State has undertaken to provide an opportunity for an education in its public schools, such an oppor-

---

[6] 311 US 693, 85 LEd 448, 61 SCt 75 (1940).
[7] 347 US 483, 98 LEd 873, 74 SCt 686 (1954).

tunity is a right which must be made available to all on equal terms.

(4) Segregation of children in public schools solely on the basis of race deprives children of the minority groups of equal educational opportunities, even though the physical facilities and other "tangible" factors may be equal.

(5) The "separate but equal" doctrine adopted in *Plessy* v. *Ferguson*, 163 US 537, has no place in the field of public education.

Brown v. *Board of Education* (1955) (Kansas, South Carolina, Virginia, and Delaware).[8] This case had to do with the implementation of the *Brown* decision in 1954. Because of the nationwide importance of the decision, the court invited the attorney general of the United States and the attorneys general of all states requiring or permitting racial discrimination in public education to present their views on the question.

After hearing a number of briefs the Court came to a decision and remanded the cases to district courts "to take such proceedings and enter such orders and decrees consistent with their opinion as are necessary and proper to admit to public schools on a nondiscriminatory basis with all deliberate speed the parties to these cases."

Cooper v. *Aaron* (1958) (Arkansas).[9] This case developed from the claim and action of the governor and the legislature of Arkansas that "they are not bound" by the Supreme Court in the holding in *Brown* v. *Board of Education.*[9a]

The state officials suspended the action of the Little Rock School Board which planned to integrate the public schools of that city. The district court upheld the action of the state officials, but that decision was reversed by the court of appeals. The case was finally appealed to the United States Supreme Court where it was ruled that a state cannot nullify directly or indirectly the supreme law of the land. The court

---

[8] 349 US 294, 99 LEd 1083, 75 SCt 753 (1955).
[9] 358 US 1, 3 LEd(2d) 5, 78 SCt 1401 (1958).
[9a] *Supra,* n 7.

emphasized that the state is primarily responsible for public education, but its actions must be within the legal limits of the federal Constitution.

Griffin v. *School Board* (1964) (Virginia).[10] In an attempt to circumvent the *Brown* decision, the state of Virginia amended its constitution to authorize the general assembly and local governmental bodies to appropriate funds to aid students to attend public or nonpublic sectarian schools other than those owned by the state.

Later the general assembly met in special session to enact legislation to close any public schools which were integrated, to cut off state funds in these schools, and to pay tuition grants to pupils in secular private schools. This legislation was declared unconstitutional by the court of appeals of Virginia.

Then the general assembly abandoned the "massive resistance" approach for "freedom of choice" by enacting a tuition grant program. At the same time the compulsory attendance law was also repealed.

In June of 1959 the United States court of appeals for the Fourth District directed the federal district court to enjoin discrimination in Prince Edward County, whereupon the supervisors of the county refused to levy taxes. Consequently the schools remained closed until the Supreme Court decision in 1964.

The United States Supreme Court ruled that the closing of Prince Edward County schools while other public schools of Virginia remained open was a violation of the state Constitution. The case was remanded to the district court with direction to enter a decree which would guarantee the petitioners the kind of educational opportunity afforded elsewhere.

4.4   U. S. Supreme Court and religion

Quick Bear v. *Leupp* (1908) (South Dakota).[11] The complaint in this case was brought by Ruben Quick Bear and

---

[10] 377 US 218, 12 LEd(2d) 256, 84 SCt 1226 (1964).
[11] 210 US 50, 52 LEd 954, 28 SCt 690 (1908).

Ralph Eagle Feathers in behalf of the Sioux Indians on the Rosebud Agency in South Dakota. The suit was brought against Francis Leupp because of his desire to make a contract with a Catholic Mission for education of Indian children.

The objection to the use of funds for sectarian education was based upon an Act of 1897 contracted with them by the federal government: "It is hereby declared to be the settled policy of the government to hereafter make no appropriation whatever for education in any sectarian school."[12]

The Supreme Court ruled that this statute must be sustained only if the money is ". . . raised by taxation from persons of all creeds and faiths, or none at all, and appropriated gratuitously for the purpose of education among the Indians, and not from 'tribal funds' which belong to the Indians themselves. . . ." Since the money was from tribal funds it was not considered a gratuitous grant and was therefore constitutional.

Pierce v. *Society of Sisters of Holy Names* (1925) (Oregon).[13] One of the most influential decisions in perpetuating nonpublic schools was that handed down by the United States Supreme Court in the Oregon compulsory public school attendance case. The litigation in this case grew out of an Oregon law enacted in 1922, which required children between the ages of eight and sixteen to attend public schools. The obvious purpose of the law was to prohibit private elementary schools. The Supreme Court referred to the provisions of the Fourteenth Amendment as nullifying legislation designed to deprive any person of life, liberty, or property without due process of law.

The notable decision in the Oregon case demonstrates the constitutional protection of parents' right to send their children to schools of their own choice. The classic statement of the court is forceful and has been generally unchallenged:

---

12 30 Stat at L 62, 79 Chap. 3.
13 268 US 510, 69 LEd 1070, 45 SCt 571, 39 ALR 468 (1925).

The fundamental theory of liberty upon which all governments of this Union repose excludes any general power of the state to standardize its children by forcing them to accept instruction from public teachers only. The child is not the mere creature of the state; those who nurture him and direct his destiny have the right, coupled with the high duty, to recognize and prepare him for additional obligations.[14]

Cochran v. *Louisiana State Board of Education* (1930) (Louisiana).[15] This case and that of *Borden* v. *Louisiana State Board of Education*, 123 So 655, are companion cases. The decision of the United States Supreme Court applied to both. They are generally credited as originating the "child benefit theory" in the expenditure of public funds to sectarian schools.

These Louisiana cases concerned the legality of expending public funds to assist nonpublic schools. The litigation in the cases followed the passage of a statute which provided for free textbooks, at public cost, to the children of the state, regardless of whether they attended nonpublic or public schools. The legality of the statute was challenged shortly after its enactment. In defending the statute, the state court made the following observations: (1) the law did not provide for the purchase of books for sectarian schools; (2) because it provided for free books for the children of the state, the law was obviously enacted for the benefit of the children and the "resulting benefit of the state"; (3) the schools are not the beneficiaries of the statute; and (4) the books furnished by the state are not sectarian books. The United States Supreme Court sustained the validity of the statute and approved the theory of the state court.

Minersville School District v. *Gobitis* (1940) (Pennsylvania).[16] The litigation in this case concerned the requirement of the flag salute as a condition for school attendance. The Jehovah's Witnesses protested the regulation because

---

[14] *Ibid.*

[15] 281 US 370, 74 LEd 913, 50 SCt 335 (1930).

[16] 310 US 586, 84 LEd 375, 60 SCt 1010, 127 ALR 1493 (1940).

their religion forbids paying homage to the flag. They contended that the flag salute was unconstitutional as applied to them because their religious belief prohibits them from "bowing down before any graven image."

After receiving an adverse decision from the state courts, Gobitis appealed the case to the United States Supreme Court. The Supreme Court upheld the lower court by ruling that it was within the rights of a school board to require the flag salute as a means of achieving a feeling of national unity. The court emphasized that the requirement did not infringe, without due process, the liberty guaranteed by the Fourteenth Amendment. According to this ruling, individual freedom could be subordinated to national unity.

West Virginia State Board of Education v. *Barnette* (1943).[17] This case developed from a regulation of the state board of education in West Virginia requiring the flag salute in all the public schools of the state. Pupils who disobeyed the regulation were subject to dismissal from the school and a penalty for "unlawful absences."

The constitutionality of the regulation was challenged. When the case finally reached the United States Supreme Court, the high tribunal ruled in favor of Barnette, a Jehovah's Witness, thereby reversing the decision of the *Gobitis* case, with three dissenting justices. In substance the Supreme Court held that a school board, in compelling pupils to salute and pledge allegiance to the American flag transcends constitutional limitations on its power and "invades the sphere of intellect and spirit which it is the purpose of the First Amendment to our Constitution to reserve from all official control."

Everson v. *Board of Education of Ewing Township* (1947) (New Jersey).[18] This is one of the landmark cases dealing with the issue of expending public funds to assist nonpublic schools. For at least a quarter-century, the lower courts had been in hopeless conflict concerning the validity of statutory provisions for pupil transportation to nonpublic schools at

---

17 319 US 624, 87 LEd 1628, 63 SCt 1178, 147 ALR 674 (1943).
18 330 US 1, 91 LEd 711, 67 SCt 504, 168 ALR 1392 (1947).

public expense. Because of the differences in state constitutions and statutes, and the various interpretations
placed upon them by the state courts, the issue was clouded.
There still is considerable doubt regarding the matter, despite the "five to four" ruling of the United States Supreme
Court that the use of public funds by school districts in New
Jersey for the transportation of children to nonpublic schools
was not in violation of any provision of the Constitution of
the United States.

The line of reasoning followed in the New Jersey bus case
was the same as that previously manifested in the Louisiana
textbook cases. It was argued that the public appropriations
for transportation of pupils to nonpublic schools was for the
benefit of the children rather than the school. This trend
of judicial reasoning might well encourage certain nonpublic
schools to pleas for the extension of public expenditures to
cover costs of textbooks, transportation, school lunches,
school health services, and the like. It is well recognized that
public assumption of any phase of nonpublic school expenses
reduces the costs which would otherwise have to be borne by
the nonpublic schools themselves.

McCollum v. Board of Education (1948) (Illinois).[19] This
is one of the most significant and oft-quoted cases concerning
religious instruction in the public schools. The case had its
beginning when a patron of the Champaign, Illinois, schools
sought a writ of mandamus to compel the school board to
discontinue the teaching of religion in the schools and to
prohibit the use of schoolrooms for that purpose. It was
charged by the plaintiffs that, since these were separate classes
for Protestant, Catholics, and Jews, the program amounted
to sectarian religious instruction, which violated the Fourteenth Amendment to the United States Constitution.

The trial court found the system of conducting religious
classes valid on the grounds that (1) the program was voluntary, (2) the use of schoolrooms for the classes did not
amount to financial support, and (3) the teachers were not
paid out of public school funds. On appeal to the Supreme

---

19 333 US 203, 92 LEd 649, 68 SCt 461, 2 ALR(2d) 1338 (1948).

Court of Illinois, the decision of the trial court was affirmed. On further appeal, however, the United States Supreme Court held that the mingling of religious education in the public schools during public school time, as was done in the Champaign city schools, was in conflict with the First Amendment to the United States Constitution and therefore invalid.

Zorach v. *Clauson* (1952) (New York).[20] The public schools of New York City devised a program of released time, patterned somewhat differently from the one involved in the *McCollum* case. Nevertheless it was litigated promptly with the charge that the school served as "a crutch" on which the churches leaned for support of their religious training.

The New York court did not agree with the allegation, and justified its decision upholding the program on the grounds that, in the New York City program there was neither supervision nor approval of religious teachers and no solicitation of pupils or distribution of cards. The religious instruction had to be outside the school building and grounds. There could be no announcement of any kind in the public schools relative to the program, and no comment by any principal or teacher on the attendance or nonattendance of any pupil.

The state court's decision was appealed to the United States Supreme Court where it was affirmed. It is significant to note, however, that three of the nine judges dissented vigorously.

Doremus v. *Board of Education* (1952) (New Jersey).[21] A New Jersey statute in question provided that "at least five verses taken from that portion of the Holy Bible known as the Old Testament shall be read, or caused to be read, without comment in each public-school classroom. . . ."

The constitutionality of the statute was challenged with the allegation that it violated both the First Amendment and the Fourteenth Amendment to the federal Constitution. The Supreme Court of New Jersey disagreed with the allegation. The state court's opinion not only upheld the constitution-

---

20 343 US 306, 96 LEd 954, 72 SCt 679 (1952).
21 342 US 429, 96 LEd 475, 72 SCt 394 (1952).

ality of the disputed statute but commented on its appropriateness.

The case was appealed to the United States Supreme Court where it was dismissed for want of jurisdiction, thus affirming the decision of the state court.

Tudor v. *Board of Education* (1954) (New Jersey).[22] This case arose in New Jersey, where at the request of Gideons International, the school board adopted a resolution permitting the distribution of Bibles to pupils. Even though the resolution stipulated that the Bibles would be given only to pupils who requested them and whose parents indicated in writing that they desired their children to have the Bibles, it met with opposition by the Catholics and Jews. A Jewish parent charged sectarianism because the Bible in question was the King James version. The state court agreed that the Bible was sectarian and that its distribution was a violation of both the federal and New Jersey Constitutions.

In appeal, the case was carried to the United States Supreme Court but was returned without further argument. The court's denial of a petition for a writ of certiorari was tantamount to affirmation of the state court's ruling.

Engel v. *Vitale* (1962) (New York).[23] The state board of regents composed a brief prayer which they recommended for the public schools of New York: "Almighty God, we acknowledge our dependence upon Thee, and we beg Thy blessings upon us, our parents, our teachers and our Country."

Shortly after the practice of reciting the regents' prayer was adopted by the school district of New Hyde Park, the parents of ten pupils brought action in a state court insisting that this official prayer in the public schools was contrary to the beliefs, religions, or religious practices of both themselves and their children. They further contended that the district's regulation ordering the recitation of this particular prayer was a violation of the First Amendment of the federal Constitution, which was "made applicable to the State of

---

[22] 348 US 816, 99 LEd 644, 75 SCt 25 (1954).
[23] 370 US 421, 8 LEd(2d) 601, 82 SCt 1261, 86 ALR(2d) (1962).

New York by the Fourteenth Amendment of the said Constitution."

The recitation of the regents' prayer as required by the school district was held legal by the Court of Appeals of New York State, whereupon it was appealed to the United States Supreme Court. In a six to one decision it was finally ruled by the Supreme Court that the prayer was unconstitutional. Justice Black, writing for the majority, noted that since all parties in the case agreed that the prayer was religious in nature, its use in the public schools was a practice wholly inconsistent with the Establishment Clause of the First Amendment to the Constitution. He stated: "It is no part of the business of government to compose official prayers for any group of the American people to recite as a part of a religious program carried on by government." Public schools are governmental institutions.

In Pennsylvania, the 1963 decision in *Abington School District* v. *Schempp*[24] also applied to *Murray* v. *Curlett*[25] a Maryland case. In both, the question was the same—the constitutionality of Bible reading in the public schools.

The litigated Pennsylvania law originally stipulated that: "At least ten verses from the Holy Bible shall be read, without comment, at the opening of each public school on each school day, by the teacher in charge. . . ." After the district court ruled against the statute, another sentence was added before it went to the Supreme Court for a ruling: "Any child shall be excused from such Bible reading, upon written request of his parents or his guardian."

The fact that the exemption clause was added to the statute did not deter the Supreme Court from declaring the law unconstitutional. On this point Justice Brennan stated:

The fact that some pupils, or theoretically all pupils, might be excused from attendance does not mitigate the obligatory nature of the ceremonies. The exercises are held in public school buildings, conducted by and under the authority of local school officials. Since the law re-

---

24 374 US 203, 10 LEd(2d) 844, 83 SCt 1560 (1963).
25 228 Md 239, 179 A(2d) 698 (1962).

quires the reading of the Holy Bible, it prefers the Christian religion. The record demonstrates that it was the intention of the state legislature to introduce a religious ceremony into the public schools of the Commonwealth.

Justice Clark, who wrote the majority opinion, stated: "The breach of neutrality that is today a trickling stream may all too soon become a raging torrent, and in the words of Madison: 'it is proper to take alarm at the first experiment on our liberties.' "

Immediately following the Supreme Court's decision in the New York prayer case, and while the Bible reading cases of Pennsylvania and Maryland were being litigated, the Florida State Supreme Court rendered a decision[26] which disregarded entirely judicial precedents of the United States Supreme Court.

The Florida court handed down a decision upholding the constitutionality of a statute that required teachers to read daily from the Holy Bible. The decision went further by approving several other educational practices with religious overtones.

After the United States Supreme Court decision in the Pennsylvania and Maryland cases, the Florida case was remanded to the Florida court for reconsideration. It refused to follow the reasoning of the United States Supreme Court, whereupon appeal was made to this high tribunal where it was declared that the Bible reading and prayers, as conducted in Dade County, were unconstitutional. As to other issues, besides Bible reading and prayers, the appeal was dismissed "for want of properly presented federal questions." These issues concerned baccalaureate services in the schools, a religious census among pupils, and a religious test for teachers.

4.5 U. S. Supreme Court and academic freedom

Meyer v. Nebraska (1923) (Nebraska).[27] This is the first United States Supreme Court decision affecting the cur-

---

[26] *Chamberlain v. Dade County Board of Public Instruction* (Fla), 377 US 402, 12 LEd(2d) 407, 84 SCt 1272 (1964).
[27] 262 US 390, 67 LEd 1042, 43 SCt 625 (1923).

riculum of a state school system. The factors leading up to the case indicate that, after World War I, a number of states enacted legislation prohibiting the teaching of German to nonpublic or public school pupils who had not completed the requirements of Grade VIII.

Although the courts of three states (Nebraska, Iowa, and Ohio) had sanctioned the legislation as a legitimate exercise of the police power, the Supreme Court ruled that the legislation was an arbitrary interference with the liberty of parents to control and educate their children, and with the liberty of teachers to pursue their lawful calling, and that it violated the liberty guaranteed by the Fourteenth Amendment to the Constitution of the United States.

Adler v. *Board of Education of City of New York* (1952) (New York).[28] This case arose from a challenge of New York legislation designed to keep subversive influences out of schools. The statute in question is generally referred to as the Feinberg law. It (1) charges the board of regents to enforce the law through necessary rules and regulations, (2) requires that the board make a list of organizations which, after inquiry, notice and hearing, are held to be subversive, and (3) requires of the board of regents to submit an annual report to the legislature on the measures taken under the law.

Irving Adler, with others, brought an action in Kings County Supreme Court to have the law declared invalid. That court granted the injunction sought. On appeal by the board of regents the state supreme court, appellate division, reversed the lower court, and this decision was subsequently affirmed by the New York Court of Appeals. Finally, Adler appealed to the United States Supreme Court with the contention that the Feinberg law and the board's rules under it abridged certain rights protected by the First Amendment.

The high court did not agree with Adler's contention. In upholding the disputed law and board regulation it said, in part, "A teacher works in a sensitive area in a school room. There he shapes the attitudes of young minds towards the

---

[28] 342 US 485, 96 LEd 517, 72 SCt 380 (1952).

society in which they live. In this, the state has a vital concern. It must preserve the integrity of the schools."

Beilan v. *Board of Education* (1958) (Pennsylvania).[29] This case concerned a teacher by the name of Beilan who had been in the Philadelphia schools for 22 years. His superintendent who claimed to have information reflecting on Beilan's loyalty, inquired as to whether or not he (Beilan) had been an officer of the Communist Political Association. Upon the advice of his attorney, Beilan stated that he would not answer that question or others of that type, as was his privilege in accordance with the Fifth Amendment.

Beilan's refusal to answer was construed by the board to constitute "incompetency." Since the Pennsylvania statutes do not have a "catch-all" phrase such as "unbecoming conduct" as a reason for dismissing teachers, the Pennsylvania courts have, on several occasions, given a broad interpretation to the word "incompetency." When the appeal reached the Supreme Court, the dismissal of the teacher was upheld by a majority of the court. Three of the judges, including Chief Justice Warren, dissented.

Elfbrandt v. *Russell* (1966) (Arizona).[30] This case involved questions concerning the constitutionality of an Arizona act requiring an oath from state employees. The oath was of conventional pattern as to the support of the United States Constitution and the constitution of Arizona. The legislature, however, "put a gloss on the oath" by subjecting to perjury prosecution and loss of job any state employee who took the loyalty oath and "knowingly and wilfully becomes or remains a member of the Communist Party" or other organizations dedicated to overthrowing the state government. However, anyone who refused to sign was not subject to dismissal but could not be paid.

Petitioner, a teacher and a Quaker, "decided she could not in good conscience take the oath, not knowing what it meant. . . ." She and her husband, teachers in separate schools in

---

29 357 US 399, 2 LEd(2d) 1414, 78 SCt 1317 (1958).
30 86 SCt 1238 (1966).

Tucson, refused to sign but continued to teach without being paid for nearly five years.

The high court ruled in favor of the teacher. Justice Douglas, announcing the 5-4 decision declaring the 1961 Arizona loyalty-oath law cannot stand, said such a requirement "rests on the doctrine of 'guilt by association' which has no place here." In explaining the court's reasoning, Douglas stated further that the law suffered from "a constitutional infirmity," since it broadly covered membership in the Communist Party and similar organizations rather than "a specific intent to further the unlawful aim" of the organizations.

The dissenting opinion in this case is significant because of the fact that it was supported by 4 of the 9 judges. Speaking for the dissenters, Justice White said Arizona has the right to "prevent its employees from affiliating with the Communist Party or other organizations prepared to employ violent means to overthrow constitutional government."

Keyishian v. *Board of Regents of Univ. of N. Y.*, 87 S. Ct. 675 (1967) (New York). Up to the time of its adjournment in June 1967 this was the last case decided by the Supreme Court that had to do with academic freedom or any other issue concerning the public schools. It is a landmark decision in that it nullified the Feinberg Law which had been held constitutional in previous cases.

The appellants in this case were notified that failure to sign an affidavit stating they were not Communists would result in their dismissal from employment. Following dismissal the appellants brought action for declaratory and injunctive relief and a three-judge federal court held the program, under which they were dismissed to be constitutional. The United States Supreme Court, however, reversed this decision.

The Supreme Court held that New York statutory provisions making treasonable or seditious words or acts grounds for removal from public school systems or barring from employment in public schools any persons willfully advocating or teaching doctrine of forcible overthrow of government 'are unconstitutionally vague and violate First Amendment."

The dissenting opinion, written by Justice Clark, with the concurrence of Justice Harlan, Stewart, and White, indicates the lack of judicial unanimity on the issue. Justice Clark states, in part: "It is clear that the Feinberg Law, in which the Court found 'no infirmity' in 1952 has been given its death blow today. . . . No court has ever reached so far to destroy so much with so little."

The cases referred to above do not constitute all of those dealing with education. They are, however, the most significant of those affecting school policy at the elementary and secondary levels. They are indicative of the powerful force the federal judiciary exerts over the public schools throughout the nation.

Members of the Supreme Court are well aware of the authority and responsibility they must assume in formulating educational policy. This is reflected in the words of The Honorable Tom C. Clark, Associate Justice of the Supreme Court of the United States, who delivered the main address at the 46th annual meeting of the National Council for the Social Studies held in Cleveland:

In short, my view is that the judiciary is one—if not the most—powerful instrument in our governmental machinery. I ask you, reflect tonight, what force in American government has triggered a more tremendous exercise of governmental power in every field of public activity, including health, welfare, education, juvenile problems, and industrial and economic relations? What power has equally and as surely curbed the excesses of legislative action?[31]

---

[31] Tom C. Clark. "The Role of Law in the School Curriculum." *Social Education*. March, 1967. p. 186.

4.6   U. S. Supreme Court cases since 1967

Pickering v. *Board of Education* (1968) (Illinois).[32] The issue as to whether public school teachers have the constitutional right to express themselves on matters which are of public concern has frequently been litigated in the federal courts. One of the most significant cases pertaining to the issue originated in Illinois and went to the highest court in the land for final settlement.

Here the board dismissed a teacher for writing a letter which allegedly contained false statements, claiming that they damaged the reputations of board members and the school administrators.

The Court weighed the allegations of the board but rejected them as being inconsequential in a case where a teacher's right of free speech is involved. The rationale of the Court for its ruling is expressed, in part, by the following statement:

> . . . the question whether a school system requires additional funds is a matter of legitimate concern on which the judgment of the school administration, including the School Board, cannot, in a society that leaves such questions to popular vote be taken as conclusive. On such a question free and open debate is vital to informed decision-making by the electorate. Teachers are, as a class, the members of a community most likely to have informed and definite opinions as to how funds allotted to the opertion of the schools should be spent. Accordingly, it is essential that they be able to speak out freely on such questions without fear of retaliatory dismissal.[33]

Epperson v. *Arkansas*.[34] After being litigated in the state courts on numerous occasions, the issue concerning a teacher's right to teach evolution was finally carried to the United States Supreme Court.

---

[32] 391 US 563, 20 LEd(2d) 811, 88 SCt 1731 (1968).
[33] *Id.,* p. 1736.
[34] 393 US 97, 21 LEd(2d) 228, 89 SCt 266 (1968).

This case was instituted by a teacher seeking a declaration that the Arkansas statute was void, and enjoining the state and defendant officials from dismissing her for violation of the statute which aimed to prohibit the teaching of evolution. First the law was decreed unconstitutional by a chancery court in 1966. Then in 1967 the Supreme Court of Arkansas reversed the decision and held that the anti-evolution law is a valid exercise of the state's power to specify the curriculum in the public schools. Finally, however, the United States Supreme Court reversed the judgment of the Supreme Court of Arkansas by concluding: "Plainly, the law is contrary to the mandate of the First, and in violation of the Fourteenth Amendment to the Constitution."[35]

Green v. *County School Board of New Kent Co.* (1968) (Virginia).[36]

Raney v. *Board of Education of Gould School District* (1968) (Arkansas).[37]

Monroe v. *Board of Commissioners of Jackson* (1968) (Tennessee).[38]

The last segregation decisions during the Warren era were rendered in May 1968. They evolved from litigation over the question as to whether or not the "freedom of choice" plan was sufficient to meet the requirements for desegregating the public schools.

In some instances the "freedom of choice" plan was found to be an effective tool in developing a unitary school system; in other instances it was found that the plan did not constitute adequate compliance.

The Court ruled, in the Virginia case, that "whatever plan is adopted will require evaluation in practice, and the Court should retain jurisdiction until it is clear that state-imposed segregation has been completely removed."[39]

---

[35] *Id.*, p. 273.
[36] 391 US 430, 20 LEd(2d) 716, 88 SCt 1689 (1968).
[37] 391 US 443, 20 LEd(2d) 727, 88 SCt 1697 (1968).
[38] 391 US 450, 20 LEd(2d) 733, 88 SCt 1700 (1968).
[39] Supra n. 36, p. 1695.

In considering the effectiveness of the "freedom of choice" plan, the Court made the following concluding statement:

> Where it offers real promise of aiding a desegregation program to effectuate conversion of a state-imposed dual system there might be no objection to allowing such a device to prove itself in operation. On the other hand, if there are reasonably available other ways, such for illustration as zoning, promising speedier and more effective conversion to a unitary, nonracial school system "freedom of choice" must be held unacceptable.[40]

Board of Education of Central School District No. 1 v. *Allen* (1968) (New York).[41]

Thirty-eight years after *Cochran,* another textbook case was brought before the United States Supreme Court for settlement. The latter case differed from the earlier one in that the issue had to do with the *lending* of the textbooks rather than the actual *giving.* "A law of the State of New York requires local public school authorities to lend textbooks free of charge to all students in grades seven through 12; students attending private schools are included."[42]

The thrust of the case, then, was whether the statute was in conflict with the First and Fourteenth Amendments to the Constitution, because it authorizes the loan of textbooks to students attending parochial schools.

In holding that the law *was not* in violation of the Constitution, the High Court applied the test of constitutionality laid down in *Everson* v. *Board of Education,* that "to withdraw the strictures of the Establishment Clause there must be a secular legislative purpose and a primary effect that neither advances nor inhibits religion."[43]

---

[40] *Id.,* p. 1696.
[41] 392 US 236, 20 LEd(2d) 1060, 88 SCt 1923 (1968).
[42] *Id.,* p. 1924.
[43] *Id.,* p. 1926.

It is significant to note that the major portion of the report for this case covers the vigorous dissents of three Justices—Black, Douglas, and Fortas.

Tinker v. *Des Moines Independent Community School District* (1969) (Iowa).[44] Symbolic expression in opposing certain governmental activities has triggered a number of court cases litigated in the federal courts. The most publicized of such cases arose when a group of adults and students in Des Moines met and decided to publicize their objections to the hostilities in Vietnam and their support for a truce by wearing black armbands. Contrary to a board policy, the Tinker children returned to school with armbands displayed, and were accordingly suspended.

In considering an injunction restraining the school officials from disciplining the offending pupils, the District Court concluded that "the action of the school authorities was reasonable because it was based upon their fear of a disturbance from wearing the armbands." That decision, however, was reversed by the United States Supreme Court in 1969.

The Supreme Court upheld the pupil's symbolic expression by application of the Free Speech Clause of the First Amendment and stated:

. . . the wearing of armbands in the circumstances of this case was entirely divorced from actually or potentially disruptive conduct by those participating in it. It was closely akin to "pure speech" which, we have repeatedly held, is entitled to comprehensive protection under the First Amendment.[45]

. . . In our system, students may not be regarded as closed-circuit recipients of only that which the State chooses to communicate. They may not be confined to the expression of those sentiments that are officially approved. In the absence of a specific showing of constitu-

---

[44] 393 US 503, 21 LEd(2d) 731, 89 SCt 733 (1969).
[45] *Id.*, p. 736.

tionally valid reasons to regulate their speech, students are entitled to freedom of expression of their views.[46]

Alexander v. *Holmes County Board of Education* (1969) (Mississippi).[47] Despite the *Brown* decision, many school boards have continued to assign pupils to schools in such a manner as to perpetuate segregated schools. Consequently an avalanche of court cases descended upon the Federal Courts of Appeals, where considerable "gradualism" had been permitted for local school boards to convert their dual school systems to unitary systems, within which no person would be excluded from any school because of race or color.

The issue finally reached a climax when, on writ of certiorari to the U. S. Court of Appeals for the Fifth Circuit, the United States Supreme Court remanded the case to the lower court which "shall retain jurisdiction to insure prompt compliance with its order." The terse statement of the Supreme Court follows:

> The question presented is one of paramount importance, involving as it does the denial of fundamental rights to many thousands of school children who are presently attending Mississippi schools under segregated conditions contrary to the applicable decisions of this Court. Against this background the Court of Appeals should have denied all motions for additional time because continued operation of segregated schools under a standard of allowing "all deliberate speed" for desegregation is no longer permissible. Under explicit holdings of this Court the obligation of every school district is to terminate dual school systems at once and to operate now and hereafter only unitary schools.[48]

United States v. *Montgomery County Board of Education* (1970) (Alabama).[49] An increasing number of cases have come before the courts in recent years regarding *faculty*

---

[46] *Id.,* p. 739.
[47] 396 US 19, 24 LEd(2d) 19, 90 SCt 29 (1969).
[48] *Id.,* p. 29.
[49] 395 US 225, 23 LEd(2d) 263, 89 SCt 1670 (1969).

desegregation. Although most of them have been settled in the lower federal courts, one such case went to the United States Supreme Court for final settlement.

Originally a federal district court had ordered the Montgomery County Board of Education to take immediate steps to further desegregate its public school system. Its order provided that the board must move toward a goal whereby the ratio of Negro-white faculty members in each school would be substantially the same as the overall ratio in the system, with a *fixed mathematical ratio* based on race for the 1968-69 school year.

On appeal, the U. S. Court of Appeals, Fifth Circuit, concluded that the standards for faculty desegregation cannot be inflexible and held that the district court decree should be interpreted to mean "substantially or approximately" the 5-1 ratio set by the lower court.

On further appeal, the Supreme Court of the United States rejected the proposed modification by the Court of Appeals and upheld the district court's original decree. Otherwise it would "take from the order some of its capacity to expedite, by means of specific commands, the day when a completely unified, unitary, nondiscriminatory school system becomes a reality instead of a hope."[50]

After expressing its reluctance to compromise the judicial intention for complete desegregation of the public schools, the Court concluded: "We hope and believe that this order and the approval that we now give it will carry Alabama a long distance on its way toward obedience to the law of the land as we have declared it in the two *Brown* cases and those that have followed them."[51]

Swann v. *Charlotte-Mecklenburg Board of Education* (1971) (North Carolina).[52]

---

50 *Id.,* p. 1676.
51 *Ibid.*
52 91 SCt 1267 (1971).

North Carolina State Board of Education v. *Swann* (1971).[53]

McDaniel v. *Barrese* (1971) (Georgia).[54]

Davis v. *Board of Commissioners of Mobile County* (1971) (Alabama).[55]

On April 20, 1971, the Supreme Court of the United States unanimously upheld the constitutionality of *busing* as a means to "dismantle the dual school systems" of the South. In a series of landmark decisions written by Chief Justice Warren E. Burger and supported by the eight other justices, the Court overrode the arguments of the Nixon Administration and the Justice Department, which had intervened on the side of the Southern school systems in four companion cases.

Under circumstances apparent in the *Charlotte* case, the Court found "no basis for holding that the local school authorities may not be required to employ bus transportation as one tool of school desegregation. Desegregation plans cannot be limited to the walk-in school."[56]

The Court, however, recognized the validity of an objection "to transportation of students when the time or distance of travel is so great as to risk either the health of the children or significantly impinge on the educational process," and that the district courts should weigh the soundness in the light of many relevant factors.

In regard to the North Carolina Anti-Busing Law the Supreme Court, Mr. Chief Justice Burger, held that the statute forbidding assignment of any student on account of race or for purpose of creating a racial balance in the schools and forbidding busing for such purpose was invalid on grounds that the proscription against assignments made on basis of race would deprive school

---

[53] 91 SCt 1284 (1971).
[54] 91 SCt 1287 (1971).
[55] 91 SCt 1289 (1971).
[56] *Id.*, p. 1283.

authorities of the one tool absolutely essential to fulfill-
ment of their constitutional obligation to eliminate existing dual school systems and that the proscription against
assignment of students for purpose of creating racial balance would conflict with duty of school authorities to disestablish dual systems.[57]

Earley v. *Di Censo* (1971) (Rhode Island).[58]

Lemon v. *Kurtzman* (1971) (Pennsylvania).[59]

Two long-awaited United States Supreme Court landmark
decisions were rendered on June 28, 1971, which invalidated
the laws of two states (Rhode Island and Pennsylvania) giving public funds to private schools for secular instruction.
The rulings constituted a serious setback for the nation's
Catholic school system, which admittedly was in dire need
for public funds to survive.

In its decisions, the Court disregarded the predisposition
of President Nixon (who had gone on record as favoring
"parochiaid") even though two of its members, Chief Justice Warren E. Burger and Justice Harry A. Blackmun,
were Nixon appointees.

In *Earley* v. *Di Censo*, which originated in Rhode Island,
the Court struck down a state law which paid 250 teachers
up to 15 percent of their salaries for treating "similar subjects." The vote was 8 to 1, with Justice White dissenting.

In *Lemon* v. *Kurtzman*, which originated in Pennsylvania, the Court struck down a statute which earmarked
$20-million a year from cigarette and horse-racing revenues
to private schools for teacher salaries, textbooks and instructional materials. The vote was 8 to 1, with Justice White
again disagreeing.

Chief Justice Burger, who spelled out the rulings in a
23-page opinion noting that parochial schools are directly
under the supervision of the Roman Catholic hierarchy,

[57] *Id.,* p. 1284.
[58] 91 SCt 2105 (1971).
[59] 91 SCt 2105 (1971).

declared: "We cannot ignore the dangers that a teacher under religious control and discipline poses to the separation of the religious from the purely secular aspects of pre-college education."[60]

Essentially, the Chief Justice emphasized that direct instructional public assistance, for which the Rhode Island and Pennsylvania educational acts provided, involved "expressive entanglements between Government and religion," and that therefore they constituted a violation of the First Amendment prohibiting official "establishment of religion."

---

[60] *Id.*, p. 2113.

Part II

THE SCHOOL IN THE STATE SPHERE

STATE CONSTITUTIONAL PROVISIONS
FOR SCHOOLS

In the early stages of our national development little attention was given to the now trite phrase that "education is the function of the state." In fact, the original schools of America represented individual or local enterprises with parental and parochial, but not public support. Decentralized control of education therefore became firmly entrenched, and it was not until the broader scope of state government was realized that any successful attempt was made to place the control of education under state government. State concern for education followed the general movement toward a social conception of government. Even then the state concern was manifested principally by aid and encouragement to the local schools rather than by an exercise of authority over them.

Local initiative with respect to education is so highly regarded in our democratic society that the state legislatures have not unduly exercised their constitutional powers to the extent of denying local communities the right to participate in the management of the schools. On the contrary, most states have enacted legislation which permits, delegates, or requires considerable local school management. In so doing the states have not surrendered their prerogatives, but have merely determined the machinery by which the state function shall be performed.

Greater state control over public education in recent decades can be attributed chiefly to increasing support of education from state funds. As the state income tax and other state taxes have generally supplanted the local property tax as a source of public revenue, local communities have had to place greater dependence upon the state for the financing of adequate school programs. Obviously and properly the granting of state funds for education has been accompanied with certain state controls designed to guarantee wisdom and economy in the expenditure of those funds. The controls are usually stipulated in the state laws and exercised through state officials, agencies, and boards.

In the evolution of governmental control over public education, the early concern was the extent to which the state was gaining authority which was originally assumed by local committees. Now there is considerable concern that state control may be supplanted by federal control. Many persons are beginning to speculate as to what effect the increasing federalization of public-welfare activities will eventually have upon education. As was indicated in the preceding chapter the federal government is already doing much to aid certain phases of public education in the various states, and much more is being contemplated and demanded.

What degree of federal control will accompany federal aid? It is highly conceivable that the same social and economic forces which have caused greater state responsibility and control over local schools are likely to develop on a still broader scope so as to bring about federal-state relations somewhat analogous to those now existing between states and local school districts.

The suggestion of such a possibility should cause no alarm. After all the federal government is—like the state government—a servant of the people. As long as it remains democratic, the people themselves shall decide the degrees of support and control of education by state governments and the federal government in accordance with the general welfare.

The original and basic authority of the state to establish, support, and control public schools may be found in the state constitutions—at least in those that were drafted or revised during the past century.

5.1 Number of provisions

If it is surprising to some that no direct reference to education is made in the federal Constitution, it should be more surprising that many of the early state constitutions made no reference to education or schools. State constitutions of New Hampshire, New Jersey, Delaware, Maryland, Virginia, South Carolina, New York, Kentucky, Tennessee, Louisiana, and Illinois—framed during the period from 1776 to 1818—all were equally silent on the matter of education.[1]

Maryland amended its Constitution four times before 1864, New York adopted a new Constitution in 1872, and Illinois in 1848, all without including any mention of education. Of the twenty-three States forming the Union in 1820, ten had by that time made no mention of education in any of their Constitutions.[2]

Now each of the fifty states has included provisions for education in its constitution. In general, there had been a tendency to increase the number of provisions dealing with education in the state constitutions. The states admitted to the Union prior to 1820 had on the average only one provision about education in their first constitution. The eleven states admitted between 1821 and 1860 had an average of about five provisions concerning education in their first constitution; the four states admitted between 1861 and 1880 averaged nine provisions; the seven admitted between 1881 and 1900 averaged fourteen provisions; and the three states admitted between 1900 and 1912 averaged approximately eighteen provisions about education in their constitutions.

The trend for increasing the number of education provisions in state constitutions was thrown into reverse with the admission of the two newest states to the Union in 1959. Alaska and Hawaii have but three and five provisions about education in their respective constitutions.[3] Many of the other constitutions referred to above have had the number

---

[1] Cubberley, *op. cit.*, p. 94.

[2] *Ibid.*

[3] *Constitutions of the United States, National and State.* New York: Oceana Publishing Co., 1962, Vol. I: *Alaska*, pp. 16-17; *Hawaii*, p. 17.

of provisions pertaining to education reduced considerably in the amended drafts. This is in line with the modern concept that state constitutional provisions pertaining to education should not be too numerous or detailed.

5.2 Basic provisions establishing public school systems

Regardless of the number of provisions in their constitutions, each of the fifty states—with one exception—has at least one provision in its constitution for the establishment of a public school system. Connecticut is the only state in the Union which does not have a general mandate in its constitution requiring the legislature to provide for a system of free public schools.

Excerpts from all the state constitutions reveal that there is considerable similarity in the basic provisions for establishing public schools. Virtually every one expresses or implies that the state legislature or assembly shall provide, from public funds, for maintenance of a public school system.

Many of the state constitutions stipulate limitations for which the mandate is applicable, such as those which have to do with age range of pupils, minimum length of school year, freedom from sectarian control, and nondiscrimination because of race, religion, or ancestry. Some of the southern states have provisions in their constitutions requiring segregated public schools. The provision in the Louisiana constitution is illustrative: "Separate free schools shall be maintained for the education of white and colored children between the ages of six and eighteen years. . . ."[4] Of course, since 1954, this provision is meaningless. Any provision of a state constitution which is in conflict with a provision of the federal constitution, as interpreted by the United States Supreme Court, is null and void.

In an exhaustive study,[5] Campbell found state constitutional provisions for the establishment and support of public

---

[4] Louisiana Constitution, Art. XII, 1.

[5] Olan Kenneth Campbell, "An Analysis of Provisions of State Constitutions Affecting Support of Public Schools," unpublished Ed. D. Dissertation, Department of Education, Duke University, 1954, pp. 23-31.

school systems. The following excerpts from Campbell's summary, plus the later provisions for newer states (Alaska and Hawaii) follow:

ALABAMA

The legislature shall establish, organize and maintain a liberal system of public schools throughout the State for the benefit of the children thereof between the ages of seven and twenty-one years . . . (Art. XIV, 256).

ALASKA

The legislature shall by general law establish and maintain a system of public schools open to all children of the state. . . . (Art. VII, 1).

ARIZONA

Provision shall be made by law for the establishment and maintenance of a system of public schools which shall be open to all the children of the State and be free from sectarian control (Art. XX, Ordinance 2).

ARKANSAS

Intelligence and virtue being the safeguards of liberty and bulwark of a free and good government, the State shall ever maintain a general, suitable and efficient system of free schools, whereby all persons in the State between ages of six and twenty-one years may receive gratuitous instruction (Art. XIV, 1).

CALIFORNIA

The Legislature shall provide for a system of common schools by which a free school shall be kept up and supported in each district at least six months in every year (Art. IX, 5).

COLORADO

The General Assembly shall, as soon as practicable, provide for the establishment and maintenance of a thorough and uniform system of free public schools throughout the state . . . (Art. IX, 2).

CONNECTICUT

The fund, called the school fund, shall remain a perpetual fund, the interest of which shall be inviolably appropriated to the support and encouragement of the public, or common schools throughout the state, and for the equal benefit of all the people thereof (Art. VII, 2).

DELAWARE

The General Assembly shall provide for the establishment and maintenance of a general and efficient system of free public schools . . . (Art. X, 1).

FLORIDA

The Legislature shall provide for a uniform system of public free schools and shall provide for the liberal maintenance of the same (Art. XII, 1).

GEORGIA

There shall be a thorough system of common schools for the education of children, as nearly uniform as practicable, the expense of which shall be provided for by taxation, or otherwise . . . (Art. VIII, 1).

HAWAII

The State shall provide for the establishment, support and control of a statewide system of public schools free from sectarian control. . . . There should be no segregation in public educational institutions because of race, religion or ancestry; nor shall public funds be appropriated for the support or benefit of any sectarian or private educational institution (Art. IX, 1).

IDAHO

The stability of a republican form of government depending mainly upon the intelligence of the people, it shall be the duty of the legislature of Idaho, to establish and maintain a general, uniform and thorough system of public, free common schools (Art. IX, 1).

ILLINOIS

The General Assembly shall provide a thorough and efficient system of free schools, whereby all children of this State may receive a good common school education . . . (Art. VIII, 1).

INDIANA

It shall be the duty of the General Assembly to encourage by all suitable means, moral, intellectual, scientific, and agricultural improvement; and to provide by law, for a general and uniform system of common schools, wherein tuition shall be without charge, and equally open to all (Art. VIII, 1).

IOWA

The Board of Education shall provide for the education of all the youths of the State, through a system of common schools, and such schools shall be organized and kept in each school district at least three months in each year . . . (Art. IX, 12).

KANSAS

The Legislature shall encourage the promotion of intellectual, moral, scientific and agricultural improvement, by establishing a uniform system of common schools, and schools of a higher grade . . . (Art. VI, 2).

KENTUCKY

The General Assembly shall, by appropriate legislation, provide for an efficient system of common schools throughout the state (Section 183).

LOUISIANA

The educational system of the State shall consist of all free public schools, and all institutions of learning, supported in whole or in part by appropriation of public funds. Separate free schools shall be maintained for the education of white and colored children between the ages of six and eighteen years; . . . (Art. XII, 1).

MAINE

The Legislatures are authorized, and it shall be their duty to require the several towns to make suitable provision, at their own expense, for the support and maintenance of public schools . . . (Art. VIII).

MARYLAND

The General Assembly, at its first session after the adoption of this constitution, shall, by law, establish throughout the State a thorough and efficient system of free public schools; and shall provide by taxation, or otherwise, for their maintenance (Art. VIII, 1).

MASSACHUSETTS

It shall be the duty of legislatures and magistrates, in all future periods of this commonwealth, to cherish the interests of literature and the sciences and all seminaries of them; especially the university of Cambridge, public schools and grammar schools in the towns . . . (Ch. V, p. 2).

MICHIGAN

Religion, morality and knowledge being necessary to good government and the happiness of mankind, schools and means of education shall forever be encouraged (Art. XI, 1).

The Legislature shall continue a system of primary schools, whereby every school district in the State shall provide for the education of its pupils without charge for tuition . . . (Art. XI, 9).

MINNESOTA

The stability of a republican form of government depending mainly upon the intelligence of the people, it shall be the duty of the legislature to establish a general and uniform system of public schools (Art. VII, 1).

The Legislature shall make such provisions, by taxation or otherwise, as, with the income arising from the school fund, will secure a thorough and efficient system of public schools in each township in the State . . . (Art. VIII, 3).

MISSISSIPPI

It shall be the duty of the Legislature to encourage by all suitable means, the promotion of intellectual, scientific, moral and agricultural improvement, by establishing a uniform system of free public schools by taxation or otherwise, for all children between the ages of six and twenty-one years, and as soon as practicable, to establish schools of higher grade (Art. VIII, 201).

MISSOURI

A general diffusion of knowledge and intelligence being essential to the preservation of the rights and liberties of the people, the General Assembly shall establish and maintain free public schools for the gratuitous instruction of all persons in this state between the ages of six and twenty years (Art. XI, 1).

MONTANA

It shall be the duty of the legislative Assembly of Montana to establish and maintain a general, uniform and thorough system of public, free common schools (Art. XI, 1).

That provision shall be made for the establishment and maintenance of a uniform system of public schools, which shall be open to all the children of said State of Montana and free from sectarian control (Ordinance I, 4).

NEBRASKA

. . . it shall be the duty of the Legislature to pass suitable laws . . . to encourage schools and the means of instruction (Art. I, 4).

The Legislature shall provide for the free instruction in the common schools of this State of all persons between the ages of five and twenty-one years (Art. VII, 6).

NEVADA

The legislature shall provide for a uniform system of common schools, by which a school shall be established and maintained in each school district at least six months in every year . . . (Art. XI, 2).

NEW HAMPSHIRE

It shall be the duty of the Legislature and Magistrates, in all future periods of this government, to cherish the interest of literature and the sciences, and all seminaries and public schools . . . (Pt. 2, Art. 83).

NEW JERSEY

The legislature shall provide for the maintenance and support of a thorough and efficient system of free public schools for the instruction of all the children in this state between the ages of five and eighteen years (Art. VIII, 4).

NEW MEXICO

Provision shall be made for the establishment and maintenance of a system of public schools which shall be open to all the children of the State and free from sectarian control ... (Art. XXI, 4).

NEW YORK

The legislature shall provide for the maintenance and support of a system of free common schools, wherein all the children of this state may be educated (Art. XI, 1).

NORTH CAROLINA

The General Assembly ... shall provide by taxation and otherwise for a general and uniform system of public schools, wherein tuition shall be free of charge to all the children of the State between the ages of six and twenty-one years (Art. IX, 2).

NORTH DAKOTA

The legislative assembly shall provide ... for a uniform system of free public schools throughout the State, beginning with the primary and extending throughout all grades up to and including the normal collegiate course (Art. VIII, 148).

OHIO

The general assembly shall make such provisions ... as ... will secure a thorough and efficient system of common schools throughout the state ... (Art. VI, 2).

OKLAHOMA

Provisions shall be made for the establishment and maintenance of a system of public schools, which shall be open to all the children of the State and free from sectarian control ... (Art. I, 5).

The legislature shall establish and maintain a system of free public schools wherein all children of the State may be educated (Art. XIII, 1).

OREGON

The Legislative Assembly shall provide by law for the establishment of a uniform and general system of common schools (Art. VIII, 3).

PENNSYLVANIA

The General Assembly shall provide for the maintenance and support of a thorough and efficient system of public schools, wherein all the children of this Commonwealth above the age of six years may be educated, . . . (Art. X, 1).

RHODE ISLAND

The diffusion of knowledge, as well as of virtue, among the people, being essential to the preservation of their rights and liberties, it shall be the duty of the General Assembly to promote public schools, and to adopt all means which they may deem necessary and proper to secure to the people the advantages and opportunities of education (Art. XII, 1).

SOUTH CAROLINA

The General Assembly shall provide for a liberal system of free public schools for all children between the ages of six and twenty-one years . . . (Art. XI, 5).

SOUTH DAKOTA

The stability of a republican form of government depending on the morality and intelligence of the people, it shall be the duty of the Legislature to establish and maintain a general and uniform system of public schools wherein tuition shall be without charge, and equally open to all; and to adopt all suitable means to secure to the people the advantages and opportunities of education (Art. VIII, 1).

TENNESSEE

Knowledge, learning and virtue, being essential to the preservation of republican institutions, and the diffusion of the opportunities and advantages of education throughout the different portions of the State, being highly conclusive to the promotion of this end, it shall be the duty of the General Assembly in all future periods of this government, to cherish literature and science (Art. XI, 12).

TEXAS

A general diffusion of knowledge being essential to the preservation of the liberties and rights of the people, it shall be the duty of the Legislature of the State to establish and make suitable provision for the support and maintenance of an efficient system of public free schools (Art. VII, 1).

UTAH

The Legislature shall provide for the establishment and maintenance of a uniform system of public schools, which shall be open to all children of the State, and be free from sectarian control (Art. X, 1).

VERMONT

. . . a competent number of schools ought to be maintained in each town, for the convenient instruction of youth; and one or more grammar schools to be incorporated and properly supported, in each county in this State . . . (Ch. II, 64).

VIRGINIA

The General Assembly shall establish and maintain an efficient system of public free schools throughout the State (Art. IX, 129).

WASHINGTON

Provision shall be made for the establishment and maintenance of systems of public schools free from sectarian control which shall be open to all the children of said state (Art. XXVI, 4).

WEST VIRGINIA

The Legislature shall provide, by general law, for a thorough and efficient system of free schools (Art. XII, 1).

WISCONSIN

The Legislature shall provide by law for the establishment of district schools, which shall be nearly uniform as practicable; and such schools shall be free and without charge for tuition to all children between the ages of four and twenty years; and no sectarian instruction shall be allowed therein (Art. I, 3).

WYOMING

The right of the citizens to opportunities for education should have practical recognition. The Legislature shall suitably encourage means and agencies calculated to advance the sciences and liberal arts (Art. I, 23).

Some authorities in the field of school law believe the constitutional provisions cited above are adequate. They contend that additional detailed provisions would be superfluous and even detrimental. Several of the constitutions do come close to having only the one provision pertaining to a public school system which mandates its establishment and support. Other state constitutions, as already indicated, have numerous detailed provisions pertaining to the public schools.

5.3 Appropriateness of constitutional provisions

Since each of the fifty states has its own constitution, considerable variation may be found in the state constitutions with respect to the public schools. Some of the provisions are well-conceived and in keeping with the times; others are antiquated and inadequate to the extent of impeding educational progress.

Any state constitution is out of tune with the times, as far as education is concerned, if it does not conform to the following stated principles: (1) The state constitution should contain the *basic* provisions for the organization, administration, and support of a state program of education. (2) It should empower and direct the legislature to establish the general plan for carrying out the basic provisions so set forth. (3) It should be broad enough to include all of the essentials for an educational program. (4) It should exclude details which tend to limit or handicap the legislature in developing an adequate school system to meet emerging needs. (5) It should include provisions which are applicable on a state-wide basis. (6) It should be uniform in its application to educational opportunities and minimum essentials. (7) It should be in harmony with the provisions of the federal Constitution.

Numerous constitutional provisions are not in accord with these principles. They are objectionable in that they are not "in tune with the times." Several of the constitutional provisions which pertain to the office of the state school executive are illustrative. At least 30 states have constitutional provisions for that office, some of which incorporate such details as method of selection, term of office, and compensation. Numerous provisions stipulate composition, selection, duties, and compensation of various state educational boards. In some instances the state constitutions even have similar provisions pertaining to county school officials and boards.

Other constitutional provisions which can conceivably stymie educational progress are those which specify the types and sizes of local school administrative units; set the tax limit for educational purposes; limit the bonded indebtedness of county, township, school district, and other political divisions of the state; and fix the age limits of those for whom free education shall be provided.[6]

5.4 Amending state constitutions

Unfortunately many of the provisions in state constitutions concerning public education were hastily drafted, without much attention to principles such as those stated above. Once a constitution is adopted it is difficult to amend it. The section of the North Carolina Constitution which stipulates how the state constitution may be altered is illustrative:

> No part of the Constitution of this State shall be altered unless a bill to alter the same shall have been agreed to by three-fifths of each House of the General Assembly. And the amendment or amendments so agreed to shall be submitted at the next general election to the qualified voters of the whole State, in such manner as may be prescribed by law. And in the event of their adoption by a majority of

---

[6] E. C. Bolmeier, "Is School Law in Tune with the Times?" *1962 Yearbook of School of Law*, ed. Lee O. Garber, Danville, Ill.: The Interstate Printers and Publishers, 1962, pp. 185-198.

the votes cast, such amendment or amendments shall become a part of the Constitution of this State.[7]

Campbell found that the procedures for amending constitutions in all the other states are equally difficult and consequently, "the states have made few changes in their own fundamental law."[8]

Nevertheless the citizens of each state would do well to evaluate the educational provisions in the Constitution and to eliminate or amend those which are objectionable. Despite the difficulties encountered in amending certain constitutions, the importance of an unhampered state educational system justifies the effort.

A complete compilation of state constitutions with articles pertaining to "Education" was published in 1962.[9] Obviously, since then, many of the constitutional provisions have required revision to meet the needs of the times. For example, amendments incorporated into the 1971 State Constitution for North Carolina "update the Constitution to current practices and conform the North Carolina Constitution to requirements of the federal Constitution."[10]

---

[7] North Carolina Constitution, Art. XIII, 2.

[8] Campbell, "An Analysis of Provisions of State Constitutions Affecting Support of Public Schools," p. 18.

[9] *Constitution of the United States, National and State.* New York: Oceana Pub. Co., 1962.

[10] "Constitutional Changes Affecting Education." *School Law Bulletin,* Vol. II, No. 2, University of North Carolina at Chapel Hill, April, 1971, p. 1.

Chapter 6

STATE LEGISLATURES AND THE SCHOOLS

Section
6.1 Scope of legislative authority over the public schools
6.2 Guiding principles in formulating school legislation
6.3 Predicament facing state legislatures

The basic authority of the state to create and govern the public schools is embodied in the various state constitutions. The primary avenue through which that authority is exercised, however, is the state legislature. In fact, the state constitution charges the legislature with the responsibility for providing a state educational system, and grants the necessary authority to do so accordingly.

6.1 Scope of legislative authority over the public schools

The legislature possesses plenary authority over all educational matters other than those restricted by federal and state constitutions. Therefore, within the constitutional limits, the legislature is empowered to determine the types of schools to be established throughout the state; the means of their support; the types of their curricula; the manner of their control; the ages of children entitled to attend; the length of the school sessions; and the qualifications, duties, and compensations of teachers and other school personnel.

That the plenary authority over the public schools resides in the legislature is firmly stated by an Ohio court: ". . . the control of schools, be they public or private, providing elementary and secondary education for the youth of Ohio, reposes in the Legislature of our state."[1]

Much of the litigation challenging state legislative authority over the public schools grows out of the erroneous contention that education is a local concern, and therefore

---

[1] *Board of Education* v. *State Board of Education* (Ohio), 116 OhioApp 515, 22 OO (2d) 393, 189 NE (2d) 81 (1963).

subject to self-government. This misconception should have been dispelled as early as 1890 after the ruling of the Indiana Supreme Court in the classic and leading case of *State* v. *Haworth*.[2] The following excerpt from the Indiana court has been quoted numerous times in other jurisdictions. It succinctly sets forth the well-established legal principle that education is a state function and not an inherent function of the local community:

> Essentially and intrinsically the schools in which are educated and trained the children who are to become the rulers of the commonwealth are matters of State, and not local jurisdiction. In such matters, the State is the unit, and the Legislature the source of power. The authority over schools and school affairs is not necessarily a distributive one to be exercised by local instrumentalities; but on the contrary, it is a central power residing in the Legislature of the State. It is for the law-making power to determine whether the authority shall be exercised by a State board of education, or distributed to county, township, or city organization throughout the state. . . .

Every year numerous cases reach the higher state courts in which the authority of the legislature to create, alter, or abolish school districts is challenged. In virtually all instances, the courts uphold the legislature's determination of any pattern of district organization it chooses—providing it is within constitutional limits. For example, a Wyoming court said: "In the absence of constitutional restrictions, the questions as to whether local boards may exercise their delegated power to change school district boundary lines, without notice and a hearing for property owners, is a matter solely for the determination of the legislature."[3] In the same year, and in the same area of litigation, a Texas court stated:

> The Legislature has the power to create school districts at will without any kind of notice. It also has the power to change the boundaries of or abolish school districts, to consolidate them, to group them for high school purposes,

---

[2] 122 Ind 462, 23 NE 946 (1890).

[3] *Marathon Oil Co.* v. *Welch* (Wyo), 379 P(2d) 832 (1963).

to annex school districts to other school districts and to provide the mode and agencies for effecting such action.[4]

One of the important reasons for leaving to state legislatures the determination of educational policy rather than having it written into the state constitution is to expedite necessary modifications. Legislative changes in plans of organization and management are generally approved by the courts unless there are constitutional provisions to the contrary. A court's statement from a previously cited case exemplifies this point:

> As the power over schools is a legislative one, it is not exhausted by exercise. The Legislature having tried one plan is not precluded from trying another. It has a complete choice of methods, and may change its plan as often as it deems necessary or expedient. . . . It is clear, therefore, that even if it were true, that the Legislature had uniformly intrusted the management of school affairs to local organizations, it would not authorize the conclusion that it might not change the system.[5]

Even the wisdom of the legislature's action in school matters is not subject to administrative or judicial decision. In this connection, the Supreme Court of Florida remarked: "It is not the province of an administrative body, nor indeed of this court, to weigh the wisdom of an enactment of the legislature."[6]

The well-established legal principle that the state legislature possesses *plenary* powers over matters concerning education is reiterated in 1968 by a federal court:

> Arkansas or any other state of the Union can set up and maintain a public school system, or can refuse to set up or maintain a public school system, or even abolish an existing state public school system within its bound-

---

[4] *Neill v. Cook* (Tex), 365 SW(2d) 824 (1963).

[5] *State v. Haworth*, 122 Ind 462, 23 NE 946 (1890).

[6] *Neal v. Bryant* (Fla), 149 S(2d) 529 (1963).

aries, but if a state elects to and does set up a public
school system, it must do so in a manner that does not
conflict with the United States Constitution as interpreted
by the U. S. courts and at the present time a segregated
school is absolutely prohibited. Since there is nothing in
the U. S. Constitution directing the establishment and/or
maintenance of a public school system, the states have
no positive guides to follow in establishing, financing and
maintaining public school systems. Each state is left to
its own ingenuity and there is no positive guide for the
exercise of constitutional and legislative ingenuity by a
state and each state must find its own money, provide its
own criteria, establish its own zones of attendance and
build, administer and maintain its own school system.[7]

In summarizing the potential of the legislature's authority
over the public schools, a single sentence from an Ohio
court is to the point: "When the General Assembly speaks
on matters concerning education it is exercising *plenary*
power and its action is subject only to the limitations contained in the Constitution."[8]

6.2   Guiding principles in formulating school legislation

In view of the fact that the legislature possesses complete
power over the public schools, it must also assume complete
responsibility for the enactment of laws which are beneficial
to the state educational system. Obviously many well-in-
tended laws are enacted which prove to be improper, inadequate, and unsatisfactory. The authority of the state
legislature to appeal and amend laws, however, places upon
it the obligation to keep school laws up-to-date to meet the
needs of the times. The great portion of time devoted to
the enactment and revision of school laws at every legislative
session is proof of the seriousness with which the legislature

---

[7] *Haney* v. *County Board of Education* (Arkansas) 284 FSupp 916, 1968.

[8] *Board of Education* v. *State Board of Education* (Ohio), 116 OhioApp
515, 22 OO(2d) 393, 189 NE(2d) 81 (1963).

assumes its authority and responsibility concerning school matters.

Most school laws are well conceived and accordingly beneficial to the educational systems of the respective states. Unfortunately, though, there are many statutory provisions pertaining to education which are poorly conceived and poorly stated and thereby detrimental to educational efficiency.

In order for school laws to promote and facilitate a good educational program, they should be enacted and organized in conformity with sound principles of school legislation. The following general principles should be considered in the enactment of school laws:

(1) The laws should be in agreement with the provisions of the state constitution, which, in turn, should be in harmony with the provisions of the federal Constitution. Disregard for this principle frequently leads to litigation.

(2) Even though statutory laws should be more specific than constitutional provisions, they should be general enough to enable state and local boards of education to function without needless handicaps and restrictions.

(3) The laws should be stated in unmistakably clear terms so as to convey the precise intent of the legislation.

(4) The laws should be codified periodically and systematically—deleting or amending provisions which are obsolete.

Some states have not re-codified their school laws within the past quarter century. [9]

In view of the numerous inaccuracies and inadequacies of certain school codes, it is no wonder that school laws are not clearly understood and interpreted by those who are expected to rely upon them. Legislatures, departments of education, and school boards would also do well to appraise their school codes with respect to timeliness, clarity, and propriety. The cost of re-codification is small when compared with the cost

---

[9] Raymond L. Klein, "A Critical Analysis of School Codes," unpublished Ed. D. Dissertation, Department of Education, Duke University, 1953, p. 112.

of litigation growing out of misunderstanding of antiquated and vaguely written statutory provisions.

6.3 Predicament facing state legislatures

Legislatures are sometimes criticized for not exerting more effectively their prerogatives for the support of education. For example, one writer states:

> The weaknesses of state government are of particular importance in a policy area like education where the states traditionally have had paramount legal responsibility and authority. . . . Indeed, the state legislature has almost complete power over public education except where there are specific restrictions implicit in the state constitution. . . .
>
> The decade of the 1970's may well see either a dynamic renaissance of the states, or if they continue not to fulfill their responsibilities, a total and perhaps irrevocable centralization of authority in the federal government. American education will be greatly influenced by the developments which will occur.[10]

The plight facing state legislatures, however, is that they do not have—and find difficulty in procuring—sufficient funds to provide for the educational needs of the state and local school systems. With the competitively high proportion of tax revenue going to the federal government, the states have to rely upon financial aid from Washington to support their school systems. And, so far, federal support has been provided only with considerable federal control.

A scheme to provide the federal funds while alleviating federal control is referred to as "revenue sharing," whereby federal tax funds would flow back to the respective states to be expended autonomously. Public officials, as well as educators, hold different opinions as to the legality and wisdom of sharing federal funds as thus proposed. Disagree-

---

[10] Michael D. Usdan, "Politics and Education," *The School Administrator,* November, 1970, pp. 7-10.

ment has been most vigorously manifested among Congress-men. Spokesmen for national organizations of teachers (NEA and AFT) are outspoken in their rejection of the proposal that federal revenues be shared with state and local districts for the operation of public education.

One renowned educator and writer (Arthur H. Rice), however, suggests that sharing would tend to lessen the "importance, power, and prestige of national groups." He challenges

> the membership of educational organizations, and all edu-cators, to go on record as to their conviction, and hope-fully their recommendations, that more of the massive amounts of tax money collected by the federal govern-ment be returned to the people from whom it is collected in the states and the communities—and by whom it should be invested for the purposes and needs of public educa-tion as the public visualizes them.[11]

[11] Arthur H. Rice, "Let's Stop Playing Politics and Endorse Revenue Sharing," *Nation's Schools*, April, 1971, p. 14.

Chapter 7

STATE JUDICIARIES AND THE SCHOOLS

Section

7.1   Hierarchy of state judiciaries
7.2   Constitutional provisions for judiciaries
7.3   Number of state court decisions
7.4   Alternatives for court procedures
7.5   Criticisms of state court rulings
7.6   Courts not legislative functionaries
7.7   Courts not bound by precedents

7.1   Hierarchy of state judiciaries

As it is with the federal judiciary, the state judiciary is also organized on a ranking basis. The highest ranked court in most states is called the *state supreme court;* in several states the highest ranking court is called the *court of appeals.* Next in descending order is usually the *intermediate courts* which function between *trial courts* of general jurisdiction and the highest courts. The intermediate courts are referred to as courts of appeals, unless that title is given to the state's highest court.

If a litigant is dissatisfied with the decision of a trial court he may appeal to a higher court which would be the intermediate where it exists, or if not, to the state supreme court or the state court of appeals. A decision of the state's highest court of the state is final unless it involves an issue over which the federal courts have jurisdiction. Most school cases which are appealed to the federal courts involve rights guaranteed by the First and Fourteenth Amendments to the United States Constitution.

7.2   Constitutional provisions for judiciaries

Each state constitution contains the basic provisions for the establishment of a judicial organization to provide a system of impartial justice and to act as a check upon the legislative and executive branches of the state government. A provision of the constitution of our newest state, Hawaii, is illustrative. "The judicial power of the State shall be vested in one supreme court, circuit courts, and in inferior courts as the legislature may from time to time establish. The several courts shall have original and appellate jurisdiction as provided by law."[1]

The above general provision is very similar to that found in each of the constitutions of the other forty-nine states for the establishment of a judiciary. From there on, however, due to independent legislative authority, the state judicial systems vary considerably with respect to organization and procedure.

Regardless of the judicial systems determined by the legislatures, within the constitutional limits, the various courts of practically every state are called upon each year to settle some case of litigation involving the authority of the state legislature, a state educational body, or the officers of a subdivision of the state with respect to educational affairs.

7.3   Number of state court decisions

The extent to which the higher state courts decide cases concerning the schools is indicated by the number of cases referred to in the *Yearbook of School Law*.[2] According to the 1971 yearbook, 420 cases were adjudicated in the courts of record. Of this number, 137 were in the federal courts, and all others (283) in the appellate courts of forty-four states. Presumably hundreds were settled in the lower courts of the states and not appealed to courts of record.

As would be expected the states with the greatest populations have the greatest number of court cases. In the 1971 yearbook, no school cases were reported for six states (Colorado, Delaware, Hawaii, Maine, New Hampshire, Virginia).

---

[1] Hawaii Constitution, Art. V, Sec. 1.

[2] Lee O. Garber and Reynolds C. Seitz, *Yearbook of School Law*. Danville, Illinois: The Interstate Printers and Publishers, 1971, pp. 323-345.

Ten states (Alabama, Alaska, Montana, Nevada, New Hampshire, North Dakota, South Carolina, Tennessee, Vermont, Wyoming) reported only one case each. On the other extreme, 65 school cases were adjudicated in the higher courts of New York state. This number becomes more impressive when it is realized that the commissioner of education in New York is authorized by law to settle many litigious issues pertaining to the schools.

7.4   Alternatives for court procedures

Due to the time and expense involved in court procedures, certain administrative agencies, such as state educational offices or the state board of education, have frequently been delegated judicial authority over routine educational issues which potentially could otherwise develop into litigation. Different opinions have been voiced with respect to the wisdom and validity of such procedures. Some claim it is justified by expediency, whereas others claim it obscures the relative functions of judicial and administrative bodies. At any rate the practice is common in certain states. For example, several hundred school disputes are settled in New York each year by the commissioner of education, or his representative.

The judicial authority granted the commissioner of education in New York is extraordinarily great. The section of the *Education Law* dealing with "Appeals or petitions to Commissioner of Education and other proceedings" stipulates:

> Any person conceiving himself aggrieved may appeal or petition to the Commissioner of Education who is hereby authorized and required to examine and decide the same: and the Commissioner of Education may also institute such proceedings as are authorized under this act and his decisions in such appeals, petitions or proceedings shall be final and conclusive, and not subject to question or review in any place or court whatever.[3]

---

[3] Art. 34, Chapter 21 of Laws of 1909, Sec. 310.

Despite the firm statement of the New York law, however, it is not *absolutely* conclusive. A number of decisions of the commissioner of education have been appealed to and ruled upon by a state court. A declaration from a 1971 decision is illustrative:

> By section 310 of the Education Law, the decision of the Commissioner of Education on an appeal to him is made final and conclusive and is not subject to question or review in any place or court whatever. However, the Court of Appeals has held that a determination of the Commissioner does not have finality and may be reviewed if such determination is shown to be "purely arbitrary."[4]

Also the New Jersey Commissioner of Education is granted by law extensive authority to render decisions concerning school disputes in New Jersey. According to correspondence with the New Jersey Department of Education in May, 1967, the authority of the New Jersey Commissioner of Education to hear and decide disputes arising under school laws is provided in New Jersey Statutes Title 18, Education, Chapter 3, Section 14 and is stated as follows:

> The commissioner shall decide without cost to the parties all controversies and disputes arising under the school laws, or under the rules and regulations of the state board or of the commissioner.

> The facts involved in any controversy or dispute shall, if required by the commissioner, be made known to him by the parties by written statements verified by oath and accompanied by certified copies of all documents necessary to a full understanding of the question.

> The decision shall be binding until a decision thereon is given by the State Board of Education on appeal.

The numerous decisions of the Commissioner are compiled and published annually as *New Jersey School Law Decisions*. Other states would do well to provide such valu-

---

[4] *Reid* v. *Nyquist*, 319 NYS(2d) 53 (1971).

able information to help school boards and administrators in dealing with the legal problems arising constantly.

In other states, court procedures are also often avoided by the opinions of the attorney general. Although his opinions are not binding, and may possibly be reversed by court decisions, they are in general adequate enough to settle minor disputes. The attorney general serves in an advisory rather than judicial capacity. His main contribution in the area of education is to advise and guide the state department of education and the state board of education in formulating legal policies and preparing legal documents so as to be in conformity with the constitutional and statutory provisions of the state.

In many states, the attorney general's office includes several assistants. Where such a situation prevails it is common and desirable for the attorney general or one of the assistant attorneys general to specialize in school cases. In virtually all the states someone in the attorney general's office will give his opinions to school administrators who raise questions regarding the legality of certain school practices. In some of the states the opinions are not given without first consulting the chief state school officers, whereas in fewer states the school officers are never consulted. Elsewhere the practices fall between these two extremes.

7.5   Criticisms of state court rulings

Although the most publicized and severe criticisms of recent court decisions are launched more against the federal courts than the state courts, the great majority of school cases are adjudicated in the state courts. Obviously this is because education is generally regarded as a state function. The express provisions for the establishment, organization, and control of public education are contained in the state constitutions and statutes, and thereby not subject to federal jurisdiction, unless colliding with provisions of the United States Constitution.

It is difficult to reconcile some of the criticism against the courts for unsatisfactory school law, rather than going to the source of that which causes the dissatisfaction. Despite the obsoleteness of many constitutional and statutory provisions pertaining to the schools, the public has been somewhat lethargic in action for repeal, amendment, or enactment of laws so as to make them more in tune with the times. Altogether too many antiquated, vague, and unconstitutional laws are retained on the statute books. Then, when the laws are violated or misinterpreted, litigation frequently follows. Since the resulting court opinions are not likely to be satisfactory to both plaintiff and defendant, the court becomes the target of criticism and blame by the dissatisfied party, and the cry is heard for "court reform," "judicial review," and even "impeachment of judges."

7.6   Courts not legislative functionaries

There would likely be less protest and criticism of court decisions on school cases if there were a better understanding of the respective responsibilities of the legislative branch and the judicial branch of our government. The state legislature possesses exclusive authority to enact laws on matters relating to the schools except so far as restrained by the state constitution and the Constitution of the United States. The state judiciary, on the other hand, has no authority or responsibility to legislate. The proper function of the courts is threefold: (1) they rule on the constitutionality of legislative enactments, (2) they interpret laws, and (3) they settle disputes.

Cognizant of the possible encroachment upon the legislature's sphere of functions, the courts are constantly guarding against interference. Time and again the courts emphasize that they are not concerned with the wisdom, reasonableness, or even the expediency of legislative acts. They accept the judgment of the legislative branch unless it is arbitrary, capricious, unreasonable, and without foundation.

Despite the courts' dicta frequently condemning or praising certain legislation, their actual rulings are generally based only upon the constitutionality of the statutes. A common statement in court decisions is that "the wisdom of the law is for the legislature, not the courts"[5] or "the wisdom or un-wisdom of the challenged statutes and the propriety of their enactments presents a legislative and not a judicial prob-lem."[6]

The courts generally apply the same policy of noninter-ference with school board rules and regulations as they do with legislative acts. That the courts' rulings are based solely upon the legality rather than the propriety of the schools' regulations is evidenced by a judicial declaration upholding a board regulation designed to prohibit boys who marry from participating in competitive sports of the high school: "The Court's duty, regardless of its personal views, is to uphold the Board's regulation unless it is generally viewed as arbi-trary and unreasonable. . . ."[7]

In a more recent case[8] dealing with the same issue the Supreme Court of Utah stated: "Courts are not concerned with the wisdom or propriety of school boards' rules and regulations prescribing the qualifications for student partici-pation in extra-curricular activities. . . ."

As a rule, the courts will not supply omissions in the law, nor will they add to the law; neither will they correct statu-tory confusion and deficiencies. They will not attempt to do in round-about fashion what they think the legislature should have done. Courts have emphasized repeatedly that if the voters are dissatisfied with the statutes they should make their appeal to the legislature and not the courts.

7.7   Courts not bound by precedents

Even though the courts will usually follow precedents in rendering decisions, it has been frequently held that they need not do so where conditions and facts are widely differ-ent because of changing times. This is well illustrated in a

---

[5] *People v. Lloyd,* 304 Ill 23, 136 NE 505 (1922).

[6] *Lederman v. Board of Education of City of New York,* 96 NYS(2d) 469 (1950).

[7] *Cochrane v. Board of Education of Messick School District,* 360 Mich 390, 103 NW(2d) 569 (1960).

[8] *Starkey v. Board of Education of Davis County School District,* 14 Utah(2d) 227, 381 P(2d) 718 (1963).

case [9] where a court held that there is no necessity or justification for perpetual immunity of school district liability. In referring to the legal principle established in an earlier case than the one at hand, the court pointed out that "the law is not static and must follow and conform to changing conditions and new trends in human relations to justify its existence as a servant and protector of the people and, when necessary, new remedies must be applied where none exist."

In almost every area of school law there is evidence that precedent is not everlasting. Although legal principles may lag in keeping pace with rapidly changing social and economic conditions, they eventually conform. In some instances, the legal principles change gradually and slowly, as exemplified by the principle of "immunity for tort liability of school districts," or the "separate but equal" principle involved in racial segregation in the public schools. In other instances, such as where anti-subversive legislation is involved, the legal principles have been modified or reversed rather abruptly. It is for the courts to determine, if, when, and how legal principles should be altered.

---

[9] *Moore* v. *Moyle*, 405 Ill 555, 92 NE(2d) 81 (1950).

Chapter 8

STATE BOARDS OF EDUCATION

Although the legislature is usually charged with the responsibility of organizing, providing for, and administering a state system of education, it is obvious that the legislature cannot perform these functions directly by itself. Even the formulation of educational policy is somewhat beyond the pale of legislative functions. Accordingly most state legislatures have delegated a good share of the responsibility of policy making, as well as other school matters, to state boards of education.

8.1   Evolution of state boards of education

The first semblance of a state board of education is credited to New York, where a board of regents was established in 1784. (This board was not given control over all the schools of the state until 1904.) Next, in 1825, a state board was created in North Carolina, for the purpose of administering what was known as the "Literary Fund." The sole responsibility of this board was to invest the funds and apply the proceeds "to the instruction of the youth of the State in the principles of reading, writing, and arithmetic to be divided among the counties in proportion to their white population."[1] Shortly afterward rudimentary state boards, with

---

[1] Edgar W. Knight, *Public Education in North Carolina.* New York: Houghton Mifflin Co., 1916, p. 80.

limited educational responsibilities, were established in Vermont and Missouri.

The first real state board of education, however, which would today be considered as such, was established in Massachusetts in 1837 with Horace Mann as its first secretary. The rapid development of this educational body was due largely to the insight and ambition of Mann. Consequently other states followed the practice of Massachusetts, and inserted provisions in their constitutions or statutes for the establishment of similar agencies.

By 1949, at least 40 states were considered to have state boards of education. Since that time 8 more states have established boards, so at the time of this writing, only 2 of the 50 states, Illinois and Wisconsin, do not have state boards of education.

8.2 Constitutional and statutory provisions

Provisions for the establishment of state boards of education are almost equally divided between state constitutions and statutes. Twenty-two of the 48 states with boards have the provisions for them contained in their constitutions; whereas the other 26 states provide for the boards in their statutes.

In general, the constitutional provisions pertaining to state boards of education are quite brief and general. The provisions of the Ohio Constitution as amended through 1959 are illustrative:

There shall be a state board of education which shall be selected in such manner and for such terms as shall be provided by law. There shall be a superintendent of public instruction, who shall be appointed by the state board of education. The respective powers and duties of the board and of the superintendent shall be prescribed by law.[2]

The provisions in some of the other state constitutions are spelled out more in detail with respect to the selection, number, and terms of office for members.

---

[2] Ohio Const., Art. VI, Sec. 4.

As in other areas of school organization and administration, it is generally considered wise and expedient to have only the basic—if any—provisions of the constitution pertaining to state boards of education. Then the legislatures are not handicapped in enacting such legislation governing the boards as may be desirable for changing conditions.

8.3   Legal authority of state boards of education

The legal authority of a state board of education is somewhat analogous to that of a local board of education—the main difference being that of geographic scope. The state board of education possesses express or implied authority over the schools of the entire state; whereas the local board of education may exercise authority only over the schools of a designated territorial subdivision of the state school district. In both instances, the legislature—or even the state constitution—may limit the authority of state boards and local boards by including provisions directly in the statutes or constitutions which govern the schools.

The legal scope of a state board's powers is succinctly stated by Remmlein:

In any phase of school management wherein the state board of education has been given powers of operation, the rules and regulations of the state board have the force and effect of law. However, being a creature of the legislature in most states, the state board has only the powers delegated to it or implied in the delegated powers. In the states where the state board is created by constitutional provision, its constitutional powers are very general, and in specific instances it depends upon the legislature for its authority to act. In either case, if the state board acts outside its delegated or implied power, the rule or regulation is void. There is, however, a presumption of authority, and until challenged in court, all rules and regulations of the state board are presumed to be valid and have effectiveness as enforceable as a statute enacted by the legislature.[3]

[3] Madaline Kinter Remmlein, *School Law.* New York: McGraw-Hill Book Co., 1950, p. 3.

Generally, state legislatures delegate to boards the duties for which *broad discretionary powers* are considered essential to good public administration. The legislatures most frequently delegate ministerial duties, or duties that require the use of little or no discretionary powers, to single officers.

The main duties and functions assigned by law to state boards of education include the following:

(1) Adoption of rules and regulations which have the effect of law.

(2) Regulation of teacher certification.

(3) Prescription of minimum standards in specified areas.

(4) Determination of educational policies.

(5) Adoption of courses of study.

(6) Determination of regulations governing apportionment of state school funds.

(7) Regulation of teacher education other than by certification.

(8) Determination of the plan of organization for the state department of education.

(9) Prescription of the duties of the chief state school officer.

(10) Adoption of textbooks.

8.4 Methods of selection

The most common method of selecting the members of state boards of education is appointment by the governor. The laws of 31 states stipulate that all or a majority of the members shall be appointed by the governor.

Only two states, Florida and Mississippi, have state boards of education composed wholly of ex officio members. In addition to these wholly ex officio boards, 14 other states have one or more ex officio members on the board. For example, in North Carolina the constitution provides for 3 ex officio members (lieutenant governor, state treasurer, and state superintendent of public instruction) plus 10 members appointed by the governor; 1 each from 8 educational districts into which the state has been divided by the general assembly, and 2 from the state at large.[4]

State board of education members are elected in 11 states by the people or their representatives. In 8 of these states they are elected by popular vote. In the state of New York, they are elected by the state legislature; in Washington, by local school board members; and in Iowa, by conventions of delegates chosen by local school boards.

In Wyoming, the members of the state board of education are appointed by the chief state school officer with the approval of the governor.

8.5   Term of office

The terms of office, as fixed by law, range from 2 years in North Dakota to 13 years in New York. A 6-year term of office is the most common, being employed in 15 states. Some of the laws fix the terms of office so that they overlap, thereby providing some stability and continuity for state educational programs and to prohibit the governor from reconstituting the entire board during any single year he is in office.

8.6   Size of boards

The number of members on state boards of education ranges from 3 in Mississippi to 23 in Ohio. Many of the laws provide for a board with an uneven number of members to preclude any possibility of a stalemate in voting. Consequently the most common size of a state board is 7, 9, or 11.[5]

8.7   Qualifications of members

A majority of the 48 states having state boards of education have provisions in the laws stipulating certain restrictions or qualifications of membership. For example, in some

---

[4] North Carolina Const., Art. IX, Sec. 8.

[5] Robert F. Will, *State Education*, OE-23038 Misc., No. 46. Washington, D. C.: U. S. Department of Health, Education and Welfare, United States Government Printing Office, 1964, pp. 15-18.

states, the laws provide that one or more of the members must be engaged in educational work. In contrast with that requirement, other states stipulate that no members shall be engaged in educational work.

Among other restrictions imposed by law are that: "not more than a certain number shall belong to the same political party; no member may be connected with any textbook publishing concern; no person shall be appointed to the board who is in any way subject to its authority; no board member shall hold any other elective or appointive office in the State."[6]

---

[6] Ward W. Keesecker, *State Boards of Education and Chief School Officers Bulletin 1950*, No. 12, Washington, D. C.: Federal Security Agency, United States Government Printing Office, 1950, p. 16.

Chapter 9

CHIEF STATE SCHOOL OFFICERS

Section

Each state has a chief school officer, usually referred to as
"state superintendent of public schools," "state superintendent of public instruction," or "state commissioner of education." Regardless of the title the school officer bears, he holds
a position which is unequaled in its potential influence over
the state educational system. The importance which the
lawmakers attach to the position of chief state school officer
is reflected in the constitutional and statutory provisions
which provide for the method of selection, qualifications,
term of office, salary, and relationship to the state board of
education.

9.1   Methods of selection

Because of the importance of the office, lawmakers consider it imperative that the chief state school officer be selected in such a manner as to procure the most capable
person possible. It is doubtful, though, that the most common method of selection (popular vote) is the most desirable
or effective. Although the trend has been away from selection by popular vote, by 1965, the laws of 21 states still provided for selection in that manner. It is obvious that this
type of selection limits the field of candidates. Not many
persons are willing to enter the campaign for election.
Moreover, after once obtaining office by election it is a
temptation to spend much of the time while in office maneuvering and scheming for the next campaign if reelection
to the office is sought.

As stated by Will:

> The elected chief State school officer is one of the anomalies of State government in our day. Students of political science and State educational administration have been in firm agreement for over half a century that it is undesirable to select the chief State school officer by popular vote. One reason for the persistence of this practice is the fact that the elected chief State school officer is generally a constitutional officer. The difficulty of amending the constitution in many States has served to perpetuate the elective method. In addition, strong resentments defending the right of the people to select the chief State school officer have developed over the years.[1]

The trend away from selection by popular vote is toward appointment by the state board of education. With an amendment to the Michigan constitution, changing the method of selection from election of the voters to appointment by the state board of education, effective in 1964, the laws of 24 states provided for the selection of the chief state school officer by appointment of the state board of education.

School administrators favor this method of selection mainly because of its divorcement from politics. The state board of education is in a free position to seek the most competent person for the office and to retain him in office as long as he is satisfactory. Moreover, appointment by the board eliminates the possibility of dualism in responsibility and authority which might otherwise exist between the board and the official.

9.2 Qualifications

The legal qualifications of the chief state school officer are lax. Approximately half of the states report no legal provisions in this respect. Where qualifications are required they pertain mainly to educational preparation and experience. The most common educational qualification stipulated in the statutes is that the chief state school officer shall be able to qualify for a teaching certificate.

---

[1] Will, *op. cit.*, pp. 20-21.

The legal requirements with respect to experience are usually vague. Some states merely specify that the chief state school officer shall be "an experienced educator." Nebraska requires four years as superintendent, principal, or supervisor; whereas Kansas requires ten years in teaching or administration. Nine other states require at least five years of teaching and administrative experience.[2]

9.3   Term of office

The constitutional and statutory provisions pertaining to the term of office for the chief state school officer vary from state to state. In 19 states the laws in this respect are inadequate. In 13 of the 19 in the inadequate category, the chief state school officer serves at the pleasure of the state board of education; in 4 states, the law is silent on the matter; in 1 state he serves at the pleasure of the governor; and in the other state in which legal requirements are vague, the term is consistent with that of the governor who makes the appointment.

In 31 of the 50 states, the laws specifically designate the term of office for the chief state school officer—ranging from 1 year in Delaware to 6 years in Minnesota. "Of the remaining 29 states, 6 provide for 2-year terms, 20 for 4-year terms, and 3 for 5-year terms."[3]

In fixing the term of office of the chief state school officer, good judgment should be exercised by the lawmakers. It is generally contended that he should have sufficient security while in office to conduct his duties without fear of dismissal at the unlimited discretion of appointive agencies or officers.

Dismissal of the chief state school officer—as any other public officer—without just cause, is in conflict with democratic ideals. Nevertheless, the laws should provide for proper procedure in dismissal of the chief state school officer for cause. The 1964 report of the Office of Education states that: "Ideally, the agency or officer empowered to appoint the chief State school officer should also be empowered

---

[2] The Council of State Governments, 1949, p. 187.

[3] Will, *op. cit.*, p. 26.

to initiate action to dismiss him under administrative procedures that make adequate provisions for notice, hearing, and appeal."[4]

9.4 Salaries

Regardless of the method of selection or required qualifications, it is not likely that the most competent person will be placed in the important office which heads up a state school system unless salaries are paid which are somewhat commensurate with the responsibilities and qualifications demanded.

Salaries, effective in 1965, for chief state school officers ranged from $9,000 in South Dakota to $40,000 in the state of New York. Ohio and New Jersey come closest to meeting the New York level, with salaries of $25,000 and $24,000, respectively.[5] Although comparable figures have not been compiled recently, according to salary increases in general, it may be estimated that the 1972 salaries for chief state school officers have increased by approximately 20 percent.

9.5 Relationship to state board of education

In 34 states the chief state school officer is designated as a constitutional officer, usually in the Education Department, but frequently in the Executive Department. The laws use different titles for the office, such as: "secretary," "executive secretary," "executive officer," "administrative officer," "executive director," "chief executive officer," "official agent," "treasurer," and "executive and administrative head."

Although the title may suggest the relationship of the chief state school officer to the state board of education, it cannot be relied upon to do so. Board rules and regulations are more likely to determine relationships.

Legal authorities express doubt as to whether the chief state school officer should be directly associated with the

---

[4] Will, *op. cit.*, p. 27.
[5] *Ibid.*

board's internal government in any capacity.

In those States in which the chief State school officer is designated by law as the executive officer of the board, it is implied that the board is responsible for both legislative and executive functions at administrative levels. One possible solution to this dilemma would be to delegate all duties in the law to a central education agency and to distribute the governmental powers needed to perform these duties between the State board of education and the chief State school officer. All legislative powers could be placed with the State board of education and all executive powers could be placed with the chief State school officer. Detailed legislation could then be enacted to resolve problems that arise relative to what constitutes an executive or legislative power.[6]

---

[6] Will, *op. cit.,* p. 28.

Part III

THE SCHOOL IN THE LOCAL SPHERE

Chapter 10

THE SCHOOL DISTRICT

Even though education is generally regarded a function of the state, there is no instance in which the public schools are operated directly by the state legislature or even a state board of education. Legislators and others realize the benefits accruing from local self-government in such matters as education, and have accordingly refrained from removing the administration of the public schools too far from the local communities. Thus their operation and control, within broad limits set by the state constitution and the legislature, have been delegated to local people.

For the purpose of exercising the delegated responsibility, local school districts have been created and clothed with the necessary administrative powers.

10.1 Legal nature of the school district

Briefly stated, a school district is a territorial subdivision of the state assuming responsibility and exercising delegated authority over education within its boundaries. According to *American Jurisprudence:* "School districts may be generally defined as local administrative authorities with fixed territorial limits, created by the legislature, and subordinate to its will, as agents of the state for the sole purpose of administering the state system of public education."[1]

Local school districts are incorporated as agencies of the state for purposes of executing the state's educational policy.

---

[1] "Schools," *Am. Jur.,* Vol. 47, sec. 42.

Therefore, a school district may be considered as a corporate entity. There has been considerable discussion and litigation, however, regarding the particular corporate status of a school district as contrasted with that of other corporations—particularly municipal corporations.

There is a distinct difference between a municipality and a school district, even though they frequently encompass the same geographical area, and are both referred to as "corporations." School districts are incomplete municipalities, and are therefore designated as "quasi-municipal corporations," or, more frequently, "quasi corporations."

State laws usually express the corporate powers conferred upon school districts. In one of the earliest publications on school law, Weltzin lists the corporate powers of school districts as found in the state laws:

1. To possess a corporate name.
2. To acquire and hold real and personal property.
3. To convey such property when necessary or expedient to the purposes of the corporation.
4. To contract and be contracted with.
5. To sue and be sued in the corporate name.
6. To receive grants, gifts, and bequests.
7. To make bylaws, rules, and regulations.
8. To exercise the right of eminent domain.
9. In general, to exercise those corporate powers usually possessed by public corporations of this rank, and to do those things necessary to the attainment of those ends for which the corporation was organized.[2]

Despite the fact that a school district is a body corporate, possesses the usual powers of a corporation for public purposes, and may sue and be sued, it has no territorial integrity.

It is subject to the reserve power of the state exercised through administrative authority to change its territory according to current educational needs and good educational principles. The state may change or repeal all powers of a school district, take without compensation its

<hr />

[2] J. F. Weltzin, *The Legal Authority of the American Public School.* Grand Forks, N. D.: Mid-West Book Concern, 1931, p. 51.

property, expand or restrict its territorial area, unite the whole or a part of it with another subdivision or agency of the state, or destroy the district with or without the consent of the citizens.[3]

The state is supreme in the creation and control of school districts and may, if it thinks proper, modify or withdraw any of their powers or destroy such school districts without the consent of the legal voters or even over their protests."[4]

10.2 Variations in school district patterns

Because of the wide latitude of choice residing in state legislatures to establish school districts, there is considerable variation among the states as to the manner in which the state is divided into geographical areas for the purpose of school control.

In an isolated case, the boundaries of the single school district are identical with those of the state (Hawaii). In most instances, however, the school district boundaries are made to coincide with those of existing political subdivisions of the state, such as county, township, city, or town. For example, in West Virginia, where the county plan prevails, there are 45 school districts identical in area with the 45 counties of the state. In North Carolina there are 100 school districts for the 100 counties of the state, plus 52 special districts, some of which are and some of which are not coterminous in area with cities.

10.3 Decrease in number of school districts

The number of school districts in the United States continues to decline. The Office of Education reports that:
in the fall of 1969 there were 19,169 public school districts—a decrease of 1,271 or six percent, from the 20,440 districts in the preceding year. . . . Three States had

---

[3] *Board of Education of School District No. 30 v. Winne,* 177 Neb 431, 129 NW(2d) 255 (1964).

[4] *Languis v. De Boer,* 181 Neb 32, 146 NW(2d) 750 (1966).

decreases of more than 100: South Dakota, 441; Nebraska, 193; and Minnesota, 146.

The 1969-70 total of 19,169 was less than one-fourth the number in 1949-50 and less than one-half the number in 1959-60. There are still four states with over 1,000 districts: Nebraska, 1820; Illinois, 1227; Texas, 1216; and California, 1082.[5]

10.4   School district and municipal boundaries

The state laws vary considerably with respect to fixing boundaries of city school districts. Consequently there is lack of uniformity as to whether or not the boundaries of the city proper and the school city coincide. Of the cities having populations in excess of 50,000, approximately 63 percent have boundaries coinciding with those of the city school district, whereas in approximately 37 percent, the boundaries do not coincide. In the very large cities having over 50,000 population, 85 percent have boundaries which are coterminous with those of the city school district.[6] That the boundaries of school districts in the largest cities are generally coterminous with those of the city may be partially due to the fact that lawmakers consider the area and population of a large city great enough for administrative effectiveness.

State legislatures have not adopted a standard pattern for fixing boundaries of city school districts. In Pennsylvania the law leaves no doubt as to how much territory the city school district shall embrace: "Each city, incorporated town, borough, or township in this Commonwealth, now existing or hereafter created, shall constitute a separate school district. . . ."[7] Consequently all the cities of Pennsylvania have identical boundaries for cities and school districts.

Some state legislatures are less specific in limiting the boundaries of a city school district. For example, in Ohio

---

[5] "Number of School Districts Continues to Decline," *American Education,* August-September, 1970, p. 37.

[6] E. C. Bolmeier, "Legal Implications of School District and Municipal Boundaries," *School Board Journal* (March, 1949), p. 29.

[7] *School Laws of Pennsylvania,* 1933, Art. 1, sec. 101.

"each city, together with the territory attached to it for school purposes, shall constitute a city school district."[8] Unlike the cities of Pennsylvania, none of the Ohio cities with population over 50,000 have boundaries identical with those of the city school district.

10.5   Alteration of school district boundaries

Since school districts are but parts of the machinery employed in carrying out the educational policies of the state, the legislature, in addition to creating school districts, may abolish them, or alter their boundaries as public policy may dictate.

In a dispute over the scope of legislative authority in determining school district boundaries, the Supreme Court of North Dakota held that:

> The inhabitants of a school district have no property rights in the boundaries thereof, but the formation or alteration of school districts and their boundaries is entirely within the power of the legislature.[9]

The courts are aware of the legislature's authority in the alteration of school district boundaries, and they show no disposition to interfere with their prerogative. For example, in a Wisconsin case the State Supreme Court stated:

> Whether the boundaries of a school district should be changed is not a question of law or fact for judicial determination, but purely a question of policy, to be determined by the legislative department. Such a matter presents a question of political expediency for the legislative department. The courts have nothing to do with the policy, wisdom, justice, fairness of such matters. They present questions for the consideration of those to whom the state has entrusted its legislative power, and their determination of them is not subject to review or criticism

---

[8] *Baldwin's 1934 Code of Ohio*, sec. 4680.

[9] *In Re Township 143, North Range 55, West Cass County* (ND) 183 NW(2d) 520 (1971).

by the court. . . .[10]

Federal courts may intervene when school district boundaries are altered for purposes prohibited by the Federal Constitution. For example, a U. S. District Court held that a public school district, under order of a federal court to desegregate its schools and operate a unitary school system, could not validly divide a school district into two separate and independent districts, where the division would result in establishing segregated school districts. The Court acknowledged that:

> Had the patrons of the school district attempted the proposed establishment of two districts at a time when there were no racial implications and prior to the district becoming involved in desegregation litigation, it may well have been that no constitutional objection would have been offered. . . .[11]

Due to the fact that municipal boundaries are frequently extended it is necessary for the legislature to determine if and how the boundaries of the school district are to be altered. Here again the statutes vary. In some instances the additional area taken into the municipality automatically becomes a part of the school district so that the boundaries of the civil city and the school district continue to be identical. In other instances the approval of a majority vote of the electors in the proposed larger school district is required.

The statutes of Mississippi illustrate the automatic extension of school-district boundaries to coincide with the expanded municipality:

> Where the limits and boundaries of any city, town or village, which constitutes a separate school district, or a part thereof, have been, or may hereafter be extended as now provided by law, so as to include therein the whole

---

[10] *Zawerschnik* v. *Joint County School Committee*, 271 Wis 416, 73 NW(2d) 566 (1955).

[11] *Aytch* v. *Mitchell* (Ark), 320 FSupp 1372 (1971).

or any part of any adjacent rural separate school district or any adjacent existing consolidated school district, such rural separate school district or consolidated school district, or such parts thereof as are incorporated within the municipal limits by reason of such extension, shall thereby be automatically merged with and become a part of such municipal separate school district. [12]

Statutes providing for the automatic extension of city school district boundaries to coincide with extended boundaries of a municipality are in the minority. The more common statutory provision requires the approval of the electorate comprising the area proposed for annexation. The statutes of North Carolina are illustrative:

> The boundaries of a district situated entirely within the corporate limits of a city or town, but not coterminous with such city or town, may be enlarged so as to make the district coterminous with such city or town. . . . The governing body of such city or town may at any time, upon petition of the board of education or other governing body of such district, or upon its own initiative if the governing body of the city or town is also the governing body of the district, submit the question of enlarging the district as aforesaid to the qualified voters of such new territory proposed to be added to such district at any general or municipal election called for said purpose. [13]

10.6 Judicial interpretations of identical boundaries

The fact that boundaries of a school district have often been superimposed upon those of a municipality has been the source of much litigation. This is particularly true where city officials have been authorized and required by the legislature to perform certain duties with respect to the establishment and maintenance of public schools, such as the appointment of school board members and the approval of the school budget. Consequently, the courts have been called upon repeatedly to interpret the intention of the legislatures

---

[12] *Mississippi Code* 1942, Annotated, Chap. V, Title 24, sec. 6428.
[13] *General Statutes of North Carolina*, 1943, Vol. III, secs. 115-197.

and to test the constitutionality of statutes pertaining to this issue.

The courts have been consistent in emphasizing the fact that, even where boundaries of the municipality are identical with those of the city school district, there is no cause to believe that in such instances the city officials have any more authority in school matters than where the boundaries are nonidentical. A school district is not a municipal corporation; it is a quasi corporation created by the legislature for the purpose of performing state functions. It is a political subdivision of the state and owes its creation to the general statutes of the state. The municipal corporation, however, is merely a local corporation for performing local functions.

In a strict legal sense there ordinarily is no such thing as a "city school district." It is called that merely because it encompasses the geographical area of the city; but, in fact, it is actually a designated division of the state performing a state function and is completely independent from municipal control.

The mere superimposition of school district boundaries upon those of the municipality does not detract from the prerogatives of the school district. The legislature frequently permits or requires identical boundaries merely as a means or basis of designating the district, classifying it, and assigning it certain powers and duties. Nevertheless, a school district with its territorial boundaries coterminous with the boundaries of a city is generally a corporate entity separate and distinct from the city.[14]

---

[14] *Board of Education of Chicago* v. *Upham*, 357 Ill 263, 191 NE 876 (1934); *McCurdy* v. *Board of Education of Bloomington*, 359 Ill 188, 194 NE 287 (1934).

Chapter 11

SCHOOL DISTRICT TORT LIABILITY*

A firmly established concept of common law in the United States is the doctrine which holds that governmental agencies are not liable for their torts (civil wrongs, other than a breach of contract, for which the court will provide a remedy in the form of an action for damages). Since school districts (school boards) are governmental agencies performing governmental functions, they are insulated from liability as much as is the state itself.

Tort liability of school districts has developed into one of the more controversial and litigious issues of school law. Perhaps there has been no more significant school matter litigated in our state courts over past decades than that of school district tort liability.

11.1 Reasons for perpetuation of immunity rule

Although there are many more important arguments in favor of abandoning the immunity doctrine as applied to school districts, there are some arguments for its retention. Fuller analyzed a number of court decisions which upheld the nonliability rule, and accordingly listed the following reasons given by the courts:

---

* Note: For an abridgment of a doctoral dissertation dealing with trends see: David v. Martin, "Trends in Tort Liability of School Districts as Revealed by Court Decisions." *Legal Issues in Education.* Chapter 18, pp. 169-81, published by the Michie Company, Charlottesville, Virginia, 1970.

1. *Sovereignty.* The school district exercises sovereign power as it acts through the board of education, and is as immune from suit as the sovereign itself. To permit actions for torts would be contrary to the theory of sovereignty of the states in the United States.

2. *Stare decisis* (principle of referring to previously judged cases for guidance in present cases). The principle of tort nonliability for school districts has been determined by the settled rule of common law that quasi-corporations are not liable for the torts of their officers, agents, and employees committed during acts performed solely for the benefit of the public except when such liability is provided by statute.

3. *Governmental function.* The school district is not liable for torts of its officers, agents, or employees analogous to the liability enforced against municipal corporations for proprietary activities because it exercises governmental functions for the benefit of the public and has no proprietary function for its own corporate benefit.

4. *Legal inability to pay.* The school district cannot be liable for torts because it has no corporation fund from which it can legally satisfy tort judgments and no method whereby it can legally raise funds for this purpose.

5. *Involuntary agency.* The school district is not liable in a tort action because it is an involuntary statutory agency, of limited powers and prescribed duties, and without choice of whether it will function.

6. *Respondeat superior.* The school district is not liable for the torts of its officers, agents, or employees because the principle of respondeat superior (owner, employee, or agent is liable for acts of his servants or employees) does not apply to school districts.

7. *Ultra vires* (an act outside and beyond the powers permitted). The school district cannot be made subject to tort liability, because any tortious act of its officers, agents, or employees is *ultra vires* the powers of the district.

8. *Immunity as charity.* School districts should enjoy the torts immunity traditionally accorded to charitable

institutions.

9. *Impairment of school functions.* School district tort liability is undesirable on the grounds of public policy because it would result in a multiplicity of suits and serious impairment of the functions of some schools.

10. *Prohibitive cost.* Tort liability of school districts is undesirable because it would increase the financial burden of maintaining the schools.[1]

11.2 Reasons for abrogating immunity rule

The main reason usually given for the abrogation of school district immunity is because it is unduly harsh and unjust in requiring the individual alone to suffer the wrong, and society should afford relief.

In the introductory paragraph of a report on the origin of governmental immunity from tort doctrine, Garber states:

> Few principles of jurisprudence have been so criticized and so castigated as the doctrine of governmental immunity from tort. It has been denounced by students of the law, textbook writers, and jurists alike. Today it is being challenged as never before, and a few states have abrogated it—some by statute and some by judicial decree.[2]

Even though courts have generally followed tradition in holding governmental agencies immune from tort liability, the dissenting opinions frequently show the reluctance of the judiciary to hold fast to the antiquated doctrine. The following bitter denunciation is illustrative:

> The whole doctrine of governmental immunity from liability for torts rests upon a rotten foundation. It is almost incredible that in the modern age of comparative sociological enlightenment and in a republic, the medieval absolutism supposed to be implied in the maxim, "the

[1] E. E. Fuller, "Reasons Given by Courts for School District Immunity," *American School Board Journal*, 103:23-25, November, 1941.

[2] Lee O. Garber, "Origin of the Governmental Immunity from Tort Doctrine," *Yearbook of School Law.* Edited by Lee O. Garber. Danville, Ill.: The Interstate Printers and Publishers, 1964, pp. 235-243.

king can do no wrong," should exempt the various branches of government from liability for their torts, and that the entire burden of damages resulting from the wrongful acts of the government should be imposed upon the single individual who suffers the injury, rather than distributed among the entire community, constituting the government, where it could be borne without hardship upon the individual, and where it justly belongs.[3]

11.3   Statutory trend concerning nonliability doctrine

Although adherence to the immunity principle was steadfast for nearly a century, a growing trend toward its abrogation is now discernible, both in statutes and court decisions.

With the early establishment of public schools, there were no specific statutes pertaining to school district liability. The common-law principle that the states or their political subdivisions (school districts) are not subject to tort action prevailed. Near the middle of the nineteenth century, however, a few states began to pass legislation intended to abrogate the governmental immunity of their school districts. Since that time numerous other states have introduced and passed legislation designed to waive the immunity rule in part or in its entirety.

This trend, however, is slow and it appears that state legislatures are not inclined to do much constructively about the matter until motivated or forced to do so by implication and consequences of judicial opinion.

11.4   Judicial trend concerning nonliability doctrine

At the very beginning of litigation concerning school district tort liability, the courts applied the rule of governmental immunity to protect school districts from tort liability. In the first school case of record, the Supreme Court of Massachusetts held, in 1860, that a town was not liable for injuries sustained by a pupil when he fell into a dangerous excavation in a school yard. Since the 1860 Massachusetts case there have been several hundred cases in which the

---

3 *Hoffman v. Bristol, City of,* 113 Conn 386, 155 Atl 499 (1931).

state courts have upheld the nonliability doctrine as applied to school districts. The main reason given by the courts why the school district should not be held liable was by virtue of its being a subdivision of the state and thereby enjoying sovereign immunity.

Over the century, then, there has been general adherence to the legal principle that school districts are immune from liability. During this period, however, it is interesting and significant to note a trend within a trend. Despite the general rule of nonliability of school districts, there has also been a trend of circumvention. That is—legal grounds have been established whereby the principle is inapplicable under certain circumstances.

There has been a growing tendency for courts to disregard the doctrine of school district immunity to liability in such instances as where the school district is (1) found guilty of trespass or nuisance; (2) found to be engaged in proprietary functions; and (3) protected from financial loss by liability insurance.

The major barriers in the judicial trend of school district immunity, however, did not develop until after 1900. Since then the courts in ten states have ruled school districts liable for their torts on the basis of legislative enactment abolishing the rule of nonliability or by judicial decision. These states, in the chronological order of court decision abrogating the immunity rule, are: Washington (1907), New York (1907), California (1928), Illinois (1959), Michigan (1961), Wisconsin (1962), Arizona (1963), Iowa (1967), Nebraska (1969), and Colorado (1971).

Court decisions in Iowa and Nebraska, presaged the enactment of legislation to abolish the immunity doctrine.[4] In *Moore* v. *Murphy*, the Iowa Supreme Court gave the assurance for a re-examination of the immunity rule at the first opportunity. Consequently, in 1967, the Iowa legislature abolished the rule of governmental immunity—making all subdivisions of the state liable for tortious acts, and authorizing purchase of liability insurance to cover officials and

---

[4] 254 Iowa 969, 119 NW(2d) 759 (1963).

employees.

Two years later, in 1969, the legislature of Nebraska did away with governmental immunity by passage of LB 154 and 155. Prior to the statutory enactments, the Nebraska Supreme Court had followed the lead of other states in removing immunity—particularly with torts arising from proprietary activities of governmental units.

At the time of this book revision, the last state to depart from the immunity doctrine was Colorado. Two different cases were decided on the same day by the Supreme Court of Colorado. In the first case,[5] the court stated: "we hold that the court-made doctrine of governmental immunity of school districts is overruled."

The other case[6] involved a county as the governmental unit, but was applicable to school districts. The opinion of this case was similar to that of its contemporary. In its dicta, however, the court emphasized that it was correcting the judicial mistakes that were made earlier. The court said, in part:

> It has been repeatedly stated that the doctrines of sovereign and governmental immunity have been made by the courts and, when it appears that these rules were wrong when made and wrong currently, the courts should abolish the rule.[7]

> The effect of this opinion and its two contemporaries is simply to undo what this court has done and leave the situation where it should have been at the beginning, or at least should be now: in the hands of the General Assembly of the State of Colorado.[8]

It is doubtful that the relatively few states in which the courts have disregarded the immunity doctrine constitute a

---

[5] *Flournoy v. School Dist. Number One in the City and County of Denver* (Colo), 482 P(2d) 966, 967 (1971).

[6] *Evans v. Board of County Commissioners of the County of El Paso* (Colo), 482 P(2d) 968 (1971).

[7] *Id.*, p. 970.

[8] *Id.*, p. 972.

marked trend. The forceful language employed by the courts (particularly in the last few instances) invalidating the old immunity rule, however, portends a significant trend.

There is now sufficient judicial evidence to indicate that the dominance of the principle that school districts are not liable in tort actions has already reached its highest point and has recently entered a period of decline.

The widely publicized *Molitor v. Kaneland* case of Illinois in 1959 marks the turning point. [9] As most students of school law are aware, the Supreme Court of Illinois abruptly overthrew the doctrine of governmental immunity, as applied to school districts, in action for tort damages. In this case, a minor (plaintiff) brought action against the defendant school district for personal injuries sustained in a school bus accident, allegedly caused by the driver's negligence.

All through the report of the case there is evidence that the court disregarded precedent in favor of fairness and timeliness. It boldly declared: "We do not believe that in this present day and age, when public education constitutes one of the biggest businesses in the country, school immunity can be justified on the protection-of-public-funds theory."

Finally in response to defendant's contention that if the immunity doctrine should be abolished, it should be by the legislature and not the courts, the Supreme Court replied:

> The doctrine of school district immunity was created by this court alone. Having found that doctrine to be unsound and unjust under present conditions, we consider that we have not only the power, but the duty, to abolish that immunity. We closed our courtroom doors without legislative help, and we can likewise open them.

11.5 Adjusting to the trend

Of course a school district cannot, of its own volition, abrogate its common-law governmental immunity. This may be done only by statutory or judicial law. As has been indicated, some states have already abrogated their school district

---

[9] *Molitor v. Kaneland*, 20 Ill 555, 155 NE(2d) 841 (1959).

immunity. In other instances, a number of states have created "save harmless" laws and "state claim boards" for the payment of damages in the event of injury caused by activities of the school district and its employees.

The procedures provided by North Carolina are illustrative. There the law provides for the payment, up to $10,000 limit, of claims of parents for pupils injured or killed in boarding, riding on, or alighting from a school bus.

In other jurisdictions—even where judicial opinion disfavors the immunity doctrine for school district liability—the courts cling to the earlier viewpoint that the change should be effected by legislative rather than judicial action. For example, after examining a number of tort cases in several jurisdictions in recent years, an Iowa court finally concluded in a 5-4 decision that "abrogation of the doctrine should come from legislative, not judicial action."[10]

With the changing trends in school district liability as determined by statute or court decision, local school boards are often perplexed as to what action should be taken against potential liability in order to protect themselves and their employees from financial loss. A likely inclination is to purchase liability insurance. There is question, however, that school boards may legally insure themselves from liability when they are immune from liability in the first place. How can one insure against something that is nonexistent?

It appears that concern over school district tort liability is restricted too much to the aspect of *indemnification*. More attention should be given by school boards to the *prevention* of tort liability. Compensatory measures can never take the place of preventive measures.

The waiving of district immunity and the legalizing of liability insurance are obligations which rest with the legislature. The safety of the pupils, however, is a matter for which the local school officials must assume responsibility. They are responsible for the careful selection of school personnel so that children are not made victims of recklessness.

---

[10] *Boyer* v. *Iowa High School Athletic Association*, 256 Iowa 337, 127 NW(2d) 606 (1964).

Moreover, it is their duty to inform school personnel of the personal liability of the latter in the event of accidents and injuries resulting from negligence. The mere fact that school officials are exempt from *legal liability* for the tortious acts of their employees imposes upon them a greater *moral liability* to avoid and eliminate, as much as possible, the dangers involved in the operation and conduct of the schools.

Chapter 12

THE SCHOOL BOARD

12.1   Legal nature of the school board

It is somewhat confusing to note in the educational literature that the terms "school district" and "school board" are
often used interchangeably. School boards and school districts do both exist for the same purpose of assuming responsibility and exercising authority over education within
legally defined boundaries. The "school district" is a territorial subdivision of the state in which the state function of
education is performed; whereas, the "school board" is an
agency, composed of citizens, representing the territorial
subdivision of the state in performing essentially the same
state function.

Since the local school board is the creature of the state
legislature, it possesses no common-law powers. The board's
only function is to carry out the will of the state toward education as expressed by the state legislature. In so doing, a
school board really functions as a legislative body itself over
school matters within the boundaries of a school district. In
general, its limitations are only those expressed or implied
in the state statutes, state constitution or the federal
Constitution.

A Mississippi court defines a school board as "an administrative agency to which certain powers have been delegated

146

by the legislature which are either administrative or legislative in nature."[1]

An Ohio court refers to the school board as "a quasi corporation acting for the public as one of the state's ministerial educational agencies 'for the organization, administration, and control of the public school system of the state.' . . . it is a body corporate and politic . . ., and, therefore, suit against board is plainly a suit against the government and its property."[2]

According to a Court of Appeals of Louisiana:

> A school board need not have specific legislative authority for every act which may be incidental or necessary to the performance of its duties. It has such implied or additional powers as are necessarily and properly incident to the performance of its statutory duties.[3]

The school board, as an agency of the state, possesses mandatory, directory, and permissive powers to perform those functions which are essential to the educational program established by the state. In so doing, however, the board may exercise its authority only as a corporate body. Its members, as individuals, possess no authority over the schools. The contrast of the legal status of the school board with that of an individual member of the board is described by the Supreme Court of Appeals of West Virginia:

> . . . a member of the board individually has no authority of any kind in connection with the schools of his country, except that the president, as such, is required to sign orders, contracts and so forth. The board of education can only act as a board, and when the board is not in session the members, severally or jointly, have no more authority to interfere with schools or school matters than any other

---

[1] *Loftin v. George County Board of Education* (Miss), 183 S(2d) 621 (1966).

[2] *Wayman v. Board of Education*, 5 OhioSt(2d) 248, 34 OO(2d) 473, 215 NE(2d) 394 (1966).

[3] *Disposal Systems, Inc. v. Calcasieu Parish School Board* (La), 243 S(2d) 915, 920 (1971).

citizen of the country [4]

It may be concluded, therefore, that in order for an action to be binding it must be taken by the school board as a whole. What constitutes "school board as a whole" will be defined more specifically later in connection with the discussion of quorums at school board meetings.

The assumption of powers to be exercised by the board is not entirely a matter of choice by the board. The school board may not divest itself of powers given to it by the legislature by delegating *discretionary* authority to committees, officers, or employees. In numerous instances, however, the courts hold that school boards may delegate *ministerial* duties. The difficulty in distinguishing between *discretionary* duties and *ministerial* duties is often the cause for disagreement and litigation. In fact, what may appear to be a single duty, sometimes has both discretionary and ministerial aspects.

Ordinarily the school board is not authorized by constitution or statute to assume professional functions of the public school. Apparently the courts are cognizant of the board's limitation in this respect as is exemplified by a judicial statement:

> The law does not contemplate that a board of education shall supervise the professional work of teachers, principals and superintendents. They are not teachers, and ordinarily, not qualified as such. Generally they do not possess qualifications to pass upon methods of instruction and discipline. The law clearly contemplates that professionally trained teachers, principals, and superintendents shall have exclusive control over these matters. [5]

12.2   Sources of laws pertaining to school boards

A study [6] of the laws pertaining to boards of education

---

[4] *State ex rel Rogers* v. *Board of Education of Lewis County,* 125 WVa 579, 25 SE(2d) 537 (1943).

[5] *State* v. *Board of Education,* 125 WV 579, 25 SE(2d) 537, 542 (1943).

[6] E. C. Bolmeier, "The Selection of City Boards of Education," *American School Board Journal* (May, 1938), pp. 41-43.

reveals many variations as to number of members, method of selection, filling of vacancies, and removal from office.

The many variations are due to the fact that each state legislature is authorized by its constitution to prescribe the conditions under which school boards shall be created and governed. Some state legislatures have exercised their prerogative by passing *general* laws which are applicable to all cities within a specified population range. Other legislatures have passed *special* laws applicable to individual cities. Still other legislatures have defined limits in which the cities themselves, through *home-rule* government, may determine the composition of the school board and the method of selecting its members.

Consequently, provisions applicable to school boards may be found in the general laws of the state, special-acts charters, and home-rule charters. In some instances the provisions pertaining to city boards of education are incorporated in both the general laws of the state and in the city charter. When these provisions are contradictory, the question may arise as to which law supersedes the other.

In general, the courts hold that home-rule charters dealing with school matters must be in harmony with, and not contrary to, statutory provisions. Where provisions of home-rule charters deny or abridge provisions contained in the general state law, "the charter provisions would be void by reason of conflict with the state law." [7] Of course this ruling stems from the well-established legal principle that education is a state and not a municipal function.

However, when a city charter is created by special acts, it does not necessarily follow that such a charter is superseded by a general state law if the two are contradictory. This is illustrated by a Connecticut case in which the court ruled that "a vacancy in the school committee is properly filled by the council; the provisions of the charter inconsistent with the general statutes controlling." [8]

---

[7] *Gerth v. Dominguez*, 1 Cal(2d) 239, 34 P(2d) 135 (1934).
[8] *State v. Hatch*, 82 Conn 122, 72 Atl 575 (1909).

12.3   Selection of school board members

The number of members which shall comprise the local school board is determined most frequently by general laws based upon a classification system. Therefore there is likely to be considerable uniformity in this respect within the boundaries of a single state. The main exceptions within a state are for city school systems. A majority of the laws referring to city boards of education stipulate specifically the number of members which shall comprise the board. This is particularly true when the provisions governing city boards of education are contained in home-rule charters, special acts, or in those portions of general laws applicable to single cities.

Under the provisions of certain general laws, the legislature fixes the limits as to number, and the voters of the school district determine the actual number of members within those limits. For example, the laws of Ohio refer to city boards of education as consisting of "not less than two members nor more than seven members."[9] Likewise the New Jersey law leaves the decision for the actual number constituting a city board of education "to the qualified voters of the municipality."[10]

Until comparatively recent years, two cities, St. Paul and Chattanooga, had no members on a school board. In fact, they had no school board at all, and the schools were governed by a "Commissioner of Education."

Over two-thirds of the large cities have school boards with 5, 7, or 9 members. Seven is the most usual number. In smaller cities and rural school districts the more prevalent number of board members is 5. Administratively and expeditiously the number of members on the school board may be important. Legally, however, it is an academic matter. The validity of board action has no relation to the size of a board, whether it has 3 or 23 members. Some persons are inclined to believe the more members who comprise the board of education, the more likely the school is to be represented adequately; others disagree.

---

[9] *Codes of Ohio*, 1934, Title XIII, sec. 4698.
[10] *New Jersey School Laws*, 1931, Art. VI, sec. 60(1).

It is rare that the laws provide for boards with 4, 6, or 8 members. This is indicative of a preference for odd numbers to avoid deadlocks in voting. In some cities, where there is an even number of board members, provisions have been made to break a possible deadlock in voting. For example, an Act of the Connecticut General Assembly provides that the mayor of the city of Bridgeport "shall cast the deciding vote" when the school board of 6 members "shall be equally divided on any issue." [11] This is a good example of questionable compromising with an unsatisfactory law instead of simply amending the law itself to make it satisfactory.

In virtually all cases where a new law is enacted or an old one amended, providing for a change in the number of members on a city board of education, the membership is decreased. The trend toward smaller boards follows a tendency to select members from the city at large in lieu of the antiquated ward basis of representation. Laws vary about as much in stipulating the methods by which school board members are to be selected as they do in specifying the number of members to constitute the board. Although in the great majority of cases boards are selected by the electorate, considerable variations exist for the larger cities. This is particularly true where the applicable laws are contained in the home-rule or special-acts charters. For cities over 50,000 population, selection by appointment is slightly greater than by election.

Public officials are not always in agreement as to which is the better method of school board selection, as was exemplified in the summer of 1966, when there were charges that the New York City Board of Education was not sufficiently attuned to the people's wishes. Governor Rockefeller expressed the opinion that one of the problems of the city was that "the people don't have the chance to elect their own representatives"; whereas State Commissioner of Education, Allen, argued that: "The system the city has now—a panel that selects a group with the mayor making his appointments

---

[11] Special Act 491 of the General Assembly of Connecticut, 1933, secs. 1, 3.

from the panel's selection—produces a better board."[12]

Where boards are selected by the electorate, the type of election at which they are elected is a matter of concern. Some contend that the election of school board members at a municipal election tends to subordinate school issues to those of the municipality and that the school elections are permeated by municipal and partisan maneuvering. Nevertheless, in cities where school boards are elected by the voters, over 60 percent are elected at city elections.

In over half of the larger cities where boards of education are appointed, the mayor is designated by city charter or statute as the sole appointing agency. The city council ranks second to the mayor as an agency for appointing members to city boards of education. In some instances the mayor and council combine as a single unit to perform the function.

Four cities have their school board members appointed by judges. In Washington, D. C., the judges of the Supreme Court of the District of Columbia appoint a board of 9 members, 3 of whom shall be women.[13] The board of education in Wilmington, Delaware, consists of 6 members "appointed by the resident judge of New Castle County."[14] Members of the boards of school directors in districts of the first class in Pennsylvania (Philadelphia and Pittsburgh) are appointed by "the judges of the court of common pleas of the county in which such school district is situated."[15]

Self-perpetuating school boards are becoming a rarity. Nevertheless an early law governing school board selection for Macon, Georgia, is still operative. There the board has "perpetual succession of members" and the board itself is authorized to "fill vacancies in the said Board, in whatever manner caused."[16] Also several of the city administrative units in North Carolina maintain the waning self-perpetuating method of selecting school board members.

---

[12] "Elect or Appoint Board?" *Nation's Schools* (November, 1966), p. 115.

[13] *Code of District of Columbia*, 1929, Title 7, sec. 1.

[14] *Delaware Laws*, 1931, H.B. 257.

[15] *School Laws of Pennsylvania*, 1933, Art. II, sec. 202.

[16] Act of the General Assembly of Georgia, approved, August 23, 1872, sec. 2.

12.4 Methods of filling vacancies

Where school board members gain office by appointment, the law usually provides that the same agency which appoints the regular members is also authorized to fill vacancies by appointment. Vacancies on elected school boards are in most cases filled by the remaining members of the board or else the vacancy is permitted to exist until the next school or city election.

The laws applicable to a number of cities where board members are originally elected provide that vacancies shall be filled by appointment. The mayor is most frequently authorized to fill the vacancy by appointment even though the board was originally elected by the people.

The matter of filling vacancies on school boards is considered so important that statutes frequently go into great detail in stipulating how the vacancies shall be filled. Also they become somewhat complicated, as may be noted by the applicable statute for North Carolina:

> All vacancies in the membership of the board of education in such counties by death, resignation, or otherwise, shall be filled by the action of the county executive committee of the political party of the member causing such vacancy until the meeting of the next regular session of the General Assembly, and then for the residue of the unexpired term by that body. If the vacancy to be filled by the General Assembly in such cases shall have occurred before the primary or convention held in such county, then in that event nominations for such vacancies shall be made in the manner hereinbefore set out, and such vacancy shall be filled from the candidates nominated to fill such vacancy by the party primaries or conventions of such county. All such vacancies that are not filled by the county executive committee under the authority herein contained within thirty days from the occurrence of such vacancies shall be filled by appointment by the State Board of Education. . . .[17]

As might be anticipated the courts will be called upon to

---

[17] *Public School Laws of North Carolina*, 1965, Chap. 115, sec. 24.

clarify such complicated legislation. In fact, the North Carolina Supreme Court did attempt to simplify the statute by explaining what the legislature had intended.[18]

12.5 Removal of school board members

With few exceptions removal of school board members is provided for in the general laws which are applicable to all school districts whether established and incorporated by special act or not. The provisions of the general laws, however, are not uniform for the different states.

Most frequently the board itself conducts the procedure whereby school board members are removed from office. A North Carolina statute is illustrative and typical:

In case the State Superintendent of Public Instruction shall have sufficient evidence that any member of a county or city board of education is not capable of discharging, or is not discharging, the duties of his office as required by law, or is guilty of immoral or disreputable conduct, he shall notify the chairman of such board of education, unless such chairman is the offending member, in which case all other members of such board shall be notified. Upon receipt of such notice there shall be a meeting of said board of education for the purpose of investigating the charges, and if the charges are found to be true, such board shall declare the office vacant: Provided, that the offending member shall be given proper notice of the hearing and that record of the findings of the other members shall be recorded in the minutes of such board of education.[19]

Removal of members from school boards in the state of Iowa may be made only by the courts.[20] Any member of the board of school commissioners of Indianapolis may be removed from office "upon petition of ten residents of said city to a superior or circuit court upon proof of either official misconduct in office or neglect of official duties."[21]

18 *State* v. *Fortner,* 236 NC 264, 72 SE(2d) 594 (1952).
19 *Public School Laws of North Carolina,* 1965, Chap. 115, sec. 30.
20 *Iowa Code,* secs. 1091, 1117.
21 *School Laws of Indiana,* 1932, sec. 496.

Also, the court of common pleas is authorized to remove school board members of Pennsylvania cities upon the receipt of a petition signed by ten resident taxpayers of the district involved.

Some laws authorize removal of school board members by means of the "recall." Thus the school laws of Oregon provide that "every school director in districts of the first class in Oregon is subject, as herein provided, to recall by the legal voters. . . ."[22] Also, Kansas school laws provide that school board members in certain cities "shall be nominated and elected in the same manner, as nearly as practicable, as are the mayor and commissioners in such cities and may be recalled in like manner."[23]

The number of cases in which city officials are authorized to remove school board members are few but significant— because of potential "municipal control" over "state officials."

A check-up by correspondence, in September, 1966, with the mayor's office in the cities of New York, San Francisco, and Baltimore reveals that the mayor in each of these cities is empowered by law to remove school board members under certain conditions.

For the city of New York, Section 523 of the New York City Charter provides that "a member of the Board of Education or a local school board may be removed by the Mayor on written charges after a hearing."

In accordance with Section 134 of the Charter for San Francisco, members of the board of education who are "nominated by the Mayor" are also "subject to recall and to suspension and removal. . . ."

The new charter for Baltimore (1964) provides that "the Mayor shall have the power to remove at pleasure, during the first six months of their respective terms, all municipal officers appointed by him. . . . This provision is rather all-inclusive and applies to many City offices in addition to the Board of School Commissioners."

Apparently there has never been sufficient cause as yet for the mayor in any city referred to above to exercise his pre-

---

[22] *Oregon School Laws,* 1931, sec. 35-1316.
[23] *School Laws of Kansas,* secs. 125, 72-1604.

rogative of removal as authorized by law. In the event, however, such action would take place, litigation would likely
follow with the charge that a municipal officer has no jurisdiction over a state officer. Then one might speculate that
the courts would uphold the laws with the interpretation that
municipal officers (mayors) are serving *ex officio* as state
officials while performing a state function of appointing and
removing other state officials (school board members).

Where the laws specifically empower city officials to remove
school board members, they possess the legal right to do so.
If, however, no law stipulates such authority, it cannot be
legally assumed. Where city officials knowingly or unknow-
ingly disregard the law, or devise their own law, by attempting to remove or control board members, their actions may
be challenged in the courts. If so, the courts will not uphold
the city official's actions because of misinterpretation or
ignorance of the law.

A 1966 case [24] illustrates ignorance of certain city officials
as to their limited authority over school board members by
virtue of their appointive function. The pertinent facts of
this case indicate that: (1) the statutes of Alabama empower
the governing body of the city (mayor and city council)
"to select a board of education of five members to exercise
the government and control of the schools of such city . . .";
(2) the school board, acting within the province of statutory
provisions fired the superintendent of schools; (3) "the action
of the board was met with strong displeasure by the Mayor
and City Council"; (4) the mayor admitted using the word
"ultimatum" when telling the board members "they had
until midnight to resign"; (5) the board refused to resign;
(6) in ruling that the city officials were acting beyond their
province of legal authority, the court emphasized that "the
legislative purpose was to invest in boards of education, when
duly and legally selected, the authority to act as free and
independent agencies of the city in the operation of the city
school system, free of interference by the governing bodies
which may have appointed the members."

---

[24] *Day* v. *Andrews*, 279 Ala 563, 188 S(2d) 523 (1966).

12.6   Trends pertaining to school board membership

Some of the data presented in the preceding sections of this chapter were obtained from research findings of several decades ago. It is noteworthy, however, that according to later research, the legal factors have remained rather constant. In a comparison of 1936 and 1968 data, Stallings found that:

Provisions for school board membership have not changed radically over the years. The most substantial changes in cities in these studies which have occurred, are large population increases, more use of the council-manager form of government and less of the commission plan, and decrease in identical boundaries of school district and city. There was a fairly large decrease in city elections of school board members, in mayors and city councilmen filling vacancies, and in school systems being city departments.

Areas in which there is little difference in the 1936 and 1968 data are use of general laws governing school board membership, size of school boards, ex officio members, and selection of school board members.[25]

12.7   Incompatible offices

Virtually all states have constitutional and statutory provisions prohibiting "double-office holding" (incompatible offices). Sometimes school board members fall under the *general* ruling without being designated as such; in other instances the laws refer to school board members specifically.

---

[25] Ann Coble Stallings, "Legal Factors Pertaining to School Board Membership in Municipalities Over 100,000 Population," Unpublished doctoral dissertation, Duke University, 1968, pp. 232-233.

"When the functions and duties of two offices are inherently such that one is subordinated to and controlled by the other, they are held to be incompatible under the common law."[26]

It is a well-established legal principle that one may not serve as a school board member while holding another public office. For example, in North Carolina where the state constitution forbids double-office holding, the court ruled that a school board member who accepts the position of mayor "automatically and instantly vacates the first office, and he does not thereafter act as either a *de jure* or a *de facto* officer in performing functions of the first office because he has neither right nor color to it."[27]

Moreover, one is *not* eligible to serve as a school board member while under contract as a public school teacher. A case in point is where a mayor appointed a school teacher to fill a vacancy on the board. The court invalidated the appointment and declared: "Common sense dictates the conclusion that being a school teacher and a member of a board of education in the same school is patently incompatible."[28]

The teacher argued that his acceptance of board membership vacated his teaching position rather than preventing his appointment to the board. The court responded by saying: "Here defendant teacher was bound by his teaching contract for the school term and was not legally free to abandon one public job for another."[29]

12.8   School board members as officers of city or state

City charters frequently refer to school board members as

---

[26] Newton Edwards, *The Courts and the Public Schools.* Chicago: University of Chicago Press, 1955, p. 121.

[27] *Edwards* v. *Board of Education of Yancey County*, 235 NC 345, 70 SE(2d) 170 (1952).

[28] *Visotcky* v. *City Council of Garfield*, 113 NJSuper 263, 273 A(2d) 597, 599 (1971).

[29] *Id.,* p. 600.

"city officers." Consequently litigation frequently develops over the issue as to whether they are city officers in the strict sense of the term as are other officers of the city.

A general ruling is that the functions performed determine whether school board members are city or state officers.[30] Where courts have ruled that education is a function of the state it obviously follows that school board members are officers of the state.[31]

In most jurisdictions it is held that school board members are state officers rather than city officers. Excerpts gleaned from a few of the leading cases dealing with the issue are indicative:

"The board of education of Port Huron is a municipal corporation distinct from that of the city, and its members are not city officers subject to removal by the city council.

The power given that body to remove officers does not reach any but city officers."[32]

"The duties and obligations resting on school boards and the purposes of the corporation they officer, we can conclude that they are not 'officers and employees of the government' of a civil city."[33]

"Obviously the Legislature, in referring . . . to officers of the cities, did not have in mind members of a city board of education. For they, or rather their predecessors, known as the city school trustees, whose powers and duties were similar, have by this court been declared state officers."[34]

"Although as a matter of first impression it might appear that all officers elected by the electors of a city were necessarily 'city officers,' upon reflection, and possibly more mature consideration of the legal aspects involved, together with authorities handed down by the Supreme and Appellate Courts of this state, it will become apparent that the election

[30] *Kahn* v. *Sutro*, 114 Cal 316, 46 Pac 87 (1896).

[31] *City of Louisville* v. *Commonwealth*, 134 Ky 488, 121 SW 411 (1909).

[32] *People ex rel. Tibbals* v. *Board of Education of Port Huron*, 39 Mich 635 (1898).

[33] *Agar* v. *Pagin*, 39 IndApp 567, 79 NE 379 (1906).

[34] *Whitt* v. *Wilson*, 212 Ky 281, 278 SW 609 (1925).

of the several members of the board of education is merely
a preliminary means of inducting such members into their
respective offices, and that, when seated therein they become,
and thenceforward are, officers of a political subdivision of
the state, separate and distinct from the municipality within
the boundaries of which the school district is located."[35]

Not only do courts rule that school board members are
state officers but go so far as to say that city officers are *ex
officio* state officers when performing school functions. A
statement by the Supreme Court of Kansas illustrates the
point: "The members of the city council, when considering
tax levies made by the board of education for school purposes, act *ex officio* as members of the school board." [36]

The adjudications referred to thus far indicate a high
degree of unanimity of judicial opinion in declaring that
school board members are "state officers." However, in
conformity with unusual legislative intent, the courts may
refer to school board members as "city officers." In the
first instance of a court following this rare reasoning, the
Supreme Court of Wisconsin held that "the members of the
board of education are city officers" and that "the board of
education is merely an arm of the city government."[37]

In a much more recent case[38] the same exceptional ruling
was followed by the Supreme Court of Alaska, which ruled
that board members are subject to recall as are municipal
officers. The court based its decision on the reasoning that
the school board is an arm or agency of the city government
and board members are municipal and not state officers.

In attempting to distinguish between the city school district and city, the court stated:

The only real distinction between the two is that the
city's normal municipal officers are regulated by a city
council, the members of which are elected to office by
the voters of the city; whereas, affairs relating to education

---

[35] *Ward* v. *San Diego School District*, 203 Cal 712, 265 Pac 821 (1928).
[36] *School District No. 76* v. *Ryker*, 64 Kan 612, 68 Pac 34 (1902).
[37] *State* v. *Racine*, 205 Wis 389, 236 NW 553 (1931).
[38] *Blue* v. *Stockton* (Alaska), 355 P(2d) 395 (1960).

in the city are managed by members of a school board who also are elected to office by the same voters.

Under the legislative plan of education in Alaska . . . the city has been designated the municipal entity for administration of school affairs. The city school board performs this function on behalf of the city by operating schools within the municipal boundaries. In so doing the board acts as a branch or arm of the city government.

The reasoning in this case, as in the *Racine* case, is in direct contrast to that followed in the great majority of other jurisdictions.

Regardless of whether school board members are held to be "state officers" or "city officers" the supreme authority of the state cannot be denied. Whenever the state sees fit to change the composition of the governing agencies it may, within constitutional limitations, do so—even to the extent of abolishing the board entirely.[39]

12.9   Liability of individual board members

In view of the fact that school board members give their services without compensation, it seems unjust that they should ever be held liable for their official actions. In fact, they need not be held liable and are not likely to be held liable providing their actions are in good faith and without fraud. Of course when an individual school board member acts maliciously and in bad faith he is likely to be held liable as would a school employee or any citizen.

Since school board members are laymen and often without much business or legal training they are likely to make mistakes in their official actions. The courts generally rule that if the mistakes are because of error in judgment the individual board member will not be held liable. As long as the board member acts honestly, in good faith, and within the scope of the corporate powers of the board he is free from liability. Gauerke cautions that "To be on the side

---

[39] *State ex rel. Smith* v. *St. Paul*, 128 Minn 82, 150 NW 389 (1914).

of prudence, a board member should name himself as a member of a board when he individually signs a contract for the board of education. The school district should be named as the contracting party."[40]

Of course an individual board member who does not vote along with the majority of the board in an illegal action would not be held liable personally. Moreover, he is not likely to be held liable for his acts of nonfeasance or for school employees' acts of misfeasance unless he participated in such acts directly.

There is the danger that individual school board members may become too complacent about their tortious acts or those of their employees in school matters because of the immunity which school districts (school boards) enjoy. School officers should be cognizant of the fact, however, that even though the school board, as a body, is immune from liability for the negligent acts of employees, individual members may be held liable individually if malicious action can be established. For example, the North Carolina Supreme Court found individual members of a school committee individually liable for the death of a child caused by the reckless driving of a bus driver who was known by the committee at the time he was hired to be a person who was "reckless and unfit for the position."[41]

12.10　School board meetings

Since a school board is a legal entity, it must act in its aggregate capacity for its actions to be legal. In some instances the statutes state specifically that the board must meet and act as a body in order to take any action where the exercise of discretionary authority is involved. Even in the absence of such statutory provisions, the courts hold that action of the board is legal only when convened as a unit. A

---

[40] Warren W. Gauerke, *School Law*. New York: Center for Applied Research in Education, Inc., 1965, p. 96.

[41] *Betts* v. *Jones*, 203 NC 590, 166 SE 589 (1932).

ruling of a Missouri court is illustrative:

> The board of directors of a school district is an entity which can act and speak only as such. The separate and individual acts and decisions of the director members, even though they be in complete agreement with each other, have no effect. They must be assembled and act *as a board.*[42]

In a 1966 case[43] a board's dismissal of a teacher for alleged incompetency was held illegal by the Supreme Court of Montana, because the school board did not follow the law which required official acts to be taken "in regular or special sessions." Although two of the three board members signed a letter purporting to dismiss the teacher on grounds of incompetency, "the record shows there was no meeting either special or regular prior to the respondent being summarily fired."

Judicial reasoning, in holding that a board's action is binding only when it meets as a body, was set forth somewhat in detail nearly a century ago. A quotation from the decision which is still applicable today follows:

> The different members of a board, scattered in the pursuit of their several vocations, are not the board. Duties are cast upon boards composed of a number of persons, in order that they may be discharged with efficiency and wisdom arising from a multitude of counsel. This purpose cannot be realized without conference between the members of the board, with reference to the matters intrusted to them, before they take action thereon. . . . The public selects each member of a board of directors, and is entitled to his services. This it cannot enjoy if two members can bind it without receiving or even suffering the counsel of the other. Two could, if they differed with the third, overrule his judgment, and act without regarding it; but he might by his knowledge and reason, change the bent

---

[42] *State v. Consolidated Sch. Dist. No. 3* (Mo), 281 SW(2d) 511 (1955).
[43] *Wyatt v. School Dist. No. 104,* Fergus County, 148 Mont 83, 417 P(2d) 221 (1966).

of their minds, and the opportunity must be given him. [44]

Disregard of the legal principle that *a school board must act in its aggregate capacity for its actions to be legal* may be costly to a school district. An example is afforded by a later Arkansas case.[45] Here a school teacher was discharged before the expiration of her teaching contract by the principal who acted under authority given by *two members of a five-member board*. She was unsuccessful, in a lower court, in her suit to recover from the school district the balance which she would have ordinarily drawn under the contract. On appeal, however, the Supreme Court of Arkansas ruled that: "Appellant's motion for an instructed verdict should have been granted and judgment entered for her April, May, and June salary. On remand the trial court is directed to enter judgment accordingly."[46]

Although court rulings serve generally as reliable precedents and guidelines for school board procedure, under extraordinary circumstances they may be ignored by the board with judicial approval. In other words, there are exceptions to the rule. For example, in a Pennsylvania case, pupils and teachers suddenly became ill, whereupon the president of the board called other members of the board by telephone, and without waiting to take action at a legal board meeting, employed the laboratory experts to investigate and discover the cause of the mass illness. When the bill for the services was presented, action was brought to test the right of the board to pay it. The court, in approving the action, reasoned as follows:

> In view of the emergency existing and the lack of knowledge as to what costs might be incurred, the defendant directors were fully justified in contracting for the services by their proper officers without waiting for a formal meeting in order to record the minutes of the action. Neither the time nor the conditions permitted any delay or discussion. Indeed, even the plaintiff should be commended

---

44 *School District* v. *Bennett*, 52 Ark 511, 13 SW 132 (1890).
45 *Farris* v. *Stone County School Dist. No. 1* (Ark), 450 SW(2d) 279 (1970).
46 *Id.*, p. 281.

for not requiring same before undertaking the investigation. . . . The safety of the school child is at all times the primary factor, and if necessary all requirements should be passed over in order to protect them [sic].[47]

Statutes vary in specificity with respect to a place where a board meeting may or must be held. In some states there are no statutory provisions designating where school board meetings may be held. Garber states that:

In the absence of a statute requiring a board to hold its meetings in a certain designated place, such as in a school building or within the boundaries of the district, a board is at liberty to choose its meeting place, and even if it holds a meeting outside the district that meeting will generally be held to be legal.

He adds that "When the statute requires that board meetings be held in the district, the statute controls, and a meeting held outside the district will be held to be illegal."[48]

An example is afforded by a Kansas case[49] where the statute provided that board meetings be held in the district. Nevertheless, a school board held a joint meeting outside its boundaries with another district. The court ruled that the meeting was illegal but conceded that had the board returned to its own district and called a meeting it could have approved the action it took outside the district and thus made it legal.

In the absence of a statute to the contrary a board may hold its meetings at such times as agreed upon by the board—providing its actions are reasonable. Litigation frequently develops where there is the question as to how far a board may depart from the statutes stipulating the time at which a regular meeting may be held. Court decisions vary in ruling whether the statutory provisions are mandatory or directory. Even though all members of the school board must receive actual or constructive notice of a meeting, it is not necessary

---

[47] *Smith Laboratories v. Chester School Board* (Pa), 33 DelCo 97 (1944).
[48] Lee O. Garber, *Law and the School Business Manager.* Danville, Ill.: Interstate Printers and Publishers, 1957, p. 296.
[49] *State v. Rural High School District,* 169 Kan 671, 220 P(2d) 164 (1950).

that *all* be present at the meeting in order to make the meeting legal. It is, however, a well-established legal principle that a meeting is not legal unless a *quorum* is present, but where a quorum is present, any action can be taken, with official sanction, that the entire board could have taken.

Hamilton and Reutter state that:

Unless an express statute provides otherwise, the common-law rule is that a majority of the authorized membership of a board constitutes a quorum, and under the common law a majority of a quorum may officially transact business. In the absence of a quorum, any action taken is that of the individual members present and does not legally bind the district.[50]

In voting, the majority of the quorum controls. Some rather litigious issues can arise, however, when some members constituting the quorum fail to vote. An applicable, but rather ludicrous, case arose in Missouri, where the school board in question consisted of three members, but only two of the members were present at the meeting when the controversy arose. When a question of calling an election to consider annexation was presented, one member voted to accept it, but the other member refused to vote. In holding that the one affirmative vote constituted legal approval of the issue the court declared:

There were two of the three members of the School Board present and by their presence constituted a quorum for the transaction of business, and it became and was the duty of each member to vote for or against any proposition which was presented to them. Mr. Eveland voted in favor of submitting the question of annexation and Mr. Williams did not vote. . . . It was his duty to vote for or against the question submitted. . . . When a member of a school board sits silently by when given an opportunity to vote, he is regarded as acquiescing in, rather than oppos-

---

50 R. R. Hamilton and E. Edmund Reutter, *Legal Aspects of School Board Operation.* New York: Bureau of Publications, Teachers College, Columbia University, 1958, p. 139.

ing, the measure, and is regarded in law as voting with the majority. . . .[51]

From the case reported above, the general rule, that one who fails to vote is considered as acquiescing with the majority, may be accepted. There is, however, an exception to the rule, where a statute *requires* an affirmative vote of all members present. In such an instance a failure to vote is tantamount to voting negatively on a question. Garber cites several applicable cases to the general rule and to the exception of the rule.[52]

Sometimes statutes stipulate the ratio of affirmative votes required to make a school board action binding. For example, a Kentucky law required that a board of education could remove a superintendent of schools from office by the affirmative vote of 4 members of the 5-member board. The court, however, did not permit the ouster by a 4 to 3 vote of the board when the board was enlarged to 7 members because of a merger. The court reasoned that the intention of the Legislature had been to require an 80 percent majority for legal action.

In support of its ruling the court stated: "We have often said that statutes will not be given a strict or literal reading where to do so would lead to absurd or unreasonable conclusions."[53]

There is a growing civic desire to know what actions are taken by public officials who represent them. This is particularly evidenced in school situations where school patrons want to know about the official activities of their representatives at school board meetings. Consequently the laws usually require that the meetings be "open" to the public. But since all conditions for "openness" cannot be spelled out in the statutes, litigation frequently arises as to what actually constitutes the "open" school board meeting,

After reviewing several applicable court cases, *Lindahl* v.

---

[51] *Mullins v. Eveland* (Mo), 234 SW(2d) 639 (1950).
[52] Garber, *Law and the School Business Manager*, pp. 300-305.
[53] *Wesley v. Board of Education of Nicholas County* (Ky), 403 SW(2d) 28 (1966).

Independent School Dist. No. 306, (Minn) (1965);[54] *Szilagyi* v. *State,* (Ind) (1967);[55] *Goldman* v. *Zimmer,* (Ill) (1965);[56] *Quast* v. *Knutson,* (Minn) (1967);[57] *Board of Education* v. *State Board of Education,* (NM) (1968),[58] Garber sets forth the following guidelines for conformance to legal requirements:

(1) Where a board holds a public-hearing, it may then adjourn to its regular meeting place to take action on the matter. Its failure to invite the public to the latter meeting will not be considered fatal.

(2) A board may hold executive sessions to study matters if it postpones action until it holds a public hearing.

(3) A board that fails to act legally by taking action at a closed meeting may rectify the error if it votes later, at a public meeting, to ratify the action.

(4) To meet requirements of the open meeting law, meetings must be held at a point accessible to the public.

(5) Unless a statute states the method of voting, action taken at the open meeting as a result of a prior secret ballot will not be considered a violation.[59]

"Open meeting" legislation has taken different forms in the several states. If a statute specifies that school board meetings shall be open to the public, any meeting, not in accordance with the specification would be considered by the courts to be illegal. For example, in a Texas case[60] the court states: "It is an anomaly to say that a meeting, the holding of which is forbidden by law, is a legal meeting."

An *open-meeting* act enacted by the North Carolina Leg-

---

[54] (Minn) 133 NW(2d) 23 (1965).

[55] (Ind) 231 NE(2d) 221 (1967).

[56] 64 Ill App(2d) 277, 212 NE(2d) 132 (1965).

[57] 276 Minn 340, 150 NW(2d) 199 (1967).

[58] 79 NM 332, 443 P(2d) 502 (1968).

[59] Lee O. Garber, "What Constitutes an 'Open' School Board Meeting," *Nation's Schools,* Vol. 87, No. 6, June 1971, pp. 10-11.

[60] *Toyah Independent School Dist.* v. *Pecos-Barstow Independent School Dist.* (Tex), 466 SW(2d) 377, 380 (1971).

islature, in 1971, specifies the subjects for which closed sessions for the board, or its committees, are permitted: (1) acquisition of property; (2) negotiations with employee groups; (3) conferences with legal counsel and other deliberations concerning prosecution, defense, settlement, or litigation of any judicial action in which the school board is a party or directly affected; (4) any matter constituting a privileged communication; (5) student discipline cases; (6) strategy for handling an existing or imminent riot or public disorder; and (7) appointment, discipline, or dismissal of personnel. As to the last item, however, final action on the discharge of an employee must be taken in open session.[61]

12.11 Recording board minutes

The continuous avalanche of court cases dealing with this issue provide ample evidence that meticulous and proper recording of the school board actions minimizes legal involvements. Professional literature in the field of school law is abundant with statements stressing the importance of making and preserving proper records of school board actions. The following excerpts gleaned from the writings of several authorities in the field of school law are illustrative:

1. It is only through the modicum of the duly kept minutes that the citizens and their instrument, the courts, can be apprised as to what their school board is doing.[62]

2. A board of education speaks only through and by its record of what was done when acting as a body in a corporate meeting.[63]

3. Ordinarily, the official records of a public corporation are *prima facie* evidence of the action taken by that corporation.[64]

---

[61] Robert E. Phay (Editor), "Public School Law: Changes by the 1971 North Carolina General Assembly," *School Law Bulletin*, Vol. II, No. 3, August, 1971, p. 7.

[62] Manny S. Brown, "Record of School Board Minutes," *Legal Problems of School Boards*. Cincinnati: The W. H. Anderson Co., 1966, p. 23.

[63] Robert L. Drury and Kenneth C. Ray, *Principles of School Law*. New York: Appleton-Century-Crofts, 1965, p. 23.

[64] Edwards, *The Courts and the Public Schools*, p. 193.

4. It is *prima facie* evidence of the facts stated therein, and it has been characterized as "the mind and memory" of a corporate body.[65]

5. Unless statutes provide otherwise, it is a general rule that minutes of board meetings are public documents or writings and thus are open to inspection by the public.[66]

6. The record of the minutes is the best evidence of the board's action. This is in accordance with the usual application of the "best-evidence rule" at common law.[67]

The above statements, based upon statutory provisions and numerous court decisions involving the records of school board minutes, are indicative of their relevance. Consequently, school boards would do well in applying, to the best of their ability, legal and sound procedure in recording their actions.

Even though the board minutes may be deficient in technical and formal style, their validity may not be impaired if they have been recorded in good faith, and if they indicate the board's intentions. A statement made by the Supreme Court of North Dakota exemplifies:

> In passing on the sufficiency of the minutes kept by a school board of a common school district consideration should be given to the fact that ordinarily the members of such a board and its clerk are not experts in the field of keeping records of proceedings and that the meetings of such boards are to a large extent conducted informally. Such minutes will therefore not be given a technical construction and irregularities and informalities will be disregarded, where the minutes are sufficient to show the board's intention.[68]

---

[65] Garber, *Law and the School Business Manager*, p. 307.
[66] Hamilton and Reutter, *Legal Aspects of School Board Operation*, p. 174.
[67] Remmlein, *The Law of Public School Administration*, p. 33.
[68] *Linden School District* v. *Porter* (ND), 130 NW(2d) 76 (1964).

Chapter 13

DISCRETIONARY AUTHORITY OF SCHOOL BOARDS OVER SCHOOL PROPERTY

Section
13.1   Ownership and title
13.2   Selection of school sites
13.3   Acquisition of school property
13.4   Control over school property
13.5   Judicial definition of a school building
13.6   Use of public school buildings for nonschool purposes

13.1   Ownership and title

A firmly-established legal principle is that education is a state function. Emanating from that principle, another is that schools are state institutions and therefore *school property is state property.*

The erroneous contention that a school district owns school property resting within its boundaries was disproved by the Supreme Court of Illinois in a convincing statement:

A frequently cited proposition is that the State may, with or without the consent of the inhabitants of a school district, or against their protest, and with or without notice of hearing, take the school facilities in the district without compensation and vest them in other districts or agencies. . . . The "property of the school district" is a phrase which is misleading. The district owns no property, all school facilities, such as grounds, buildings, equipment, etc., being in fact and law the property of the State and subject to the legislative will.[1]

One reason why school boards frequently contend that the school property belongs to the school district is because the laws often designate the school district or some other politi-

---
[1] *Pritchett v. County Board of School Trustees,* 5 Ill(2d) 356, 125 NE(2d) 476 (1955).

cal agency as the holder of the title to school property. Some of the most significant litigation concerning this issue is where municipal officials attempt to exercise control over school property by virtue of the fact that the laws occasionally designate the municipality or its officers as title holders or trustees of school property.[2]

In general, the courts rule that since a school city has no vested interest in public school property, the city holds the property merely as a trustee for the public, subject to change any time by act of the legislature.[3]

13.2   Selection of school sites

As a general rule, the school board is vested with authority to select a school site. Where the school board's authority to select the site has been challenged, the courts have usually held that the school board has the discretionary authority to do so. Numerous exceptions, however, exist in cities where there is considerable commingling of school and municipal functions.

In a number of the larger cities, the authority to select the site for a school is granted to city officials, such as the municipal building commissioner. In a few instances the school and city officials concur in selecting the site. Where city officials are authorized to select sites, the sites so selected usually require the approval of the board of education. Conversely, in some cases the selection of sites by school boards requires the approval of designated city officials.[4]

Frequently municipal authorities challenge the authority of a school district to determine the construction and location of a school building which might jeopardize the municipality's ability to secure revenue from a common tax base. Such was the case in Pennsylvania where a municipality at-

---

2 E. C. Bolmeier, "Municipal Participation in the Control of City School Property," *American School Board Journal* (September, 1938), pp. 47-49.

3 *City of Jeffersonville* v. *Jeffersonville School Township of Clark County,* 77 IndApp 32, 130 NE 879 (1921).

4 Bolmeier, "Municipal Participation in the Control of City School Property," p. 47.

tempted to delay plans by a school district for the construction of a school building until approval by a referendum. In holding that the "municipality lacked standing to maintain such an action," the Supreme Court of Pennsylvania declared:[5]

> As long as we have a system where the board of the school district has the exclusive duty and authority to determine the necessity and location for school buildings and the city has the exclusive power to determine questions concerning municipal services, neither can be said to have the pecuniary interest necessary to have standing to challenge the other's activities.

Outside of cases involving city versus school authority over school property, the courts have been reluctant to infringe upon the prerogative of a school board to select the school site, unless an abuse of the board's discretionary authority is manifest. For example, in 1961 an Alabama court held that "the matter of locating, constructing and maintaining buildings for public school purposes is not a function of the courts." [6]

13.3 Acquisition of school property

The issue of acquiring public school property constitutes one of the most prolific areas of school litigation. This is attested by the fact that, in a comprehensive study, approximately 500 appellate court decisions, from the published records of the 50 states, were found to be applicable to the problem. [7] The following brief conclusions are based upon the analyses of the case reports:

1. The issue of a school district's authority for acquiring and owning public school property has been definitely

---

[5] *City of Hazleton* v. *Hazleton Area School Dist.* (Pa.), 276 A(2d) 545, 547 (1971).

[6] *Smith* v. *City Board of Education of Birmingham*, 272 Ala 227, 130 S(2d) 29 (1961).

[7] Jesse L. McDaniel and Edward C. Bolmeier, *Law Governing Acquisition of School Property.* Cincinnati: The W. H. Anderson Co., 1966.

settled.

2. School boards have the authority to provide reasonable and necessary facilities for a legally-authorized program of public education.

3. Neither necessity, profit, nor convenience will substitute for legal authority in the acquisition of property for public school use.

4. The law governing the acquisition of school property is grounded in common-law principles and is characterized by a history of legal precedent.

5. The acquisition of public school property is subject to the same legal principles that govern the acquisition of property for any other public use.

6. The courts have allowed school boards broad discretionary powers in the acquisition of property.

7. Public school agencies have, on occasions, benefited from a "halo" effect where their authority for property acquisition has been challenged in the courts.

8. Most jurisdictions are in substantial agreement in regard to many aspects of school property law.

9. The only question which does not show a high degree of agreement among the states is that concerning the use of state school building authorities.

10. The expanding scope of public education has created property needs which were not envisioned when statutes were written many years ago.

11. The courts have interpreted the broad, general powers of school boards to include the authority to provide the more comprehensive school facilities of today.

12. Public school property is state property and a school district holds title as trustee only.

13. Community rights have been held to be subordinate to a state's rights in the task of legally redefining district lines and apportioning school property.

14. The school district taxpayer has no property interest in the assets of a district, nor vested property rights of any kind.

15. Where authority for the acquisition of property

has been clear-cut, court action has usually been concerned with an alleged improper method of acquisition.

16. Most public school property has been acquired by simple purchase or by purchase through condemnation.

17. The acquisition of property through donation is not as common today as in the earlier years of the public school system.

18. The power to take land by condemnation under the right of eminent domain is a sovereign right and is not restricted to public school agencies.

19. In condemnation action, the courts may consider only the questions of authority and purchase price.

20. As population growth and building congestion increase, one may assume that a greater proportion of school-site needs will be met through condemnation action.[8]

13.4 Control over school property

Basically the state has control over public school property. This power, however, is usually delegated to the school district which is a territorial subdivision of the state. The governing body, then, is the local board of education.

Limited rights of citizens to use public school property are expressed by the Supreme Court of Washington in a 1971 case[9]

   . . . it is essential to recognize the fact that while school properties are public in the sense that they are endowed and operated with taxpayers' money, they are not public in the sense that any member of the general public may, when and if he pleases, use such properties for his own personal objectives or the dissemination of his own personal views. Accordingly, the uses to which such properties may be put by members of the public, otherwise unaffiliated with the school operation, are properly subject to reasonable statutory, as well as administrative, regulation and proscription.

---

[8] McDaniel and Bolmeier, *Law Governing Acquisition of School Property,* pp. 153-154.

[9] *State* v. *Oyen* (Wash), 480 P(2d) 766, 769 (1971).

Protests by taxpayers or civic groups do not diminish the discretionary authority of school boards in the control of school property. Of course, any taxpayer is privileged to take legal action against the board for alleged abuse of authority. In virtually all instances, however, the court will uphold the board's actions in controlling the use of school property within the limits of constitutional and statutory provisions and bounds of reasonableness.[10]

Much of the litigation stems from the attempts of municipal officers to infringe upon the rights of school boards in exercising control over public school property located within the boundaries of the municipality. The issue is particularly evident in recent years when a municipality attempts to administer zoning plans which are designed to exclude certain schools from certain residential areas. Garber states that "The courts are in disagreement regarding the validity of such action," and cites several corroborate court cases.[11]

Numerous court cases have also been triggered by municipal school disputes over the control of fire hazards of public school buildings. Strong arguments have been presented, in some instances, indicating that the control over "state property" belongs exclusively to "state officers" (school board). In other instances, equally strong arguments support "municipal control" (city ordinances) designed to promote the "public safety, health and welfare."

In support of the school board's supremacy in such matters, the Court of Appeals of Kentucky ruled, in an early case, that an educational institution was not legally bound by a city ordinance requiring fire escapes on all buildings of three or more stories. The reasoning of the court was portrayed in its query: "How can the city have ever a superior authority to the State over the latter's own property, or in its control or management?"[12]

---

10 *Demers* v. *Collins* (RI), 201 A(2d) 477 (1964).
11 Garber, *Yearbook of School Law*, pp. 105-108.
12 *Kentucky Institution for Education of Blind* v. *Louisville*, 123 Ky 767, 97 SW 402 (1906).

A different line of reasoning is reflected in a more recent case in which the issue was whether or not a "school district" must comply with a "fire district" in affording fire protection to municipal and school territory. In this instance, the court ruled in favor of the fire district on the ground that the fire district was "a municipal corporation endowed with police powers in the field of fire prevention"; whereas, the school district was "a quasi-municipal corporation without police power with only the limited power of public education." Since the fire district was a creature of the state legislature, the court reasoned that the school district was as subservient to the authority of the fire district as it would be to the action of the state itself, and concluded that subservience of the school district to the fire district in this particular matter was "more likely to promote the public safety, health and welfare." [13]

In 1965, the Supreme Court of Pennsylvania ruled that the municipality had the power to regulate by means of zoning ordinances the construction of public school buildings by the school district within the municipal limits. In so ruling, the court concluded:

> We therefore find that the City of Philadelphia has been empowered to prescribe reasonable ordinances for the protection of safety, health and the general welfare, which, in regard to municipal functions, shall have the force of legislative enactment. . . . The School District is not immune from such ordinance and that it must comply therewith. [14]

The school board's limitation in exercising police power was further substantiated in a Minnesota case, where the court stated:

> . . . the school authorities are supreme in all matters directly or by implication, involving the subject of education, but with the matter of governmental police regulations, having to do solely with the maintenance of public

---

[13] *Community Fire Protection Dist. of St. Louis County v. Board of Education of Pattonville* (Mo), 315 SW(2d) 873 (1958).

[14] *School Dist. of Philadelphia v. Zoning Board of Adjustment,* 417 Pa 277, 207 A(2d) 864 (1965).

order and peace, the health, safety and freedom from violence of the citizens of the state and protection of property from destruction by violence, the school authorities have nothing to do. And it is well for them that they do not.[15]

13.5   Judicial definition of a school building

As the concept for the "school curriculum" has broadened within recent years, so has the concept for a "school building" in which certain "extracurricular" activities are conducted. Consequently, litigation frequently develops where school boards, which are authorized by statute to issue bonds for the construction and maintenance of school buildings, use the funds for benefit of gymnasiums, stadiums, swimming pools, etc.

An example is afforded by a New Jersey case in which a statute authorizing the expenditure of funds for repairing and enlarging school buildings was interpreted and acted upon by the school board to provide for a stadium. In upholding the board's litigated action, the court followed the rationale of previous cases, declaring: "competitive athletic games are no less fitted for furthering the ultimate purpose of public schools, i. e., the making of good citizens, physically, mentally, and morally, than the study of other subjects."[16]

In the same year, a decision in an Oregon case further supported the judicial interpretation as to what constitutes a "school building." The issue in point was whether or not a school board could apply a statute authorizing indebtedness for school buildings to include indebtedness for swimming pools. The court, in supporting the board's action, defined a school building thusly: "A building is a 'school building' if it is designed to carry out a part of the instructional program authorized by the district."[17]

---

[15] *Village of Blaine* v. *Independent School Dist. No. 12,* 272 Minn 343, 138 NW(2d) 32 (1965).

[16] *Board of Education* v. *Hoek,* 38 NJ 213, 183 A(2d) 633 (1962).

[17] *Petition of School Board,* 232 Ore 64, 377 P(2d) 4 (1962).

13.6   Use of public school buildings for nonschool purposes

Within constitutional limits, state legislatures may enact direct legislation to prohibit or permit the use of school buildings for any purpose, whatsoever, other than education, or to delegate the authority to school boards.

Litigation frequently develops in instances where the statutes are silent on the subject and thereby necessitate the board to exercise discretionary authority which may be challenged. The court's rulings are in variance as to whether or not the school board may permit the use of school buildings for other than purposes of education. Based upon a number of court decisions that have been rendered in recent years, it appears that the trend is to permit the use of school buildings for social, political and even religious gatherings in accordance with reasonable regulations determined by the local school board.

The most significant cases have to do with the use of public school buildings for *religious* purposes. In such cases the First Amendment of the Constitution of the United States is involved as well as are constitutional and statutory provisions of the various states.

A decision by the Supreme Court of Florida typifies the majority of decisions in other jurisdictions on the issue. The court opined as follows:

> While admittedly, there are some differences of view regarding the matter of religious meetings in school houses during nonschool periods, we think that logic, as well as our traditional attitudes toward the importance of religious worship, justifies our alignment with those courts which permit such use. . . .

> We, therefore, hold that a Board of Trustees of a Florida School District has the power to exercise reasonable discretion to permit the use of school buildings during nonschool hours for any legal assembly which includes religious meetings, subject, of course, to judicial review should such discretion be abused to the point that it could be construed as a contribution of public funds in aid of a

particular religious group or as the promotion or establishment of a particular religion. [18]

In an exhaustive study by Griffiths it was concluded that:

Where the statutes vest authority in local boards of education to permit the use of public-school buildings for religious purposes, it has generally been held that such enactments confer considerable discretion and, in the absence of abuse, the exercise of such discretion will not be reviewed by the courts. It has been emphasized repeatedly by the courts that a school board may not, in its discretion, authorize one group to use school property for religious purposes while denying use to others similarly situated. In other words, if a board of education opens the doors of a schoolhouse to one religious group it must open them equally wide to all. [19]

Even students may be denied the use of school property for religious activities if in conflict with school board regulations. For example, in a federal case originating in West Virginia a complaint by public high school students against a school board regulation prohibiting them to meet *voluntarily* in premises of the public school for purposes of engaging in group prayer was dismissed by a United States district court. In finding that the state law did not grant use of school property for religious purposes, the court stated: [20]

It should be noted that the regulation of the Board of Education denies to anyone, regardless of sect, the use of public school property for religious purposes. There is no invidious discrimination in the regulation, and it relates only to the use of school facilities and not to religious affiliations of the users.

---

[18] *Southside Estates Baptist Church* v. *Board of Trustees* (Fla), 115 S(2d) 697 (1959).

[19] William E. Griffiths, *Religion, the Courts, and the Public Schools.* Cincinnati: The W. H. Anderson Company, 1966, p. 191.

[20] *Hunt* v. *Board of Education of County of Kanawha* (WV), 321 FSupp 1263, 1266 (1971).

On the basis of recent decisions by the United States Supreme Court, concerning religious activities in the public schools, reported elsewhere in this publication, it may be conjectured that the issue is far from being resolved permanently.

Chapter 14

DISCRETIONARY AUTHORITY OF SCHOOL
BOARDS OVER SCHOOL FINANCE

Section
14.1   Authority to tax for school purposes
14.2   Managing the school money
14.3   School versus municipal control over the school budget
14.4   Diminishing reliance on local property tax

Since *education* is conceived by the courts to be a *state function*, it follows that *school money* is *state money*. This does not mean, however, that school boards are denied participation in the acquisition and management of school funds. In fact, some of the authority is delegated to school boards, who, after all, are state officials selected to provide for the schools within the boundaries of that portion of the state they represent.

14.1   Authority to tax for school purposes

The power to tax for the support of schools is not inherent in school districts, or even in all state legislatures. Some state constitutions authorize or mandate state legislatures to levy taxes for school purposes. In some instances, the state may act through direct legislative enactments; in other instances, it may delegate the authority to school districts, or other governmental units such as the county or municipality.

Sometimes school boards levy taxes for school purposes beyond what taxpayers consider to be within constitutional and statutory allowances. Consequently litigation is likely to ensue. In this connection, Garber and Edwards state that: "So long as school boards act within the scope of their statutory authority, the courts will not control their discretion with respect to the amount of taxes to be levied and collected or with respect to the purpose for which the taxes may be applied."[1]

---

[1] Lee O. Garber and Newton Edwards, *The Law Governing the Financing of Public Education*. Casebook No. 8. Danville, Ill.: Interstate Printers and Publishers, 1964, p. 3.

14.2 Managing the school money

The authority to manage school funds, after they are allocated, may be exercised by the local school board, but only in accordance with constitutional and statutory provisions. Morphet and Wardle state that:

> . . . No school board has an inherent right to collect, hold, or disburse funds for schools. The legislature of the state, subject to state and federal constitutional limitations, has the right to determine what funds from state and local sources are to be made available for schools and how they are to be allocated and disbursed. In practice, every state legislature has delegated some power for management of certain school funds to local school systems or districts. The amount and extent of power thus delegated vary considerably among the states, and may vary even among different types of districts in the same state.[2]

14.3 School versus municipal control over the school budget

Innumerable court cases have arisen over the limits of the school board's discretionary authority over the school budget because of municipal interference.

The courts have been consistent in denying municipal officers any control over the public school budget unless such is authorized by statute. The following statement is just one of many confirming this contention: ". . . the board of education is beyond control by the town or any of its officers except as limitations are found in statutory provision."[3]

Only "those agents specifically named by law can exercise fiscal control over the policies and practices of a school board and even when a state delegates certain powers of supervision to local agencies, they must exercise exactly the authority which they are given by law—and no other."[4]

---

[2] Lee O. Garber, editor, *Law and the School Business Manager*. Danville, Ill.: Interstate Printers and Publishers, 1957, pp. 72-73.

[3] *Board of Education* v. *Town of Ellington*, 151 Conn 1, 193 A(2d) 466 (1963).

[4] "Fiscal Dependence and Independence of Local School Systems," *NEA Research Memo* (mimeographed). Washington: the Association, August, 1966, p. 77.

Where the law specifically authorizes the school board to prepare and adopt its own budget without municipal interference there is little cause for dispute. Even when the law provides that the budget estimate be submitted to city officials for informative but not discretional purposes, there is no need for discord, providing such laws are stated in terms so clear that there is no question as to the school board's exclusive dominance over the budget.

Litigious controversies, however, develop when the law permits or requires commingling on the part of two distinct corporative bodies in determining the school budget. Even where such laws exist, there would be no conflict if school and municipal officials cooperated conciliatorily rather than prerogatively in the cause of economy and public welfare.

There are almost as many degrees of municipal fiscal control over the school budget expressed in the laws as there are cities governed by special acts. Discrepancies are further accentuated by the different interpretations placed upon these special provisions by school and city officials. Although court decisions have tended to set aside many of the unusual prerogatives assumed by city officers in revising the school budget, many of the questionable practices still exist.[5]

Revision of the budget estimate by striking out or changing amounts to be allotted for specific items is the most rigid type of control city officers may hold over the school budget or, in effect, over the school program, since the extent to which a particular activity may be performed is limited by the funds available for that activity. Very few laws, however, specifically grant that much authority to city officials over the school budget estimate. Most notable of those which have granted such authority are those of Detroit where "the budget shall specify the amount required for salaries of teachers and other employees of the board, repairs, fuel, supplies, and general current expenses. . . . So much of said budget as the appropriating bodies of said city school approve shall be levied and collected the same as city taxes."[6] The

---

[5] E. C. Bolmeier, "Variations in Control over City School Budgets," *American School Board Journal* (September, 1946), pp. 23-25.

[6] Bolmeier, "Variations in Control over City School Budgets," p. 23.

school budget of Baltimore is subject to review by the board of estimates and the city council. Both agencies may reduce specific items of the estimate.[7]

A more common and justifiable type of budget control is where city officials are authorized to revise the school estimates as applied to the total amount or general categories and not to specific items. After the budget has once been approved by the designated reviewing body the board of education is free to transfer amounts from one item to the other as they see fit, providing the total amount approved is not exceeded.[8]

In general, school administrators believe that the nature and importance of education are such as to warrant complete fiscal control by the board of education, free from control or influence of municipal (or county) officials. The majority of political scientists, however, favor fiscal dependence of school boards, or, at least a closer coordination of schools and municipal governments in the administration of the school's finances.[9]

Some political scientists go so far as to suggest that a solution to the conflict of decision-making at the local level would be to "abolish school systems as separate units of government, putting them under the policy direction of municipalities and counties."[10]

When and if fiscal dependence of school boards has a detrimental effect on the school system, the patrons of the schools are not denied recourse in rectifying conditions.

1. In instances where the school board is subordinated to municipal (or county) officials in fiscal affairs of the schools without explicit statutory authorization of such subordinations, the recourse of the school board or any taxpayer is by court action. The courts have been practically unanimous in denying municipal officials the authority to interfere with

---

[7] *Ibid.*

[8] *Ibid.*

[9] E. C. Bolmeier, "Legal, Illegal, and Extra-Legal Degrees of Fiscal Dependence," *American School Board Journal* (August, 1949), pp. 22-24, 68.

[10] "School Boards in an Era of Conflict," *Education U.S.A. Special Report*, 1966, p. 16.

the state function of public education in the absence of specific charter or statutory provisions which are constitutional.

2. When the laws specifically authorize municipal (or county) officials to make revision in the budget estimate formulated and submitted by the school board, and when the revisions are considered injurious to the administration of an adequate school program, recourse may be by exercise of the franchise. In virtually every instance where municipal or county officials are legally authorized to exercise discretion in controlling the fiscal affairs of the schools, such officials hold their offices by the choice of the voters at elections. Their obligation to the school community in making adequate financial allowances for the schools are just as great as they are for either "fiscally independent" or "fiscally dependent" boards of education.

3. Finally, the people, through their congressmen, have considerable influence over legislation which determines degrees of fiscal independence or dependence of a local board of education. If existing statutes permit pernicious mingling of municipal or county officials in the affairs of the public schools, repeal or amendment to such legislation may be sought.[11]

14.4 Diminishing reliance on local property tax

Since the beginning of public education, most states have relied upon the local property tax as a source of revenue for public education. There has been a growing tendency, however, to question the propriety, as well as the legality, of the local property tax for financing public education, because of the inequities it fosters.

Suits have been filed in recent years in several states challenging the constitutionality of the local property tax as a source of public school revenue. Not until August 30, 1971, were the suits successful. On that date, however, the Cali-

---

[11] Bolmeier, "Legal, Illegal, and Extra-Legal Degrees of Fiscal Dependence," p. 65.

fornia Supreme Court [12] struck down as unconstitutional that state's entire system of financing public schools, implying that its effect was to provide more money for children of the rich than for those of the poor.

The California court noted that about 50 percent of the school funds raised by each California district comes from local property taxes, which, in effect, makes it impossible for districts with small tax bases to produce sufficient revenue that more affluent districts produce with minimum effort. In its 6 to 1 ruling, the court held that "such a system must fall before the equal protection clause" of the Fourteenth Amendment to the United States Constitution, which guarantees every citizen "the equal protection of the laws."

In its 25-page report, the court stated:

Obviously, the richer district is favored when it can provide the same educational quality for its children with less tax effort. Furthermore, as a statistical matter, the poorer districts are financially unable to raise their taxes high enough to match the educational offerings of wealthier districts. Thus, affluent districts can have their cake and eat it too: they can provide a high quality of education for their children while paying lower taxes. Poor districts, by contrast, have no cake at all. [13]

At the time of this writing the effects of *Serrano* on the financing of public education is highly speculative. The court has indicated that the decision is not a final judgment and that the case should be returned to a trial court. If the trial court should find that the California school financing is unconstitutional, it would likely outline a method of orderly transition. In the transition, some authorities in school law see a shift of the school revenue burden from the local to the state and federal level, where less reliance is placed upon the local property tax as a source of revenue. In the meantime much more legal action may be anticipated before final rulings resolve the problem.

---

[12] Serrano v. Priest, 96 CalRptr 601, 487 P(2d) 1241 (1971).

[13] *Id.* at 1251-2 of P(2d).

Chapter 15

DISCRETIONARY AUTHORITY OF SCHOOL BOARDS OVER TEACHER PERSONNEL

15.1   Legal status of the teacher

As has been inferred, a *school board member* is, in the eyes of the law, a public official; he is definitely considered a school official and not a school employee.

The legal status of the *superintendent of schools,* however, is less certain. Courts have varied in classifying the superintendent as a school officer or a school employee. Although there apparently has never been a count to determine which title has been attributed to him more often by the statutes and courts, it is generally conceded that he is an employee of the school board with delegated duties and responsibilities emanating from his board of education, a state agency, or the state legislature.

In most instances, the *school principal* is conceived as a teacher and therefore considered by the courts to be a school employee, rather than a school officer. For example, an Alabama court identified the school principal's status as commensurate with that of a teacher with the following words: "The principal is a teacher who is the chief executive officer and head of the teaching faculty of a particular school."[1]

---

[1] *White* v. *State*, 42 Ala 249, 160 S(2d) 496 (1964).

The *teacher* is less likely to be classified as a school officer than any of the other professional personnel. Even though the teacher is subjected, by law, to many of the same requirements and qualifications as those of public officials, the courts generally hold that there is a distinct difference, in that "an employment does not authorize the exercise in one's own right of any sovereign power as any prescribed independent authority of a governmental nature."[2]

In discussing the subject, Remmlein concludes by stating: "As far as public school teachers are concerned, absence of the authority to exercise sovereign power has been one of the chief distinguishing marks of the position. The courts have been almost unanimous in classifying teachers as employees rather than officers."[3]

In legal theory, therefore, a teacher is a public employee of the school district by which he is employed and not a public officer exercising, by virtue of his office, discretionary and quasi-judicial power.[4]

15.2 Teacher employment

Before one can enter into a valid contract to teach in the public schools, he must possess a certificate of qualifications as is required by law. The teacher's certificate is, in essence, a document indicating that the holder has met legal qualifications required by a particular state to follow the teaching profession in that state. It does not, by itself, give the holder the right to demand a teaching position.

Garber and Edwards describe, most completely, the teacher's certificate to teach:

> The state may prescribe such qualifications for teachers as it deems necessary, and it may require that a teacher hold a certificate which indicates that he possesses the prescribed qualifications. Those to whom the state has dele-

---

[2] *State ex rel. Holloway* v. *Sheats,* 78 Fla 583, 83 So 508 (1919).

[3] Madaline Kinter Remmlein, *School Law.* Danville, Ill.: Interstate Printers and Publishers, 1962.

[4] *Eastman* v. *Williams,* 124 Vt 445, 207 A(2d) 146 (1965).

gated authority to determine whether a prospective teacher has met the statutory requirements for a certificate and to issue a certificate in case the requirements have been met, perform a discretionary duty and the courts will not control their discretion unless it is abused. But the officer or agency authorized to issue certificates may not refuse to issue a certificate without good cause. A teacher's certificate is not a contract between the state and the teacher; it is a license. Since it is a mere privilege conferred by the state, the state may revoke it. Likewise the state may impose additional qualifications upon those who already possess certificates. A certificate issued by the proper authorities is in the nature of a commission and is not subject to collateral attack; a board may not, therefore, dismiss a teacher and then set up the defense that his certificate was illegally issued.[5]

Since a teacher cannot enter into a legal contract without a certificate, if he assumes teaching duties without either a certificate or a valid contract he does so in the capacity of a "volunteer," and cannot recover for services rendered.

Statutory provisions outlawing the employment of persons to teach without certificates is exemplified by North Carolina statutes:

It shall be unlawful for any board of education or school committee to employ or to keep in service any teacher, supervisor, or other professional school personnel who does not hold a certificate in compliance with the provisions of law or in accordance with the regulations of the State Board of Education governing emergency substituted personnel.

The county or city superintendent, or other official, is forbidden to approve any vouchers for salary for any personnel employed in violation of the provisions of this section and the treasurer of the county or of the city

---

[5] Lee O. Garber and Newton Edwards, *The Law Governing Teaching Personnel.* Casebook No. 3. Danville, Ill.: Interstate Printers and Publishers, 1962, p. 3.

schools is hereby forbidden to pay out of school funds the salary of such person.[6]

Whether or not the certificate is held at the time of signing a contract is sometimes an important factor.

In case the statutes specifically require that a teacher have a certificate in order to enter into a contract, he must possess it at the time of signing the contract. Where, however, the statutes make the possession of a certificate a condition of employment, the courts are divided with respect to the time at which the teacher must have the certificate. Some hold that he must have it at the time of signing the contract; others hold—and it seems the better law—that it is sufficient if he has the certificate at the time he begins to teach.[7]

If a teacher does hold a valid certificate it cannot be revoked merely because a course which she had been hired to teach had been cancelled because of insufficient number of students. In an applicable case,[8] the North Dakota Supreme Court stated: "We believe that it is immaterial whether a sufficient number of pupils were enrolled. . . . To hold otherwise would permit school districts to arbitrarily avoid commitments which teachers may have been induced to rely on to their detriment."

Within the limits of the state constitution the state legislature has the authority to prescribe the qualifications necessary for teaching in a particular state. This authority may be exercised directly, or it may be delegated to the state board of education, or conferred upon local boards within constitutional and statutory limits.

Where statutes vest sole authority in the state board to determine the qualifications of teachers, the local school board is without power to prescribe qualifications for teachers.[9] Usually, however, the statutes permit local boards of education to prescribe qualifications beyond the minimum

---

6 *Public School Laws of North Carolina*, 1965, Chap. 115, sec. 155.

7 Garber and Edwards, *The Law Governing Teaching Personnel*, p. 4.

8 *Meier v. Foster School Dist. No. 2* (ND), 146 NW(2d) 882 (1966).

9 *Coleman v. School Dist. of Rochester*, 87 NH 465, 183 Atl 586 (1936).

state requirements. Therefore, local school boards often prescribe certain qualifications and standards for the employment of teachers.

The courts are reluctant to rule against the school board requirements unless they are unreasonable. They generally rule that "unless the standards applied by the appointing body are so clearly irrelevant and unreasonable as to palpably be arbitrary and improper, they are to be sustained."[10]

15.3   Teacher tenure

Nearly all states have statutes which provide tenure rights for teachers; North Carolina is a notable exception. However, "on July 1, 1972, the state's continuing-contract statute will be replaced by a teacher tenure act."[11]

A tenure right is construed to mean the right of employment for a continuing or indefinite period of time, subject to removal only for a cause prescribed by state law. Tenure laws are justified on the theory that they serve the best interests and welfare of the state by preventing school boards and others from removing capable teachers for unjust reasons.

In explaining the purposes for which a teacher tenure act was designed, a Louisiana court stated:

> The teacher tenure act was designed to accomplish a laudable purpose. . . . It was intended, inter alia, to protect the worthy instructors of the youth of the parish from enforced yielding to the political preferences of those therefore having the power to grant or withhold employment and to vouchsafe to such teachers employment, after a long term of satisfactory service to the public, regardless of the vicissitudes of politics or the likes or dislikes of those charged with the administration of school affairs.[12]

A Pennsylvania court also made a succinct statement indi-

[10] *Tripp* v. *Board of Examiners of City of New York*, 44 Misc(2d) 1026, 255 NYS(2d) 526 (1964).

[11] "Public School Law: Changes by the 1971 North Carolina General Assembly," *School Law Bulletin*, Vol. II, No. 3, August 1971, p. 2.

[12] *Andrews* v. *Union Parish School Board*, 191 La 90, 184 So 574 (1938).

cating the purpose for which teacher-tenure legislation was enacted: "To maintain an adequate and competent teaching staff, free from political and personal and arbitrary interference, whereby capable and competent teachers might feel secure, and more efficiently perform their duty of instruction."[13]

In a more recent Pennsylvania case, the court interpreted the purpose of a teacher-tenure law by this brief phrase: "to obtain a better education for the children of the Commonwealth."[14]

School boards are without authority to take away tenure that has been granted by the state. Of course there is no such thing as a "permanent tenure law," even though that term is frequently used. A school board may discontinue the employment of a teacher on tenure for a number of reasons expressed or implied in the statutes.

The degree of discretion which a school board attempts to exercise in taking tenure away from teachers is the cause for much litigation. For example, in the analysis of court cases dealing with teaching personnel, the Research Division of the National Education Association found that out of a total of 97 cases reported in the National Reporter System during the calendar year 1968: "Issues relating to teacher tenure were again the most numerous with 32 cases appearing in this category in 1968."[15]

15.4   Teacher dismissal

The courts are called upon perennially to determine whether or not a school board's dismissal of teachers is legal. So many different factors are involved in teacher-dismissal cases that it is impossible to lay down a single rule defining the school board's legal latitude in the dismissal of teachers. Analysis of the many court decisions in past cases do provide some legal principles which may serve as guides to school

---

[13] *Bragg* v. *School Dist. of Swarthmore,* 337 Pa 363, 11 A(2d) 152 (1940).
[14] *Johnson* v. *United School Dist.,* 201 Pa 375, 191 A(2d) 897 (1963).
[15] *The Teacher's Day in Court: Review of 1968.* Research Division, National Education Association, May, 1969, p. 5.

boards, and thereby minimize litigation. The following principles are gleaned from *American Jurisprudence* and *Corpus Juris Secundum:*

1. A school board's power to dismiss a teacher may be derived from statute, or in the absence of statute, it may stem from an implied authority to dismiss for adequate cause.

2. The power to dismiss for just cause is absolute and may not be limited by contract.

3. A teacher (as a general rule) may not be dismissed without a justifiable cause before the expiration of a contract.

4. Where the method of dismissal is prescribed by statute, such method must be followed in order for the dismissal to be valid.

5. Even though no method of procedure is set out, the teacher is entitled to notices of charges against him and to a fair hearing before an impartial board.

6. As a general rule, a removal for a cause not authorized by statute or contract and outside the discretionary powers of the school authorities is invalid.

7. The burden of proof rests upon the school board in proving incompetency, because the teacher's certificate is *prima facie* evidence of competency.

8. The teacher has the right to have competency determined on the basis of service.

9. The board can demand of teachers only average qualifications, not the highest, in determining incompetency.

10. The teacher may seek redress in the court if he feels that the evidence presented by the board is not sufficient to establish his incompetency and if he has exhausted all administrative remedies prior to this.

11. The courts are inclined to accept the testimony of superintendents, supervisors, and principals as to a teacher's ability to perform his duties.

12. Where school board's action appears to be for the welfare of the children the dismissal of a teacher is likely to win judicial approval.

Statutes vary considerably in stipulating the causes for

dismissal of teachers. Causes most frequently mentioned in the statutes are incompetency, immorality, insubordination, and neglect of duty. These reasons are sometimes supplemented in the statutes by adding the clause "and for other good and just cause" which in itself covers all the ground.

Where a statute does not have a "catch-all" phrase such as "good and just cause" a specific word may be construed as being that inclusive. For example, the Pennsylvania courts have, on several occasions, given a broad interpretation to the word "incompetency" which is the only cause for dismissal stipulated in the Pennsylvania statutes. In a case that was finally settled in the United States Supreme Court, a teacher was lawfully dismissed for "incompetency" because he refused to answer questions regarding his alleged affiliation with a subversive organization.[16]

Somewhat similarly the word "immorality" was given a broad interpretation by an Alaska court. The court ruled that two teachers were legally dismissed for *immorality*, as defined in the statute, when they solicited a labor union and fellow teachers in an attempt to remove from office the superintendent and members of the school board.[17]

In a Wisconsin case for which there was rather lengthy and sensational testimony, the court ruled that "There was sufficient evidence to support finding of school board as to activities of school teacher relating to discussion of sex matters in class and such findings were sufficient to support conclusion of lack of good behavior."[18]

Also in an Illinois case[19] a 14-year-old girl testified that her band instructor had molested her on several occasions. Although the teacher vehemently denied the charges in a display of emotional instability, the Appellate Court of Illinois upheld the dismissal of the teacher after finding it was "correct and in no wise arbitrary or capricious."

---

[16] *Beilan* v. *Board of Education, School Dist. of Philadelphia,* 357 US 399, 2 LEd(2d) 1414, 78 SCt 1317 (1958).

[17] *Watts* v. *Seward School Board* (Alaska), 395 P(2d) 372 (1964).

[18] *State* v. *Board of Directors of Milwaukee,* 14 Wis(2d) 243, 111 NW(2d) 198 (1961).

[19] *Lombardo* v. *Board of Education of School Dist. No. 27,* 100 Ill App(2d) 108, 241 NE(2d) 495 (1968).

The mere allegation of immorality or poor behavior, how-ever, or even a "forced admission" thereto is not sufficient cause for a lawful dismissal of a teacher. A case in point is where action was taken against a school board by a teacher for rescission of his resignation submitted after he had been ar-rested on criminal charges of homosexual activity. The charges were subsequently dismissed because the court con-cluded that, in upholding the teacher, his apparent consent to the charges had been obtained through the use of undue influence. Representatives of the school board had advised him that "if he didn't resign at once the school district would suspend and dismiss him from his position and publicize the proceedings, but if he did resign the incident wouldn't jeopardize his chances of securing a teaching post else-where." [20]

What constitutes "proper conduct" of a teacher is por-trayed by an excerpt from an early Pennsylvania case: "It has always been the recognized duty of the teacher to con-duct himself in such way as to command the respect and good will of the community." [21]

"The statutory power of a school board to discharge teachers is always freely construed and good cause includes any grounds which is put forward by board in good faith. . . ." Therefore, a school board's dismissal of a teacher, following his plea of guilty to charges of "disturbing the peace by being under the influence of intoxicants, attempting to fight and by the display of a gun . . ." was held by the court as "not an abuse of discretion." [22]

Of course there are limits to what constitutes "just cause" in the dismissal of teachers. For example, in a 1966 case, the Supreme Court of New Hampshire held that dismissal of a plaintiff teacher for "budgetary reasons constituted violation of statute providing that school board may dismiss any

[20] *Odorizzi* v. *Bloomfield School Dist.*, 246 CalApp(2d) 123, 54 CalRep 533 (1966).

[21] *Horosko* v. *Mount Pleasant Township School Dist.*, 335 Pa 369, 6 A(2d) 866 (1939).

[22] *Williams* v. *School Dist. No. 40 of Gila County*, 4 ArizApp 5, 417 P(2d) 376 (1966).

teacher found to be immoral or incompetent or one who does not conform to regulations prescribed."[23]

Since the Civil Rights Act of 1964, some teachers, who have not been rehired, charge they have been discriminated against. A case in point arose in North Carolina in 1965 and was settled in a federal court. There a Negro teacher charged that she was not rehired because of her participation in the civil rights movement and conspiracy of the school committee. The school board denied the allegation and stated that "the inability to perform extracurricular duties promptly and cooperatively" was the reason for not rehiring the teacher. The school board's action was upheld by a federal district court.[24]

On appeal to the United States Supreme Court the decision of the lower federal court was reversed in early 1967. The Supreme Court ruled that "refusal to renew her yearly employment contract shows that refusal was based on her civil rights activities and not for good cause as found by district court; on remand, district court must direct committee to renew her employment contract."[25]

In another North Carolina case, nine Negro teachers and the North Carolina Teachers Association alleged that the school board refused to hire the teachers because of their race. A federal district court admitted that the board's failure to reemploy Negro teachers was cause for careful scrutiny but emphasized that "the employment of teachers involves appraisal of intangibles which cannot be reduced to slide rule formula." Since the court found no evidence that the Negro teachers had been wrongfully refused employment, and moreover, under North Carolina law, the board need not give reasons for not reemploying teachers, the court decided in favor of the board's action.[26]

A teacher's right to engage in civil rights activities is legally allowable up to the extent of exercising "free speech"

---

[23] *Spencer* v. *Laconia School Dist.,* 107 NH 125, 218 A(2d) 437 (1966).

[24] *Johnson* v. *Branch* (NC), 242 FSupp 721 (1965).

[25] Case No. 719, 35 L W 3215-3216.

[26] *Buford* v. *Morganton City Board of Education* (NC), 244 FSupp 437 (1965).

rights, but not to the point where it is detrimental to the school and disruptive to the educational purpose. A case in point is that of *Cooley* v. *Board of Education of the Forrest City School District* (Ark) (1971),[27] where the contract of a teacher was terminated for alleged excessive activism.

In reviewing the case the court reasoned that "If school teacher's discharge was a result of his own public expression of views and civil rights and advocacy, he would be entitled to reinstatement."[28] Here, however, the court *upheld* the action of the school board on the grounds that testimony revealed the teacher's:

> failure to cooperate; fostering of organizations in classroom sponsored by outside adult persons and agencies; refusing to comply with requirements of the superintendent of schools, rules, regulations and guidelines of the schools; accusations against the superintendent and certain of the black community; threats; intimidation; and insubordination.[29]

15.5   Grooming regulations

Contemporaneously with all the "pupil appearance" cases, a number of cases have been adjudicated which involve *grooming regulations* for teachers. Despite the allegations that the appearance of the teacher has "a definite effect on student dress by way of example and in turn has a definite correlation with student behavior," the courts appear to be more lenient toward teachers than pupils with regard to grooming regulations.

In a California case[30] an appellate court ruled against a school board for transferring a teacher to a less desirable job of home teaching because he wore a beard in violation of administrative policy. A lower court had upheld the

---

27 327 FSupp 454 (1971).
28 *Id.,* p. 455.
29 *Id.,* p. 456.
30 *Finot* v. *Pasadena City Board of Education,* 250 CalApp(2d) 189, 58 CalRptr 520 (1967).

board on the basis of the school principal's testimony that it would have "a definite effect on student dress by way of example." The Court of Appeals, however, reversed the lower court decision and agreed with the teacher's claim that depriving him of the right to wear a beard "was a denial to him of his constitutional guarantees against deprivation of his life, liberty or property without due process of law. . . ."[31]

In another case[32] which went before a federal court because racial overtones were involved, a United States District Court ruled in favor of a teacher who allegedly failed reappointment "solely because he refused to shave his goatee." No evidence was introduced by the defendant school committee to indicate that the wearing of a goatee tended to disrupt discipline or encourage inappropriate dress by students. Consequently the court found that the principal's action "was arbitrary, unreasonable and based on personal preference."[33]

One year later, a federal court again invalidated a school principal's rule prohibiting the wearing of a mustache by a teacher. In ruling on this case the court commented:[34]

> This is indeed a gross example of a rule based upon personal taste of an administrative official which is not a permissible base upon which to build rules for the organization of a public institution. . . . When complaint reaches the Board over such rules or their enforcement, the Board, as here, will have to take a position— and be prepared to accept the consequences of the decision.

In contrast to grooming regulations favoring the teacher, a decision of a Louisiana case[35] upheld a school board regulation requiring men teachers to *wear a necktie*. The

---

[31] *Id.*, p. 523.
[32] *Braxton* v. *Board of Public Instruction of Duval County* (Florida), 303 FSupp 958 (1969).
[33] *Id.*, p. 959.
[34] *Ramsey* v. *Hopkins* (Ala), 320 FSupp 477, 482 (1970).
[35] *Blanchet* v. *Vermilion Parish School Board* (La), 220 S(2d) 534 (1969).

teacher claimed that the regulation was unrelated to any educational aim as well as being an unreasonable infringement upon his liberty of dress. The court, however, went along with the contention of the Board that "wearing neckties enhanced the image of the teacher as a professional man, leading to more community and student respect for him."[36]

15.6   Teacher leaves of absence

A teacher's leave of absence may be defined as the teacher's right or privilege of absence from a school for a limited period of time, with or without pay, and with or without effect upon tenure and contract, as authorized under state statute, or under adopted rules and regulations of local boards of education.

Teachers' leaves of absence, which are most frequently the subject of legislation, board rules, and litigation, may be classified as sick leaves, maternity leaves, and sabbatical leaves. In granting teacher leaves of these types, the school board may exercise considerable discretion. In fact, within constitutional and statutory limits, the school board has complete authority to grant leaves of absence for school personnel.

The great majority of statutes, as well as court cases, in the area of leaves of absence, deal with *sick leave*. The justification of sick leave is evidenced in dictum from the Supreme Court of Pennsylvania:

> If the state as an employer chooses to grant sick leave with pay, for limited periods . . . the action does not involve an unconstitutional misuse of public funds. When a person enters into the service of the state at a weekly or annual salary he contracts to give his employer all the services required of him during working days, subject only to occasional interruptions by the illnesses common to man. . . .[37]

---

36 *Id.*, p. 538.

37 *Kurtz* v. *Pittsburgh*, 346 Pa 362, 31 A(2d) 257 (1943).

A typical statutory provision for sick leave is found in the school laws of North Carolina.

> The Board is authorized and empowered, in its discretion, to make provision for sick leave with pay for any teacher or principal not to exceed five days per school term and promulgate rules and regulations providing for necessary substitutes on account of said sick leave. . . .[38]

Not only is a school board authorized to *grant* sick leaves; it may *require* a teacher to take a leave of absence if the cause is illness or any type of physical or mental disability.

When statutes provide for sick leave, a proper diagnosis of the claimed sickness may be required before the leave is granted. A case in point is where a teacher's application for sick leave was supported only by a certificate of a licensed chiropractor that the teacher had been treated for "lumbo sacral sprain discogenic origin." The court upheld a medical director's testimony who pointed out that the condition treated by the chiropractor necessitated a diagnosis "for which a chiropractor was not equipped or authorized by law; and that a condition such as this could be ascribed to a variety of underlying conditions which only a medical doctor could properly diagnose," and that the school board did not act arbitrarily or without reason in requiring diagnosis by properly accredited expert, and in refusing the teacher's application for sick leave.[39]

Court decisions, statutory provisions, and board policies concerning *maternity leaves* are of comparatively recent origin. This is due to the fact that until several decades ago, married women teachers were not generally considered eligible to assume teaching positions in the public schools. Now, however, not only married women, but mothers and expectant mothers are permitted to hold teaching positions. Consequently school boards find it necessary to exercise their prerogatives in establishing rules and regulations for maternity leaves. Some of the court cases arising from such

---

[38] *Public School Laws of North Carolina,* 1965, Chap. 115, sec. 13.

[39] *Garber v. Board of Education of City of New York,* 50 Misc(2d) 711, 271 NYS(2d) 329 (1966).

leaves can become rather complicated as exemplified by a Louisiana case involving the following factors: (1) a statute required school boards to grant leaves of absence to regularly employed women teachers for a reasonable length of time before and after childbirth; (2) defendant board passed a regulation that any teacher who was an expectant mother should ask for a maternity leave upon becoming aware of the pregnancy, and that one taking such leave should absent herself from school for at least 15 months and then not return except at the beginning of school in the fall or at mid-term; (3) plaintiff teacher, with tenure status, did not advise school officials of her pregnancy, but when the board found out, it granted (and required) her a 15-month leave of absence; (4) while on leave she became pregnant again; (5) second baby was born about 6 weeks after her leave had expired; (6) while mother was on leave, the board adopted a policy prohibiting a teacher to return sooner than 6 months after birth of child; (7) another board policy required a teacher to vacate her position for 24 months of continuous absence; (8) when refused permission to return to work, plaintiff claimed unlawful removal from position; (9) court ruled that since she was an employee of board during the time she was on leave, she was required to request a leave for second pregnancy; and finally, (10) the court in disposing of the case in the board's favor stated: ". . . we think the school board properly considered the welfare not only of the teacher but of the school children and the school system, and we see nothing unreasonable or arbitrary in the time fixed for such leaves of absence both before and after childbirth."[40]

For an exhaustive treatment of the subject of "leaves of absence for teachers" see study by Nelson.[41]

---

[40] *State ex rel. Sapulvado* v. *Rapides Parish School Board*, 236 La 482, 108 S(2d) 96 (1959).

[41] Robert Nelson, "Legal Aspects of Leaves of Absence for Professional Public School Personnel," unpublished doctoral dissertation, Duke University, 1967.

The main legal principles derived from cases reported since Nelson's study are that: (1) a provision for sick leave is not a gift but a benefit ;[42]   (2) a probationary teacher is entitled to a maternity leave as much as is a tenured teacher;[43]   (3) a teacher who voluntarily absents himself from duty without a leave of absence from the school board surrenders his tenure status.[45]

15.7   Extra assignments for teachers[46]

There is comparatively little litigation concerning the assignment to teachers of classroom activities. This is due to the fact that they are usually stipulated in the contract upon which there is mutual agreement. The assignment of duties for teachers beyond actual classroom teaching, however, is likely to cause dissatisfaction leading to litigation—particularly when there is no extra pay for the extra work.

Although the state legislature is empowered to prescribe the duties of teachers, it is very unusual for the legislature to spell out in detail what the teacher may or must do in or out of the classroom. Usually the statutory provisions pertaining to duties of teachers are stated in broad terms with express or implied delegation of authority to local school boards to determine the assignment of duties for teachers. Not only is a school board given authority to determine the duties of teachers; it is usually authorized to redelegate such functions to the proper school administrators, such as the superintendent of schools or the school principal who ultimately determines, with the board's approval, what the "regular" and "extra" assignments of teachers shall be.

---

[42] *Teachers Association, Central High School Dist. No. 3 v. Board of Education, Nassau County* (NY). 312 NYS(2d) 252 (1970).

[43] *Board of Education of City of School Dist. of Poughkeepsie v. Allen,* 52 Misc(2d) 959, 277 NYS(2d) 204 (1967); *Amster v. Board of Education of Union Free School Dist. No. 22,* 55 Misc(2d) 961, 286 NYS(2d) 687 (1967).

[45] *Miller v. Noe* (Ky), 432 SW(2d) 818 (1968).

[46] The contents of this section are extracted from E. C. Bolmeier, "Legality of Extra Assignments for Teachers," *Law and the School Principal,* Chap. 10, Cincinnati: The W. H. Anderson Co., 1961.

Usually such matters as teachers' extra-classroom responsibilities are referred to in the board's rules and regulations. If they are within the scope of the statutory provisions, and if they are reasonable, they will be binding. In some instances, however, teachers have challenged the legality of the school board rules. Courts have generally ruled that if the extra-classroom duties are reasonably interrelated with the other duties of the teacher and his position they are binding, even though they may not be specifically stated in writing.

Only in rare instances are such matters as extra-classroom assignments referred to specifically in the contract; usually they are left to the discretion of the school principal. When teachers believe the principal assigns duties beyond those written into or implied in the contract they may carry their grievances to the superintendent of schools or to the school board, and if they do not obtain satisfaction there, they may carry the dispute all the way to the courts. Where the disputes have gone that far, the courts have been quite consistent in holding that teachers are bound by *express* provisions in the contract, and even where contractual obligations are only *implied* the courts have manifested reluctance in the interference of school board discretion. Therefore there is not likely to be judicial disapproval of school officials reading into the contract the right to assign extra-classroom duties to teachers, providing they are within statutory limits and reasonable in amount and nature.

Litigation regarding the legality of assigning extra-classroom duties for the teacher is usually focused on the question of *reasonableness* of the extra assignment. In rendering a decision on the unreasonableness of an extra assignment, the court will consider questions such as the following: Does the assignment require excessive hours beyond the normal teaching period? Does the assignment have some relation to the teacher's interests, abilities, and certification? Is the assignment made because of its intended benefit to pupils? Is the assignment discriminatory? Is the assignment professional in nature?

Relatively few cases regarding legality of extra-classroom

assignments have reached the higher state courts. Only a couple of those which have produced legal principles are referred to here. (1) A leading case on the issue arose in New York City where the school board adopted resolutions governing service of teachers outside of regular classroom instruction. Among the resolutions was one which authorized the principal to fix the duties and hours of the teachers with-out providing for adequate protection of the teachers. Although the court upheld the legality of the board's resolution, it cautioned that any bylaw of a board authorizing teachers' duties must stand the test of reasonableness. Pertinent, in the court's dicta, was the statement that "the board may not impose upon a teacher a duty foreign to the field of instruction for which he is licensed or employed. A board may not, for instance, require a mathematics teacher to coach intramural teams." The court stated in conclusion that "in a matter within the tutelage of the internal management of the board of education and the discipline of working hours, their length, or its lack prescribed for the various teaching staffs, the court ought not to interfere with the authority primarily responsible for the conduct of the schools unless there is palpable discrimination or arbitrary action detrimental to the individual or class." [47]

(2) Another leading case on the issue of extra-classroom duties which was greatly publicized was decided by a District Court of Appeal in California in 1955. Here the school authorities required male teachers in the Sacramento Senior High School to attend certain nonclassroom activities and to supervise student behavior at such activities. The activities were school football and basketball games, which were under the auspices and control of the school authorities. Six of the athletic assignments were made to each male teacher during each school year. The stipulated duties at these games "consisted of maintaining order in the student sections of the stands, sitting in the student section, reporting disturbances to the police, preventing spectators from going on the play-

[47] *Parrish v. Moss,* 106 NYS(2d) 577 (1951).

ing field, clearing the way for the band and drill teams . . ." and several other comparable tasks. The teacher (plaintiff) involved in this case had not objected to performing these extra duties while he served for three years as a probationary teacher. Shortly after attaining permanent status, however, the teacher sought delaratory relief against the school authorities. He claimed that the nonclassroom assignments "did not fall within the scope of his duties as a teacher under the terms of his contract of employment, and that such duties were unprofessional in nature." In refusing the plaintiff's contention, the court pointed out that his contract specifically stated that it was subject to the laws of the state and the rules of the state and local boards of education. It also emphasized that, even though the duty of supervising extra-classroom activities was not mentioned in the contract, the specific duty in question was in the contemplation of the position at the time the contract was entered into.[48]

(3) In Pennsylvania, a school principal brought an action for extra pay for extra services. In ruling against him the court said:

> The principal's work is never done, just as a captain of a ship never really sleeps. Of course, with that extra responsibility goes a stipend which exceeds that of a person who has little or no responsibility. The school principal is entitled to great respect, people tip their hats to him, or should; he has an office, he makes out his own schedule, which is all that it should be. The plaintiff wishes all the prerequisites, honors and attention which go with the principal's position, but he wants to observe a time-clock schedule and be paid additionally for every fragmentary hour he applies to his responsibilities after the blackboard dust of the day has settled. This is not only not fitting from a professional point of view; it is not in accordance with the law.[49]

---

[48] *McGrath* v. *Burkhard*, 131 CalApp(2d) 367, 280 P(2d) 864 (1955).

[49] *Taggart* v. *Board of Dir. of Canon-McMillan J. Sch. Sys.*, 409 Pa 33, 185 A(2d) 332 (1962).

(4) In order to dispel the erroneous idea that the courts will always and everywhere and under all circumstances uphold a school board's requirements for extra-classroom duties of teachers, one more case is cited. The teacher involved in this case sought a preliminary injunction to restrain school officials from compelling him to take tickets at a football game without additional compensation. He alleged that he was threatened with dismissal if he failed to do so. Moreover, he contended that the assignment constituted a demotion in salary and type of position. The petitioner (teacher) appealed to the superintendent who dismissed his appeal and sustained the action of the board, whereupon it was brought before the court of common pleas. At first the court appeared to be following the reasoning in other jurisdictions as indicated in the following comment:

Modern day schools are more and more offering to their students opportunities to participate in extra-curricular activities, most, if not all, of which broaden the experience and knowledge of the pupils participating therein. The assignment of teachers to supervise such activities is well within the power of the school boards.

The court then took a quick turn-about as is reflected in its concluding statement:

However, we cannot see how an assignment to collect tickets at a football game can be considered in such a category. Were the petitioner assigned to sit with the students in a cheering section to help to inculcate in them the attributes of loyalty and good sportsmanship, we might regard such an assignment as having some direct relation to the education of his pupils but the assignment to sit beside a gate and collect tickets bears no such relation. It is a task which any adult could perform and can only be motivated by the desire of the school board to cut down the expenses of the game. We feel that such an assignment is not within the field which a teacher must perform and to require him to do so is a demotion in type of position. [50]

---

[50] *Todd Coronway* v. *Landsdowne School District, Number 785*, in the Court of Common Pleas of Delaware County, Pennsylvania, June Term (1951).

Later, a somewhat similar decision was rendered in Pennsylvania[51] where a social studies teacher refused an assignment to supervise a boys' bowling club which met once a week away from school at a local bowling center. After the teacher's refusal to take on the extra assignment, the board dismissed him. On appeal, the case finally reached the Supreme Court of Pennsylvania, where a decision was rendered in favor of the teacher, with the following comment:

> School teachers must realize that they are subject to assignment by the school board to any activity directly related to the school program; classroom duties in school hours do not constitute *all* their duties. On the other hand, school boards must realize that their power of assignment of school teachers to extracurricular duties is not without limitation and restriction; the activity to which a school teacher is assigned must be related to the school program and the assignment must be fairly and reasonable made.[52]

15.8 Scope of teachers' freedoms[53]

Generally, a public school teacher possesses certain freedoms enjoyed by all citizens. As a citizen he has the right to speak, think, and believe as he wishes. He may, with rare exceptions, affiliate with groups of his choice. He may run for and hold office, campaign for a candidate of his choice, and present his political philosophies far and wide. As a public school teacher, however, he must exercise these and other legal rights with restricted discretion, and with due consideration of the effects upon others—particularly school children. Moreover, by virtue of his position, performing a governmental function, he must conform to certain laws, rules, and regulations not equally applicable to citizens outside the teaching profession. Of course when the restrictions

[51] *Pease* v. *Millcreek Township School Dist.*, 412 Pa 378, 195 A(2d) 104 (1963).
[52] *Id.*, p. 108.
[53] E. C. Bolmeier, "Legal Scope of Teachers' Freedoms," *The Educational Forum* (January, 1960), pp. 199-206.

and regulations imposed upon the teacher appear to be unnecessary, unreasonable, or in conflict with constitutional guarantees and statutory provisions, a teacher possesses a legal right to seek relief.

Frequently there is lack of agreement among teachers and school boards as to what is reasonable and legal. When the disagreement develops into litigation, the courts determine the reasonableness and legality of the school board restrictions and requirements placed upon the teacher. Ultimately then, the courts determine the legal scope of teachers' freedoms.

15.9   Teacher latitude in using alleged obscene expressions

The extent to which teachers may use alleged obscene expressions in the classroom has come into focus with the changing social and judicial attitude toward sex and the liberal classroom treatment thereof.

A much publicized case[54] is illustrative, where an English teacher was dismissed for the reading assignment to a senior English class of a controversial article, entitled "The Young and the Old." In reviewing the facts of the case, the court noted that the teacher discussed the article, and made particular reference to a word that was used therein, and explained the word's origin and context, and the reasons the author had included it. The word, admittedly highly offensive, is a vulgar term for an incestuous son. The liberal viewpoint of the court in this case is reflected in its concluding statement:

> Hence the question in this case is whether a teacher may, for demonstrated educational purposes quote a "dirty" word currently used in order to give special offense, or whether the shock is too great for high school seniors to stand. If the answer were that the students must be protected from such exposure, we would fear for their future. We do not question the good faith of the defend-

---

[54] *Keefe v. Geanakos* (Mass), 418 F(2d) 359 (1969).

ants in believing that some parents have been offended. With the greatest of respect to such parents, their sensibilities are not the full measure of what is proper education.[55]

One year later, a somewhat similar case[56] grew out of a dismissal of a teacher for assigning, as outside reading in an English class, a story entitled "Welcome to the Monkey House," which was a comic satire written by a prominent author to explain "one particular genre of western literature." School officials described the story as "literary garbage" because it condoned "the killing off of elderly people and free sex."

Plaintiff teacher asserted in her complaint that her dismissal for the reading assignment violated her First Amendment right to academic freedom. The court ruled in favor of the teacher and emphasized that "the right to teach, to inquire, to evaluate and to study is fundamental to a democratic society."

The court concluded by stating:

When a teacher is forced to speculate as to what conduct is permissible and what conduct is proscribed, he is apt to be overly cautious and reserved in the classroom. Such a reluctance on the part of the teacher to investigate and experiment with new and different ideas is anathema to the entire concept of academic freedom.[57]

The issue was again litigated in a federal case[58] when a U. S. District Court upheld a teacher's action against a school board which discharged him for writing a slang word for sexual intercourse on the blackboard, and in discussing such word as a taboo word before his eleventh grade class.

The court, finding that the teacher's method had a "seri-

---

55 *Id.,* pp. 361-362.
56 *Parducci* v. *Rutland* (Ala), 316 FSupp 352 (1970).
57 *Id.,* p. 357.
58 *Mailloux* v. *Kiley* (Mass), 323 FSupp 1387.

ous educational purpose," commented as follows:[59]

> We do not confine academic freedom to conventional teachers or to those who can get a majority vote from their colleagues. . . . The teacher whose responsibility has been nourished by independence, enterprise, and free choice becomes for his students a better model of the democratic citizen. His examples of applying and adapting the values of the older orders to the demands and opportunities of a constantly changing world are among the most important lessons he gives to youth.

15.10   Teacher affiliation with subversive political organizations

Most of the litigation concerning teacher affiliation with subversive organizations stems from state statutes rather than from school board policies. For several decades legislators have attempted to safeguard national unity and security by enacting legislation which would help prevent subversive activities and influences in the schools. The severity of the statutes range from mild provisions merely requiring teachers to take an oath and to swear to support the Constitution, to provisions designed to identify and dismiss teachers holding membership in subversive organizations.

The most stringent and litigious law designed to purge the school system of subversive teachers was the Feinberg law of New York State.[60] In several cases growing out of the Feinberg law, the lower courts declared the law unconstitutional. The lower-court rulings, however, were reversed during the 1950's by higher courts and the contested law was held to be constitutional until January 24, 1967, at which time the United States Supreme Court declared unconstitutional the New York State laws designed to keep subversives

---

[59] *Id.*, p. 1391.

[60] For detailed treatment see: E. C. Bolmeier, "Judicial Interpretations of Legislation Designed to Prevent Subversive Activities in Schools," *The Yearbook of School Law* (edited by Lee O. Garber), 1951, pp. 73-89.

off the faculties and staffs of public schools.[61] Judging from the strong dissents in the 5 to 4 decision, it may be speculated that the issue is not permanently and satisfactorily settled yet.

Oath requirements for public school teachers particularly have been the cause for litigation. Bryson found that forty states, the District of Columbia and Puerto Rico have con⸀ itutional or statutory provisions affecting loyalty requireme⸀ts for teachers.[62]

In thirty-six states, District of Columbia and Puerto Rico public school teachers must sign some type of loyalty oath provision in order to teach in their respective states. In thirty-four of these thirty-six states the loyalty oath provisions are either constitutional or statutory in nature. In the other two, Rhode Island and Virginia, loyalty oath provisions are prescribed by the State Department of Education as part of certification requirements. Four other states, North Carolina, Ohio, Alabama and Wyoming, have some type of nonoath provision for loyalty requirements.[63]

It should not be inferred that a school board is powerless to eliminate subversive persons from the teaching staff without expressed statutory or constitutional provisions to that effect. The school board has considerable discretionary authority to make and enforce rules preventing persons with subversive ideas from teaching, as is illustrated by a case where action was brought against the Cleveland Board of Education to enjoin the board from enforcing a resolution requiring the signing of "loyalty" affidavits and oaths.[64]

The court upheld the board in this case by a broad interpretation of the Ohio statute that "the board of education shall make such rules and regulations as it deems necessary for its government and the government of its employees and

---

[61] *Keyishian* v. *Board of Regents of Univ. of N.Y.*, 385 US 589, 17 LEd(2d) 629, 87 SCt 675 (1967).

[62] Joseph E. Bryson, *Legality of Loyalty Oath and Non-Oath Requirements for Public School Teachers.* Asheville, N. C.: The Miller Printing Co., 1963.

[63] *Id.*, p. 1.

[64] *Dworken* v. *Cleveland Board of Education*, 42 OO 240, 94 NE(2d) 18 (1950).

the pupils of the schools." [65]

In recognizing the discretionary authority of school boards within this general statute, the court concluded: "Thus the law gives a school board broad discretion in the determination of its policies and with that discretion no court will interfere unless the regulation involved is contrary to the letter and spirit of our law." [66]

The court's contempt for those who seek shelter under the Constitution, while attempting at the same time to abuse it, is reflected in the following excerpts from the court's dicta:

The Cleveland Board of Education . . . has not legally violated any one of our sacred instruments. The only thing it has violated is the sensibilities of those who do not wish their treachery in embryo to be noticed; because those who could create danger to our nation are incensed whenever their motives are exposed. [67]

With the right of the Board to express tribute to our Constitution we shall not interfere; with its right, power, and duty to accept such expression from its teachers we will not interfere. Such expressions never harmed the sensibilities of the Presidents, Governors, Senators, Congressmen, Judges, Mayors or other public officers privileged to take them, nor will they harm the teachers whose precept and good example will influence the future public officers who take them. [68]

Not only have the courts upheld legislation and school-board regulations requiring oaths of nonaffiliation with subversive organizations—they have upheld school authorities in disqualifying detected members of such organizations from teaching in the public schools. [69]

---

[65] *Page's Ohio General Code,* sec. 4834-5 (now Ohio Revised Code, sec. 3313.20).

[66] *Dworken v. Cleveland Board of Education,* 42 OO 240, p. 244, 94 NE(2d) 18, p. 22 (1950).

[67] *Id.,* 42 OO 246, 94 NE(2d) 24.

[68] *Ibid.,* 42 OO 254, 94 NE(2d) 32.

[69] *Adler v. Board of Education of City of New York,* 342 US 485, 96 LEd 517, 72 SCt 380 (1952).

But in a Florida case[70] a teacher was successful, who sought, on behalf of herself and others similarly situated, to have declared unconstitutional a Florida statute requiring the taking of an oath which stipulated in part: "I am not a member of any organization or party which believes in or teaches, directly or indirectly, the overthrow of the Government of the United States or of Florida by force or violence."

The United States District Court ruled that the statute "unduly infringes upon the right of free association granted by the First and Fourteenth Amendments, and those clauses must be stricken from the oath."[71] On appeal, the United States Supreme Court upheld the decision of the District Court.[72]

There has been a pronounced trend in recent years for individuals to attempt to hide behind the Fifth Amendment by way of refusing to testify before legislative committees investigating subversive activities on the ground that to do so might incriminate them. In such cases involving teachers, the courts have held that school boards are justified in removing teachers who refuse to testify. An illustrative case arose in California where the court said:

> When defendant refused to answer questions asked of her she was guilty of unprofessional conduct as an employee of the school system. A teacher's employment in the public schools is a privilege, not a right. A condition implicit in that privilege is loyalty to the government under which the school system functions. It is the duty of every teacher to answer proper questions in relation to her fitness to teach our youth when put to him by a lawfully constituted body authorized to propound such question.[73]

Even though teachers may be required to answer questions concerning their own affiliation with the Communist party,

---

[70] *Connell* v. *Higgenbotham* (Fla), 305 FSupp 445 (1969).

[71] *Id.*, p. 452.

[72] 29 LEd(2d) 418 (1971).

[73] *Board of Education of Los Angeles* v. *Wilkinson*, 125 Cal 100, 270 P(2d) 82 (1954).

they may not be required to disclose the names of other presently employed teachers known to be or to have been members. For example, in New York City, the superintendent, under authority delegated to him by the board, suspended certain confessed members who refused to disclose names of others. They appealed to the commissioner of education who enjoined the board and superintendent from requiring these teachers to identify those they knew to have been members of the Communist party. On appeal to the courts, the commissioner's decision was upheld.[74]

15.11   Teacher participation in political affairs

State laws vary with respect to the extent to which teachers may take part in political affairs. In some instances, detailed statutory provisions prohibit public officials and employees from political activities. In other instances, the laws are silent on the matter. Still others stipulate certain areas in which public employees, including teachers, may participate. Although the controversy of school employees participating in political campaigns has not often reached the stage of litigation, there have been enough cases to establish some guiding legal principles on the subject.

In 1932, a school board in Kentucky was enjoined from dismissing a teacher for campaigning against the election of a school trustee. In ruling against the board's action, the court contended that "the teacher had done nothing wrong or corrupt or anything else that any good citizen had no right to do in support of a candidate." [75]

A teacher's freedom to engage in political campaigning does not have similar judicial sanction when carried to the classroom. An oft-quoted case is illustrative. A teacher mentioned to her students that a certain candidate would be more helpful to the school than would be an opposing lady candidate, and suggested that the students inform their par-

---

[74] *Board of Education of City of New York* v. *Allen*, 6 Misc 453, 167 NYS(2d) 221 (1956).

[75] *Board of Education for Logan County* v. *Akers*, 243 Ky 177, 47 SW(2d) 1046 (1932).

ents accordingly. The teacher was suspended on the ground of unprofessional conduct and the court upheld the suspension. This case indicates that it is not so much the words of the teacher that count as the place where they are uttered. The courts frown upon a teacher's influential comments upon controversial matters before students who constitute a "captive audience." [76]

In view of the fact that a large majority of the states allow teachers to serve in the legislature, and that in most states they do serve, the legality of the practice may be questioned. A case in point arose in Oregon where a teacher's right to serve as a member of the state house of representatives was contested on the ground that the teacher's serving in a dual capacity contravened the principle of separation of powers contrary to the Constitution of Oregon. Although the teacher contended that as a teacher he performed no "official duties" in connection with the school, the court concluded that the teacher nevertheless was performing "functions" of the executive department as a teacher and "official duties" of the legislative department, which was contrary to the constitutional provision and therefore illegal. [77]

The issue of a teacher's legal right to serve as a legislator was involved in an Alaska case[78] where a superintendent and two teachers were serving as legislators while holding their professional positions—which under provisions of the state constitution was prohibited. In commenting on the case, the Supreme Court of Alaska stated:

> The rationale underlying such prohibitions can be attributed to the desire to encourage and preserve independence and integrity of action and decision on the part of individual members of our state government. On the other hand, we recognize that citizens should be interested in and seek public office. Public service and concern for the welfare of our citizenry is essential if we are to

---

[76] Goldsmith v. Board of Education of Sacramento, 66 Cal 157, 225 Pac 783 (1924).

[77] Monaghan v. School District No. 1, 211 Ore 360, 315 P(2d) 797 (1957).

[78] Begich v. Jefferson (Alaska), 441 P(2d) 27 (1968).

have a viable state government.

Teacher participation in political activity was the cause for a case[79] which went to the United States Supreme Court for final settlement. In the proceedings, the court reversed a judgment of the Supreme Court of Illinois, which upheld the dismissal of a teacher (Pickering) by the school board for sending a letter to a local newspaper concerning a recently-proposed tax increase. The letter was critical for the manner in which the school board and superintendent had previously handled proposals to raise and use new revenue. Consequently the board dismissed the teacher with the claim that the criticism would disrupt faculty discipline and tend to foment controversy and conflict among the teachers, administrators, board members and residents of the school district.

After weighing the allegations of the board, the High Court rejected them as being inconsequential where a teacher's right of free speech is involved. The court commented as follows:

. . . the question whether a school system requires additional funds is a matter of legitimate public concern on which the judgment of the school administration, including the School Board, cannot, in a society that leaves such questions to popular vote, be taken as conclusive. On such a question free and open debate is vital to informed decision-making by the electorate. Teachers are, as a class, the members of a community most likely to have informed and definite opinions as to· how funds allotted to the operation of the schools should be spent. Accordingly, it is essential that they be able to speak out freely on such questions without fear of retaliatory dismissal.[80]

---

[79] *Pickering v. Board of Education* (Ill), 391 US 563, 20 LEd(2d) 811, 88 SCt 1731 (1968).

[80] *Id.*, p. 1736.

15.12   Teacher activities outside the classroom

In addition to limitations of teachers participating in political activities, there are numerous other situations where the extent of teachers' freedoms are reviewed by the courts.

One has to do with the activities of teachers outside the classroom and after school hours.

Apparently there are no statutes that stipulate specifically what a teacher may or may not do outside of school hours and away from the school grounds. There are general statutes, however, which authorize such boards to dismiss teachers for a host of acts committed outside the school. If the outside activity is of such a nature as to give a bad reputation to the teacher, a school board would be within its rights in dismissing the teacher on the grounds of "incompetency," "conduct unbecoming a teacher" or "for other good and just cause." An excerpt from just one of the many cases dealing with the subject illustrates:

> It has always been the recognized duty of the teacher to conduct himself in such way as to command the respect and good will of the community, though one result of the choice of a teacher's vocation may be to deprive him of the same freedom of action enjoyed by persons in other vocations.[81]

There is general judicial agreement that the peculiar relationship between the teacher and his pupils is such that it is highly important that the character of the teacher be above reproach. The view that teachers should not only have good characters but also good reputations has found universal judicial support.

The courts are rather reluctant to assume responsibility for that which a teacher does or does not do in or outside the classroom. Such prerogatives belong to legally-constituted school boards. The courts are likely to interfere only when school boards act unreasonably.

---

[81] *Horosko* v. *Mount Pleasant Township School Dist.*, 335 Pa 369, 6 A(2d) 866 (1939).

15.13   Teacher strikes

Definition of the teacher's strike. A teacher's strike is the cessation of work by a body of teachers for the purpose of forcing from the school board certain concessions pertaining to working conditions, salaries of other aspects of teacher welfare. It is more than just the refusal of several teachers to perform their duties because of unsolved grievances. It constitutes stoppage of work by an entire organized group of fellow teachers usually referred to as a "union." The teacher's strike differs from outright resignation in that it does not anticipate severance of the employer-employee relationship or discontinuance of the tenure status of the teachers.

Because of the unpleasant connotation of the word "strike," less offensive words, such as "sanctions," have been used. The courts, however, are not particularly concerned about the terminology. The determinant in ruling upon the legality of concerted work stoppage is the effect it has on the educational opportunities for the pupils, regardless of terminology.

Causal factors. Despite widespread disapproval of teacher strikes, they persist in increasing numbers. The main reasons for their increase are that: (1) statistical reports indicate that teacher salaries have been relatively lower than those for other professional workers; (2) salary increases have been disproportionately lower for teachers than for those in labor groups; (3) teachers have observed the success that labor groups, teacher unions, and even other governmental employees have had with work stoppage until concessions were granted; (4) the unavailability of qualified teachers to replace striking teachers has deterred school boards from employing retaliatory and punitive measures, such as dismissal, which would, in effect, result in teacherless classrooms; (5) the NEA has been slowly but surely moving toward a policy of condonement of teachers' strikes where milder methods fail in attaining demands. A nine-day strike, in 1971, by approximately 600 staff members against the National Education Association was condoned on the grounds that NEA is *not* a governmental organization. And

(6) the judiciary appears to be moving toward a more liberal viewpoint regarding the legality of forced negotiations.

Judicial view of teacher strikes. As early as 1951 a Connecticut court ruled that the *teachers' strike is illegal.*[82] No case has been reported since which specifically authorizes the teachers to strike. Opinion of the courts emphasize that a teacher has a right to resign but not to strike. Judicial explanation is that (1) education is a public (governmental) function; (2) teachers are governmental employees; and (3) governmental employees do not have the right to strike.

The Supreme Court of Kansas stresses the point that a teacher's strike is illegal because teaching is a governmental function:

> The objects of a political subdivision are governmental—not commercial. It is created for public purposes and has none of the peculiar characteristics of enterprises maintained for private gain. . . . Strikes against a political subdivision to enforce collective bargaining would in effect amount to strikes against the government.[83]

The same legal principle was reiterated by the Supreme Court of Florida when it upheld a statute which stipulated:

> This statute, in effect prohibits governmental officers and employees from participating in strikes against the government. It states that "no person shall accept or hold any . . . employment in the service of the state, of any county or of any municipality . . ." who participates in any strike against the governmental employer. The statute guarantees the right to bargain as a member of a union or labor organization but precludes the right to strike against government.[84]

[82] *Norwalk Teachers Assn.* v. *Board of Education,* 138 Conn 269, 83 A(2d) 482 (1951).

[83] *Wichita Public School Employees Union* v. *Smith,* 194 Kan 2, 397 P(2d) 357, 360 (1964).

[84] *Pinellas County Classroom Teachers Assn.* v. *Board of Public Instruction* (Fla), 214 S(2d) 34, 36 (1968).

Judicial view of "sanctions." Teacher groups sometimes contend that "sanctions" differ from "strikes" and are therefore legal. That the courts do not go along with such contention is evidenced by statements of the Supreme Court of New Jersey:

> Defendants deny there was a "strike". . . . But the subject is the public service, and the distinctions defendants advance are irrelevant to it, however arguable they may be in the context of private employment. . . . If individuals enter into a union or association on terms that upon the occurrence of some stipulated event or signal they will impede government in its recruitment of services, that very arrangement constitutes an agreement the law denounces. An agreement not to seek, accept, or solicit employment in government whenever the upper echelon of the union makes a prescribed pronouncement is, no less than an accomplished shutdown, a thrust at the vitality of government, and comes within the same policy which denounces a concerted strike or quit or slowdown or other obstruction of the performance of official duties.[85]

Imposition of penalties. Only a few cases[86] have been reported which indicate that penalties have been imposed upon those who strike. The obvious reason is that punitive measures such as dismissal would deplete the school of teachers, for which replacements would be difficult to secure. It is also doubtful that fines would constitute an effective deterrent to teacher strikes. Certainly they would not result in a favorable climate in the school community for a harmonious employer-employee relationship.

Negotiation as a deterrent. Even though teachers do not have a legal right to strike, the unpleasant truth is that teachers *do* strike—and in increasing numbers. The detrimental effects of the strikes in recent years is inestimable.

---

[85] *Board of Education* v. *New Jersey Education Assn.*, 53 NJ 24, 247 A(2d) 865, 872-873 (1968).

[86] *In re Brown*, 50 NJ 435, 236 A(2d) 142 (1967); *National Education Assn.* v. *Lee County Board of Public Instruction* (Fla), 299 FSupp 834 (1969).

A legal deterrent for the teachers strike is to grant public school teachers the right to negotiate with school boards on such matters as salaries, work conditions or anything else in which teacher welfare is involved.

Experts in the field of school law believe there are no necessary legal barriers for teachers and school boards to engage in collective bargaining. It is generally agreed that it would be better for school authorities to formulate reasonable procedures for teacher-board negotiations, in advance, under amicable atmosphere, rather than to be forced into bargaining situations by teachers' strikes or threats to strike which generate injury to the school and animosity in the community.

If the school board were blessed with unlimited funds to meet fiscal expectations of the teachers, the threat to strike would likely be averted. Certainly, during an inflationary economy, that situation does not exist. Mutual understanding of the predicament is necessary. In this connection, a noted authority states:

> There will be occasions when school officials can sincerely say the money is not available. In such instances, if the school board honestly feels there is fairness in the demands of teachers, good faith bargaining should dictate making that fact known and offering to join the teachers to work for some increase in available public funds.[87]

---

[87] Reynolds C. Seitz, "Teacher Negotiations, the Legal Issues." *Nation's Schools,* March, 1971, p. 51.

Chapter 16

DISCRETIONARY AUTHORITY OF SCHOOL BOARDS OVER PUPIL PERSONNEL

16.1   Legal status of the pupil

Like any other citizen, the pupil is a subject of the state, and entitled to the rights and freedoms thereof. At the same time he is subject to the regulations of the state which are designed for the health, safety, progress and general welfare of the populace.

A pupil is also a member of a family, and, in this capacity, is subject to the care and control of parents. As long as the parent provides for the proper care and control of the child, and in conformity with constitutional and statutory provisions designed for the *general* welfare, the state is not likely to interfere with the parents' natural right over the child. When the parents fail, however, to provide properly for the welfare of the child, who is unable to do so for himself, the state may legally exercise any power necessary to secure the protection and welfare of its minor subjects, as well as all other citizens. This point of view is given strong support by the declaration of an early Wisconsin court:

Where parental duty for any cause is not performed, the state, through its appropriate agencies succeeds thereto, not as an original right, but a resumption of a right delegated to parents as the natural guardians of their children, the persons under natural conditions having the most effective motives and inclinations and in the best position and under the strongest obligations to give to such children proper nurture, education and training. In cases of necessity, however, children become the wards of the people as a whole, with the duties that spring from that relation. . . . In its capacity of *parens patriae* the state can and should make provisions for the care and education of these wards of society, not only for the protection of society, but also for the benefit of the children themselves.[1]

Numerous problems in our public educational system are of concern to both the parent and the state. The ultimate authority over the pupil in such matters as admission, attendance, placement, transportation, control and curriculum is frequently the subject of dispute and litigation. An excerpt extracted from the foreword of what is perhaps the first symposium, prepared jointly by legal experts and educators, indicates the basic issue concerning the allocation of authority over the pupils:

. . . these problems are perhaps but aspects of a still more basic one—the clash between the individual and the state—the conflict between the rights of an individual family group to educate its offspring as it wishes, and the requirements of the state, whether democratic or autocratic, that its future citizens must be so educated as to fulfill certain minimum requirements for the preservation of the nation as a whole. All of us surely recognize both the right and the duty of parents to train their children according to their individual needs and desires, but few of us today would deny the necessity of the state, especially in a democracy, to be certain that all its citizens have sufficient education to discharge the responsibilities

---

[1] *Wisconsin Industrial School for Girls v. Clark County*, 103 Wis 651, 79 NW 422 (1899).

imposed and take advantage of the opportunities offered by our society.[2]

The state's responsibility for and authority over the pupil is expressed in the state constitutions and in the statutes. In many instances, the legislature acts directly in enacting laws pertaining to the pupil; in some instances, the state authorizes or mandates a state board of education to formulate policy and regulations governing the pupils; and in still other cases, the local school board, which legally is a state agency, is given discretionary authority over the pupil. It is the exercise of that discretionary authority which is of legal concern here on issues which follow.

16.2   Admission requirements

Generally a child has the right, or at least the privilege, to attend a public school. The right for a child to be admitted to the public school, however, is not absolute. It is subject to reasonable restrictions and regulations. If the statutes do not state specifically what the restrictions and regulations are which limit admission, the school board is clothed with the discretionary authority to so determine within reasonable bounds. In the words of a Connecticut court: "This is a privilege or advantage, rather than a right, in the strict sense of the term. The privilege is granted, and it is so enjoyed, upon such terms and under such reasonable conditions and restrictions as the law-making power, within constitutional limits, may see fit to impose. . . ."[3]

Age limit is a determining factor in the admissibility of children to the public school. Virtually all states have statutes stipulating the required age for a child to be admissible to the public school. There is considerable variability, however, as to the age so stipulated. Moreover, the specificity of the age varies from state to state. In some states, the statute is so specific that a local school board need

---

[2] "School Pupils and the Law," *Law and Contemporary Problems* (Editor, Robert Kramer), School of Law, Duke University, vol. 20, Winter, 1955, No. 1, p. 2.

[3] *Bissell* v. *Davison*, 65 Conn 183, 32 Atl 348 (1894).

not elaborate on the requirement. For example, the North Carolina statute states that:

> Children to be entitled to enrollment in the public schools . . . must have passed the sixth anniversary of their birth before October first of the year in which they enroll, and must enroll during the first month of the school year: Provided, that if a particular child has already been attending school in another state in accordance with the laws or regulations of the school authorities of such state before moving to and becoming a resident of North Carolina, such child will be eligible for enrollment in the schools of this State regardless of whether such child has passed his sixth anniversary of his birth before October first.[4]

In certain other states, however, the age is stated in such vague or general terms that the school board may or must determine the exact admission age.

Frequently the board's rules regarding admission age are challenged in the courts on the ground of unreasonableness. It then becomes the duty of the court to resolve the issue. Because of the numerous variables in different cases, no clearly-defined legal principles have, as yet, evolved from the decisions. Whether or not a court will uphold a board regulation regarding admission age will depend upon slight margins of differentiation. For example, in a West Virginia case, the court ruled that a board regulation providing that children who attain "the age of six years subsequent to the first day of November after the commencement of a school term shall not be enrolled for the remainder of such term" was neither unreasonable nor arbitrary.[5]

16.3   Vaccination requirements

Even though the statutes frequently provide for health and safety measures for the pupil, the school board is given considerable discretionary authority in the matter. The board may exercise this authority by making rules or regula-

---

4 *Public School Laws of North Carolina*, 1965, Art. 19, secs. 115-162.
5 *Detch* v. *Board of Education*, 145 WVa 722, 117 SE (2d) 138 (1951).

tions excluding children from school if their presence is considered to be dangerous or injurious to themselves or other pupils. For example, a board may pass a rule requiring physical examinations and health certificates, with the authority to expel pupils who refuse to comply with the rule.[6] In commenting on the exercise of this authority, the court stated: "a thing may be reasonable, though it conflicts with the individual views of the few, if it conforms to that of the many."[7]

The most frequently litigated aspect of health regulations for pupils has to do with *vaccination* as a prerequisite for admission to the public schools. Where the statutes stipulate the requirements, the courts have consistently upheld the constitutionality of the statutes, on the ground that the welfare of the many should take precedence over the individual's liberty of conscience and right of religious freedom. The judicial reasoning on the issue is reflected in a court's statement:

> Religious freedom embraces two conceptions, freedom to believe and freedom to act. The first is absolute but, in the nature of things, the second cannot be . . . the constitutional guarantee of religious freedom does not permit the practice of religious rights dangerous or detrimental to the lives, safety or health of the participants or to the public. . . .[8]

The courts are not quite so consistent in upholding vaccination requirements made by a local board as when required by statute. Even though the school board generally has the right to pass a rule requiring vaccination as a condition to admission or attendance it may, in some jurisdictions, be dependent upon the existence of an epidemic or an emergency.[9]

---

[6] *Streich* v. *Board of Education of Aberdeen,* 34 SD 169, 147 NW 779 (1914).
[7] *Ibid.*
[8] *Mosier* v. *Barren County Board of Health,* 308 Ky 829, 215 SW (2d) 967 (1948).
[9] *Rhea* v. *Board of Education of Devils Lake Special School Dist.,* 41 ND 449, 171 NW 103 (1919).

In a contrasting ruling, however, a North Carolina court ruled that a school board had as much right to take action to prevent the occurrence of an epidemic as it had to hold it after it had once started.[10]

Also an Illinois court upheld a school board which required vaccination of *all* pupils during an epidemic whether they had been exposed or not. By way of dicta, the court stated: "No child has a constitutional right to carry to others in school the loathsome disease of smallpox."[11]

Parental objection to vaccination requirements is usually based on religious grounds. Nevertheless, unless the statutes specifically exempt persons whose religious beliefs are contrary to the requirement, a school board's requirement for the vaccination is likely to be upheld by the court. For example, an Alabama court, in reasoning that the right to practice religious freedom does not confer upon the individual the right to refuse vaccination, stated: "a person's right to exhibit religious freedom ceases where it overlaps and transgresses the rights of others."[12]

Whether exemptions from the vaccination requirement will be granted by the courts may depend upon extenuating circumstances. For example, in a North Carolina case[13] a parent was *exonerated* for violation of the vaccination requirement on religious grounds; whereas, in a New York case[14] a parent was *held guilty* for not conforming to the vaccination requirement, despite religious objections.

The decisive difference in the two cases was that, in *Miday,* the parent was exempted from having his child vaccinated by virtue of a statutory clause which exempted those who belonged to a religious organization (Miracle Revival Fellowship) whose teachings were in opposition to vaccinations and immunizations, whereas, in *McCartney,* where a

---

[10] *Hutchins* v. *School Committee of Durham,* 137 NC 68, 49 SE 46 (1904).
[11] *Hagler* v. *Larner,* 284 Ill 547, 120 NE 575 (1918).
[12] *Cude* v. *State,* 237 Ark 927, 377 SW(2d) 816 (1964).
[13] *State* v. *Miday,* 263 NC 747, 140 SE(2d) 325 (1965).
[14] *McCartney* v. *Austin,* 57 Misc(2d) 525, 293 NYS(2d) 188 (1968).

similar exemption clause was advanced as a defense, it was found that the parent's faith (Roman Catholic) "does not have any proscription against inoculation."

16.4 Nonresident tuition

The school board frequently grapples with the question as to whether or not a child from one school district may attend school in another district without paying tuition. Unless there is a statute to the contrary, the school board has the discretionary authority in such a matter. The courts are generally agreed that the board need not admit a child from a different district in the absence of a statutory mandate.

Usually a child is entitled to attend a school in the district of his or her parents' residence, without paying tuition. This right, however, raises the question as to what constitutes "legal residence." Simply stated, the legal residence of a pupil is at the domicile of his parents or legal guardian. The courts, however, place various interpretations on the words "resident" and "residence." One court states that they "are words having various meanings dependent upon the context of the statute in which they occur" and "they must be construed in light of the purpose of the statute in which they appear."[15] The court further ruled that a legal domicile is not required and that "for school purposes the term residence signifies the place where a child lives with some degree of permanency."

Some courts, however, are not so lenient in the matter, as is exemplified by an Oklahoma case where the question arose as to whether children who had lived with their grandparents were entitled to attend school free of tuition in the district of the grandparents instead of the district where their parents lived. In this case the court ruled that where parents have the legal control of the children and contribute to their support substantially, the residence of the child, for

---

[15] *School District v. McCormmach,* 238 Ore 51, 392 P(2d) 1019 (1964).

school purposes, is that of the parents, and consequently the children involved were not entitled to attend school free of tuition in the district where the grandparents resided.[16]

In an Arizona case[17] a statute provided for free tuition for those students residing in a district and authorizing a tuition charge for those students who were nonresidents of the district. The court did not construe this to mean that a parent could appoint a district resident as guardian of a nonresident child merely to avoid payment of tuition. It stated that the statute "presupposes that the children are living within the district, with legal sanction for their presence there. Any other interpretation would be an absurdity, and courts will avoid such an interpretation."[18]

16.5   Summer school tuition

Due to the fact that the summer session is usually in excess of the minimum school program required by statute, and that attendance is not directly compulsory, the legality of charging summer tuition in the public schools has not, as yet, been vigorously challenged. Moreover, there are few, if any, specific statutory references prohibiting the charging of summer tuition. In this connection, however, there are no specific statutory requirements to charge summer tuition in the public school. The practice originated and continues on a somewhat extralegal basis.

In the absence of express or implied statutory provision dealing with summer tuition fees in the public schools, clarification of the issue might require judicial interpretation. In fact, a test case in the courts to determine the constitutionality of the practice would not be out of order.

Most state constitutions are in agreement in stipulating that the General Assembly shall provide by taxation for a

---

16 *Gray* v. *Board of Education* (Okla), 389 P(2d) 498 (1964).
17 *School Dist. No. 3 of Maricopa County* v. *Dailey*, 106 Ariz 124, 471 P(2d) 736 (1970).
18 *Id.*, p. 739.

free and uniform system of public schools. The provision in the North Carolina Constitution is illustrative: "The General Assembly, at its first session under this Constitution, shall provide by taxation and otherwise for a general and uniform system of public schools, wherein tuition shall be free of charge to all children of the State between the ages of six and twenty-one years."[19]

Although the state constitution expressly prohibits the charging of tuition in the public schools, a statutory provision, which permits a local supplement for a higher standard than that provided by the state, limits its use to a term not to exceed 180 days.[20]

It appears then that, in North Carolina, the constitution prohibits the charging of summer school tuition while the statutes prohibit expenditure for education beyond 180 days per year. It is a well-established legal principle that where a constitutional provision and a statutory provision are in conflict, the constitutional provision takes precedence over the statutory provision. Therefore, in states where there is a constitutional prohibition against charging summer tuition, the legislature should provide for expenditure of *public funds* to operate a summer school program if a summer program is desired. At any rate the legality of charging summer school tuition in many states is questionable. This contention is supported by the fact that fourteen out of seventeen attorneys general who gave opinions on the issue believed that charging summer school tuition was illegal; whereas only three believed the practice was legal.[21]

16.6 Compulsory school attendance

Much litigation has evolved over the issue of whether the state, in compelling parents to place their children in school

---

[19] *Constitution of North Carolina*, Art. IX, sec. 2.

[20] *Public School Laws of North Carolina*, 1943, Chap. 115, sec. 361.

[21] Frederick W. Kirby, "Legal Aspects of Tuition." Unpublished doctoral dissertation, Duke University, 1957, pp. 212-213.

and in regulating the schools which they attend, unnecessarily infringes upon the legal rights of parents. Some parents contend that they have a natural and constitutional right to determine the manner and place of their children's education. Consequently they resist state interference with that right. Others, however, believe that education is of such importance to the welfare of the individual and the security of the nation, that the state has both the right and obligation to take such action as is reasonable and necessary to provide every child with adequate educational opportunity. On that basis, state authorities contend that it is within their power to compel attendance in such manner and places as is deemed most beneficial to the child.

Because of the question as to whether the state or the parent has authority in determining school attendance, school boards are confronted with the problem of action when a child of school age is not attending school in accordance with state requirements.

Legal principles evolving from judicial opinion on the issue serve as guidelines for school boards to follow. Of course it would be impossible for a board to review all court opinions concerning parent versus state authority over school attendance whenever an individual controversy arose. A knowledge of the general principles, however, would be helpful in guiding school board action. In an objective, scholarly and exhaustive study[22] of the legal aspects of compulsory school attendance as revealed in over a hundred court cases, Benton sets forth the following pertinent conclusions:

1. Within certain limitations, states have the authority to compel parents or other persons in parental relationship to place their children in attendance at school.

2. While the federal Constitution and the constitution of each state guarantee certain rights to the individual, parental rights to the care and custody of their children are

---

[22] Thomas Malcolm Benton, "Legal Aspects of Compulsory School Attendance." Unpublished doctoral dissertation, Duke University, 1965, pp. 219-224.

not absolute. Rather, there are conditions under which such rights are subordinate to the authority of the state.

3. States may restrict parental rights to any extent necessary to the welfare and progress of the public generally or to the well-being of children. The only significant constitutional restrictions upon such actions are that: (a) they must apply equally to all individuals or classes of individuals under like circumstances, (b) the established processes of law must be followed, and (c) they must not interfere with religious liberties.

4. Judicial authorities regard education as a necessary purpose, vital not only to the well-being of the child but to the welfare of society generally and to the very survival of the democratic way of life. Thus, statutes compelling attendance at school are both reasonable and necessary; and, so long as such laws do not violate the constitutional guarantee of individual rights, they are valid exercises of state authority. As far as can be determined by this study, all compulsory school attendance statutes challenged to date have been held to be constitutional.

5. There are circumstances under which it would be unreasonable or arbitrary to compel particular individuals to attend school. For instance, judicial authorities will not support states in demanding school attendance where there is substantial authoritative evidence that the child's attendance at school will (a) endanger the well-being of or work an undue hardship upon the child or any member of the child's immediate family, or (b) compel the child to accept an educational opportunity inferior to that provided other children within the district, particularly where such inferior opportunity results from discriminatory action on the part of school officials.

6. While there are special conditions under which particular individuals may be declared exempt from the requirements of school attendance laws, exemptions are not easily gained. There is strong evidence that the courts will not declare a child exempt from his state's attendance law even when (a) the mental or physical condition of the child

is such that the child is required to attend a special state-maintained school—or equivalent private school—where facilities, equipment, and personnel are especially suited to the needs of the child; (b) the religious convictions of the child and/or his family are such that they are opposed to secular education; or (c) the child has been excluded from the assigned public school for failure to comply with the valid rules and regulations of the school.

7. In complying with the compulsory school attendance laws of the various states, parents or other persons to whom such laws apply have at least two choices as to the type of instructional program their children will attend. They may elect to place their children in attendance at (a) the assigned public school, or (b) the private school of their choice, so long as the selected school meets the requirements of the school attendance law. The courts fully agree that private schools have the right to teach and that parents have the right to place their children in attendance at such schools.

8. There are no uniform minimum standards for private schools. Such standards vary from state to state, depending upon the provisions of the school attendance law and the attitude of the courts as they interpret the meaning of such provisions. Where the school attendance law clearly establishes standards, the private school attended must meet all reasonable requirements. . . .

9. In certain states, (a) where the compulsory school attendance law of the state voluntarily permits such, and in others (b) where the courts hold that programs of instruction conducted within the home qualify as private schools, parents may comply with their state's compulsory school attendance law by having their children instructed at "home schools." There is substantial evidence that states may, where they elect to do so, demand attendance at either a public or formally organized private school, thereby denying to parents the opportunity to satisfy the requirements of the school attendance law through programs of home instruction.

10. There are no uniform standards for home schools. Such standards vary from state to state, depending upon the

provisions of school attendance laws and the attitude of the courts as they interpret the meaning of these laws. In states where home school attendance is accepted, and the school attendance law clearly establishes standards to be/maintained by such schools, the home instructional program must meet all the reasonable standards demanded by the law. Where the law simply provides that children may receive instruction outside public or private schools, failing to specify requirements for such instructional programs, the home school attended must meet only those standards demanded by the courts. Although judicial authorities are not in complete agreement on this issue, there is substantial evidence that the courts of a majority of the states will approve home instructional programs where the following minimum requirements are met: (a) instruction is provided in the subjects required by law to be taught—or those commonly taught—in the public schools of the district, (b) such instruction is given in the English language, (c) instruction is given by a reasonably competent teacher, and (d) the education provided, as measured by the child's attainments in the basic academic subjects, is comparable to that provided children of corresponding age and grade in attendance at the public schools of the district. As suggested, however, the courts of certain states may demand higher standards. The judicial authorities of at least one state have insisted that home instructional programs be fully equivalent to and meet all the requirements established for the public schools of the district, even to the extent of providing group activities and social opportunities.

A case litigated since Benton's study indicates that compulsory school attendance laws of some states are rather stringent and do not allow alternatives for attendance *at a school*. For example, the law of Kansas provides: "exemption from school attendance is only on the basis of physical or mental incapacity." Consequently a parent (member of Old Order Mennonite Church) of a 15-year-old daughter, was found guilty of violating the compulsory school attendance law, even though the child was given home instruction in lieu of *school* instruction. By way of comment, the court stated:

> Even if a system of education, consisting essentially of home instruction was considered as instruction equivalent to that given in public, private, denominational or parochial school, as required by compulsory school attendance law, such would not constitute excuse for nonattendance at latter, in view of fact that Legislature made no provision for such equivalent instruction as basis for exemption. [23]

Whether home instruction, in lieu of public or nonpublic school instruction, is accepted by the courts as fulfilling requirements, depends, in large part, on the phrasing of the applicable statutes. Leading court cases indicate that home instruction will have judicial sanction as an alternative for school instruction, providing the home instruction is *equivalent* to that which would be obtainable in a public school, and if there are no statutory restrictions.[24]

In some instances, however, courts have held that home instruction *cannot* be "equivalent" to that of public school instruction in *social* development. In an applicable case a judge stated: "I cannot conceive how a child can receive in the home instruction and experience and group activity and in social outlook in any manner or form comparable to that provided in the public school."[25]

In a 1971 decision[26] which is somewhat in variance with the majority of decisions on the same issue, the Supreme Court of Wisconsin declared unconstitutional a compulsory school attendance law as applied to members of the Amish religion. The court minimized the effect of exemptions to the compulsory attendance law in their particular case as indicated by the following statements:

> Granting an exemption from compulsory education to the Amish will do no more to the ultimate goal of edu-

---

[23] *State* v. *Garber*, 197 Kan 567, 419 P(2d) 896 (1966).
[24] *State* v. *Massa*, 95 NJSuper 382, 231 A(2d) 252 (1967).
[25] *Stephens* v. *Bongart*, 15 NJMisc 80, 189 Atl 131, 137 (1937).
[26] *State* v. *Yoder,* 49 Wis(2d) 430, 182 NW(2d) 539 (1971).

cation than to dent the symmetry of the design for enforcement.[27]

We conclude that although education is a subject within the constitutional power of the state to regulate, there is not such a compelling state interest in two years' high school compulsory education as will justify the burden it places upon appellants' free exercise of their religion.[28]

16.7   Shared-time enrollment

"Shared time," frequently referred to as "dual enrollment" is an arrangement whereby a child regularly and concurrently attends a public school for a part of the school day and a nonpublic school for the remaining portion of the school day. Presumably, while in the public school, the pupil pursues such studies as are strictly secular; whereas in the nonpublic school he engages in activities where religious elements are or may be stressed.

Although shared-time education is not exactly a new concept, it has received increased consideration and publicity in recent years. In all probability the sudden stimulus for broadening the scope of shared-time programs springs from recent court rulings of the United States Supreme Court limiting sharply the extent to which religious instruction may be provided in the public schools. Another explanation is the admitted financial difficulty parochial schools are encountering in providing a complete educational program for their pupils.

The specific question on the legality of shared-time programs has not been litigated very frequently. Therefore, in order to determine what rulings would likely be made in the event more cases are adjudicated, it would be necessary to analyze decisions which have already been rendered in related cases involving the relationships and commingling of public and nonpublic educational programs. The most applicable of those cases deal with the furnishing of free

27 *Id.*, p. 545.
28 *Id.*, p. 547.

textbooks to parochial school pupils, providing free transportation to parochial school pupils, released time programs, prohibition of Bible reading, prayers, and other religious activities in the public schools.[29]

Although these cases do not deal directly with the issue of shared time, they do have some significant implications. First, they indicate quite emphatically that religious instruction in the public schools is unconstitutional. And, second, some of the cases indicate circumstances under which public funds may be expended for the benefit of parochial school pupils.

Whether or not school boards have the discretionary authority to promote or permit shared-time programs will depend upon a number of variables. Since there are no specific United States Court decisions on the issue, school boards must turn to constitutional and statutory laws of their respective states. In discussing the constitutionality of shared-time programs, a governmental publication states:

> Each State is free to determine its position under its own constitution. State courts, legislatures, or legal officers have expressed varying points of view on the constitutionality of dual enrollment, ranging from a clear-cut affirmative position as in Pennsylvania and Michigan, to a negative ruling as in New York.[30]

Since the legality of share-time programs is so frequently questioned, it is surprising that the issue has not been litigated more extensively than it has. In fact, on the basis of the writer's research to date, there are but few cases on record which deal with the question of shared time, the first one being adjudicated over a half century ago.

The facts in the early case indicate that the guardian of a parochial school child sought admission for him to a manual training program in a public school. Admission was denied and the guardian sought a writ of mandamus which was

---

29 These cases are discussed in Chapter 1 of this publication.

30 *Dual Enrollment in Public and Nonpublic Schools.* U. S. Department of Health, Education, and Welfare. OE-24014, Cir. No. 772, 1965, p. 83.

granted by the court upon order to permit the child's admission. In granting the writ, the court stated:

A student in a private school has the right to attend an additional school or department established by a board of directors in a school district, provided he has the other qualifications of a student in the public schools in the district, and mandamus will lie to enforce his right.

Accordingly the public school officials were ordered to receive and admit the child to the public school for a manual training class.[31]

The second case,[32] coming over a half century later, may or may not portend the future judicial view on shared-time enrolments. In this case the appellate court of Illinois dismissed a complaint for an injunction to restrain the school board from maintaining an experimental dual-enrollment program wherein children enrolled part-time in a public school and part-time in a nonpublic school. In defending its position for dismissing the complaint the court concluded: "The experimental plan adopted by the Chicago School Board is merely an attempt to find a better method for the education of the Chicago public school children at the option of the parents or legal guardians of those children."

Another applicable case [33] was adjudicated in the Supreme Court of New York in 1963. It grew out of a denial of a public school to provide home teaching for a parochial school girl who was suffering from a rheumatic heart condition which would confine her to her bed approximately a half year. In ignoring the contention of the board that the instruction sought was for the benefit of a nonpublic school, the court declared: "Patently the furnishing of home teaching to Kathleen Scales is not directly in aid or maintenance of her parochial school. . . . It is difficult to conceive how the parochial school will obtain any real advantage from it."

---

[31] *Commonwealth* v. *School Dist. of Altoona*, 241 Pa 224, 88 Atl 481 (1913).

[32] *Morton* v. *Board of Education of Chicago*, 69 IllApp(2d) 38, 216 NE(2d) 305 (1966).

[33] *Scales* v. *Board of Education*, 41 Misc 391, 245 NYS(2d) 449 (1963).

The laws of some states are rather specific in requiring that enrollment be restricted to *one* school during the regular school period. For example, the statutes of Missouri stipulate "Every parent, guardian or other person in this state having charge, control or custody of a child between the ages of seven and sixteen years shall cause the child to attend regularly some day school, public, private, parochial or parish. . . ." Therefore, where a school district

> provided speech therapy for parochial school children in buildings maintained by school board, and parochial children who desired such therapy were released from school for part of their regular six-hour day in violation of statutes which require all school children to regularly attend school six hours in school day, school district practice was invalid. . . .[34]

In a declaratory judgment in 1971, the Supreme Court of Michigan held that:

> Shared time can be provided by a public school system only under conditions appropriate for a public school. This means that the ultimate and immediate control of the subject matter, the personnel and premises must be under the public school system authorities, and the courses open to all eligible to attend a public school.[35]

As shared-time programs increase, it is likely that litigation on the issue will increase accordingly. Whether the courts will declare the shared-time programs legal or illegal will depend upon varying circumstances in the school districts where they are conducted, as was the case for contrasting court decisions pertaining to released-time programs under varying conditions.

16.8 Pupil placement

Until 1954, pupil placement was not a very litigious

---

[34] *Special Dist. for the Education and Training of Handicapped Children of St. Louis County* v. *Wheeler* (Mo), 408 SW(2d) 60 (1966).
[35] *In re Proposal C* (Mich), 185 NW(2d) 9, 20 (1971).

issue. School boards were generally permitted to exercise their discretion in placing pupils in schools according to their needs and the facilities of the school district. After the *Brown* decision, however, many school boards assigned pupils to schools in such a manner as to perpetuate segregated schools. Of course the placement of pupils in particular schools because of race was in conflict with constitutional law as interpreted by the United States Supreme Court. Nevertheless, states continued to enact pupil placement laws. Some of them were designed to circumvent the court ruling so as to perpetuate segregation in the public schools, whereas others were for the purpose of expediting a transition from a segregated to a desegregated placement plan within the meaning of the United States Supreme Court decision.

Two states, Louisiana and Mississippi, in anticipation of the forthcoming *Brown* decision, enacted pupil-placement statutes in 1954. Alabama and North Carolina passed pupil-placement laws the following year; and the next year, 1956, Florida, South Carolina, Virginia, and Arkansas enacted similar laws. Tennessee and Texas followed in 1957. Of the eleven states of the South, Georgia was the only state that had not enacted a statute for a pupil-placement plan to effect a transition from a segregated to a nonsegregated school system. The statutes of the border states, Delaware, Kentucky, Maryland, Oklahoma, and West Virginia contain provisions for the enrollment of pupils in the public schools and establish authority of the boards of education for the assignment of pupils, "but these statutes are of long standing and are not related to the racial issue." [36]

The state pupil-placement laws vary with regard to the degree of authority delegated to local school boards in assigning pupils to certain schools. For example, the statute of Virginia created the Pupil Placement Board to handle all transfers of pupils for the entire state and further provided that "local school boards and division superintendents are

---

[36] Harold L. Tyer, "The Legal Status of Pupil Placement in the Public Schools of the United States." Unpublished doctoral dissertation, Duke University, 1965.

hereby divested of all authority now and at any future time to determine the school to which any child shall be admitted."[37] In contrast the North Carolina Placement Act provided ". . . each county and city board of education shall make assignments of pupils to public schools so as to provide for the orderly and efficient administration of the public schools."[38]

As was anticipated, many of the pupil placement laws and the manner in which school boards attempted to apply them were challenged on the ground of unconstitutionality. Ensuing cases were carried eventually to the federal courts. At first the federal courts refused to rule upon them and remanded them to lower courts or boards of education until all administrative remedies had first been exhausted. For example, in a case originating in North Carolina and carried to the Court of Appeals, Fourth Circuit, the court declared: "An administrative remedy is thus provided by state law . . . and it is well settled that the courts of the United States will not grant injunctive relief until administrative remedies have been exhausted." The court continued:

> The federal courts manifestly cannot operate the schools. All they have the power to do in the premises is to enjoin violation of constitutional rights in the operation of schools by state authorities. Where the state law provides adequate administrative procedure for the protection of such rights, the federal courts manifestly should not interfere with the operation of the schools until such administrative procedure has been exhausted and the intervention of the federal courts is shown to be necessary.[39]

Tyer cites 17 cases in which the courts have sustained the doctrine of "exhaustion of administrative remedies" and the same number in which the courts have not sustained the doctrine.[40]

---

[37] *Code of Virginia*, Chap. 22, sec. 230.2.

[38] *General Statutes of North Carolina*, Chap. 115, sec. 176.

[39] *Carson* v. *Board of Education of McDowell County* (4th Cir), 227 F(2d) 789 (1955).

[40] Tyer, *op. cit.*, pp. 243-245.

Until recently some of the federal courts continued to hold that one complaining of segregation practices must first exhaust all administrative remedies provided in the laws of the state before appealing to the federal courts. In 1963, however, the United States Supreme Court settled the matter when it said: "relief . . . may not be defeated because relief was not first sought under state law which provided a remedy."[41]

Although school boards have considerable discretion in the placement of pupils, the assignment of pupils to particular schools must not be for the purpose of evading or circumventing the law. Placement of pupils, like any other phase of board action which cannot be done in direct compliance with the law, cannot be accomplished by subterfuge. Any pupil placement plan must apply to all pupils and not just to those of one particular race; otherwise it will be declared to be discriminatory and illegal.[42]

In a case which originated in Louisiana, a federal court stated:

> . . . if it is "discrimination in its rawest form" to assign pupils to segregated schools solely on the basis of race in an attempt to maintain segregation, then surely it is the rawest kind of disregard for the rights of all students, both white and Negro, to arbitrarily assign them to schools on a purely geographical basis, thus, in effect, *compelling* integration in the schools, contrary to law. . . .[43]

Federal court decisions indicate clearly that school boards not only possess discretionary authority to adopt plans for desegregation (pupil placement) but to also assume responsibility for doing so. It is the school board and not the Negro pupils who must initiate plans for desegregation. A federal court stresses this point in the following manner:

> In light of the Supreme Court's explicit holding that it is the obligation of local school authorities to take affirma-

[41] *McNeese* v. *Board of Education* (Ill), 373 US 668, 10 LEd(2d) 622, 83 SCt 1433 (1963).

[42] *Blakeney* v. *Fairfax County School Board* (Va), 226 FSupp 713 (1964).

[43] *Davis* v. *East Baton Rouge Parish School Board* (La), 219 FSupp 876 (1964).

tive action to "make a prompt and reasonable start toward
full compliance" . . . it would be unreasonable for the
court to require the plaintiffs to formulate plans for desegregation. . . . It is these school officials, not the infant
plaintiffs or their parents, who are familiar with the
operation of the school system and know the administrative problems which may constitute the only legitimate
ground for withholding the immediate realization of constitutionally guaranteed rights. [44]

Moreover, school boards cannot expect the courts to
initiate desegregation (pupil placement) plans. That responsibility rests squarely upon the school board. In stressing
this point a federal court stated:

The burden of initiating desegregation in the public
schools rests upon the school authorities, who have the
primary responsibility for assessing and solving the varied
local school problems arising as a result of implementing
the decision in *Brown*, . . . and the courts must determine whether the action of the school authorities constitutes good faith implementation of those constitutional
rights. [45]

The cases referred to above merely illustrate the responsibility of school boards to conform to the *Brown* decision in
the desegregation of the public schools. There are many
more cases dealing with the issue but all of them give evidence that pupil placement policies planned by school
boards must be made in good faith and in conformity with
the law.[46]

From the many court decisions dealing with desegregation
and the pupil-placement plans for the public schools, certain
legal principles have evolved and are gradually becoming
solidified. In the concluding statements of an exhaustive
study of the legal aspects of pupil-placement laws, Tyer states

---

[44] *Buckner* v. *County School Board* (Va), 332 F(2d) 452 (1965).

[45] *Downs* v. *Board of Education* (Kan), 336 F(2d) 988 (1965).

[46] For thorough and objective treatment of all applicable cases see the
Yearbooks of School Law (edited by Lee O. Garber), under the title of
"Racial Discrimination and Segregation."

that: "These principles gained strength with the passing of each year of the decade and have become safe guidelines for school administrators who are faced with the problem of desegregation of their schools in compliance with the mandate of the Supreme Court."[47]

Tyer lists the following twelve principles derived from court decisions as being the most significant:

1. Classification to serve the objectives of the state is permissible but race cannot be a factor.

2. Negro plaintiffs do not have to exhaust administrative remedies which are designed and administered in such a manner as to preserve and maintain segregated school systems.

3. School boards have a constitutional obligation to inaugurate plans for pupil placement without putting Negro students in the position of having to seek relief in the courts.

4. Voluntary segregation is constitutional in the absence of force or coercion and the individual must be absolutely free to choose separation.

5. Dual school districts must give way to the drawing of unitary district lines; moreover, race may be considered in order to avoid segregated districts within reason and without gerrymandering.

6. The constitutional rights of plaintiff Negroes and others of their class cannot be yielded to violence and disorder.

7. "With all deliberate speed" can no longer be used as an excuse for delay in compliance with the mandate of the Supreme Court.

8. Academic achievement, psychological, and other such tests cannot be used in the placement of Negro students in white schools where white children are not required to take the same tests as conditions for admission.

9. Crowding of schools and classrooms cannot be an excuse for denying Negro children the freedom to choose the schools they are entitled to attend.

10. The "neighborhood school" concept has judicial

---

[47] Tyer, *op. cit.*, p. 229.

standing when honestly and reasonably administered but cannot be the means whereby Negro children are denied the right to a nonsegregation education.

11. Pupil placement laws are operative only in situations where segregated school systems do not exist.

12. Although school boards do not have a clear affirmative duty to correct racial imbalance by busing students to schools outside their home districts, courts have sustained such positive actions when performed for the furtherance of integrated education, even though the rights of white children may seem to have been violated.[48]

After a period of six undecisive years, however, the United States Supreme Court[49] *did affirm* the duty of school boards to employ busing of students as a means of correcting racial imbalance. The High Court emphasized that it found "no basis for holding that the local school authorities may not be required to employ bus transportation as one tool of school desegregation. Desegregation plans cannot be limited to the walk-in school."[50] It said further that "the proscription against assignment of students for purpose of creating racial balance would conflict with duty of school authorities to disestablish dual systems."[51]

Following the confusion arising from the landmark decision, Chief Justice Burger has explained, since, that the decision *does not* require "a fixed racial balance."

16.9 Pupil transportation

"Since pupil transportation has developed into one of the most important, costly, and hazardous of the auxiliary services of the schools, it is not surprising that it should be the

---

[48] Tyer, *op. cit.,* pp. 229-230.
[49] *Swann* v. *Charlotte-Mecklenburg Board of Education,* 91 SCt 1267 (1971).
[50] *Id.,* p. 1283.
[51] *Id.,* p. 1284.

subject of much legislation and frequent litigation." [52]

In some of the earlier court cases, the constitutionality of pupil-transportation laws was challenged on the ground that they were discriminatory in providing transportation for some people and not for others. Now, however, the legal principle is well established that the laws are not discriminatory, nor do they violate uniformity of public school operation. Consequently every state now has statutes authorizing the expenditure of public funds for the transportation of pupils. There is great variation, however, in the applicability of the statutes to particular states and circumstances. In some instances the law specifically requires a district to furnish free transportation for pupils; in other instances the law makes the furnishing of transportation optional with the school board; and in still other cases the duty is mandatory upon the board only under certain conditions.

Under statutes where the duty to transport pupils to and from school is mandatory the law must be reasonably construed so that no child entitled to transportation will be denied the privilege. "No discretion is conferred upon the board to expand the delegation of power. The power actually conferred is extraordinary from any point of view. It has been carefully hedged about so as to forbid, rather than to invite expansion." [53] Consequently, a federal court held that Virginia laws providing transportation grants were administered in violation of the Fourteenth Amendment where a private school was organized to which all white pupils, but no Negro pupils, applying were admitted, and its pupils received transportation grants. [54]

Litigation has frequently developed where school boards have attempted to evade the statutory requirement of furnishing transportation to certain children because of the undue expense which would be involved. Unless the statutes

[52] E. C. Bolmeier, "Legal Issues in Pupil Transportation," *Law and Contemporary Problems*. School of Law, Duke University, Vol. 20, No. 1. Winter, 1955, p. 45.

[53] *Schmidt* v. *Blair*, 203 Iowa 1016, 213 NW 593 (1927).

[54] *Pettaway* v. *County School Board* (Va), 230 FSupp 480 (1965).

specifically authorize board discretion in such matters, the courts will not permit it. As one court reasons: "It is not a question of how much it will cost the district to transport this child or that child. The district has no right to say it will transport certain children but to transport the remainder will be too costly."[55]

In a 1966 case,[56] it was shown without question that eight children in a school district in California were being totally deprived of education because the school board refused to authorize transportation. The board's refusal to furnish the transportation was because of the excessive cost which would be involved. The court ruled the board's action as illegal, contending that it was "arbitrary and unreasonable to refuse to do so simply because it may be more expensive to transport these children than others in the district."

Transportation laws which are most mandatory on the part of local boards are those in which the state board of education is authorized by law to specify the regulations under which transportation is to be provided. In at least five states (Delaware, Minnesota, New Mexico, New Jersey, and North Carolina), the state boards are so empowered. Although much of the authority may be discretionary for the state board of education, it is usually mandatory for the local boards. Any regulations which the local school board may specify must conform to those of the state board of education.[57]

In certain instances the law makes the furnishing of transportation optional with the local school board. In approximately two-thirds of the states some degree of discretion is allowable.

Where the law is clear and specific in its delegation of discretionary authority to school boards for the furnishing of transportation, there is little likelihood of litigation. If the board exercises its discretionary authority honestly, it

[55] *Mumm* v. *Troy Township School Dist.*, 240 Iowa 1057, 38 NW(2d) 583 (1949).

[56] *Manjores* v. *Newton*, 49 CalRep 805, 411 P(2d) 901 (1966).

[57] *Rankin* v. *Board of Education*, 135 NJ 299, 51 A(2d) 194 (1947).

will be upheld in court even though there is evidence that
the board's action might not have been satisfactory or beneficial to certain residents of the school district. It is not
likely that the courts will interfere unless there is evidence
that the board acted in an arbitrary and capricious manner.
Numerous cases may be cited to bear out this contention.
By way of illustration, a 1966 case [58] may be cited where a
board of education acted to have children transported to a
certain school even though some parents protested and contended it would be much better to transport them to another
school. The Tennessee court ruled that, since the board
acted to avoid danger with the possibility of overcrowding
a certain school, the discretionary authority of the board
was not abused.

By way of dicta, the court then added a pertinent statement that is applicable to most court cases where the discretionary authority of the school board is challenged:

> Boards of Education, rather than the courts, are
> charged with the important and difficult duty of operat-
> ing the public schools. So, it is not a question of whether
> this or that judge or court considers a given regulation
> adopted by the board as expedient. The Court's duty,
> regardless of its personal views, is to uphold the Board
> regulation unless it is generally viewed as being arbi-
> trary and unreasonable. Any other policy would result
> in confusion detrimental to the progress and efficiency
> of our public school system.

Many laws place distance limitations on the furnishing
of pupil transportation. Although most of the laws specify
"two miles" as the distance limitation, there are wide variations. For example, Indiana makes transportation of pupils
aged 6 to 12 mandatory if they live at least five-eighths of a
mile from school, whereas Washington permits transportation to union high schools only if the pupils live four miles
from school. [59]

[58] *Davis* v. *Fentress County Board of Education*, 218 Tenn 280, 402
SW(2d) 873 (1966).

[59] Madaline Kinter Remmlein, *The Law of Local Public School Administration* (1953), p. 141.

Sometimes the legality of distance limitations is measured not only by miles but by feet. For example, in a Wisconsin case, a school board refused to furnish transportation to some children because they lived eleven feet less than two miles from the school. Plaintiff complained of the measurement because it deviated from the path traversed by the children due to the fact that it cut across the lawn, whereas the path usually travelled by the children was from the door directly to the driveway and thence to the highway. The distance by this route was a few feet beyond the two-mile limit, and consequently the Court held that the children involved were entitled to transportation costs.[60]

The importance of the manner in which distance is measured in determining eligibility for transportation is reflected in a more recent case where a Mississippi court ruled that the distance must be measured from the door of a child's house and not from the end of the driveway.[41]

Where the distance limitation is specified in terms of miles, the school board's authority to furnish transportation is accordingly limited and decisive. Arriving at a decision is more difficult when the distance limitation is stated in such vague terms as "unreasonable," "remote," or "inaccessible." In the several states where no definite distance limitation, in terms of miles, has been placed on pupil transportation, the board's decisions in determining what is "reasonable" or "unreasonable" have been challenged frequently in the courts as abuses of discretion. In all cases the decisions have been based upon a composite of existing factors rather than upon the single one of distance. The school board as well as the court takes into consideration such factors as age of the children to be transported, climate, width and surface of the passageway, traffic hazards, amount of traffic, and even the acquaintance and experience of the children with traffic situations.[62]

---

[60] *Gandt v. Joint School District*, 4 Wis(2d) 419, 90 NW(2d) 549 (1958).

[61] *Madison County Board of Education v. Grantham*, 250 Miss 767, 168 S(2d) 515 (1964).

[62] *Schmidt v. Payne*, 304 Ky 58, 199 SW(2d) 990 (1947); *Board of Education of Clay County v. Bowling*, 312 Ky 749, 229 SW(2d) 768 (1950).

The use of student bus drivers constitutes a controversial issue. Some states—particularly North Carolina, South Carolina, and Virginia—rely heavily on youths to drive the school buses. North Carolina employs over 9,000 student bus drivers under 18 years of age.

The issue was aggravated by the Fair Labor Standards Act as amended by the 89th Congress to extend its provisions to public school personnel.[63] The modified standards of the act provide that the minimum age of 16 be extended to 18 for occupations which are hazardous. The Secretary of Labor declared school bus driving a "hazardous occupation." Consequently, North Carolina would have had to replace approximately 9,000 student bus drivers by adult drivers with considerably higher wages.

Two North Carolina officials—the Governor and Superintendent of Public Instruction—conferred with the Secretary of Labor and won temporary exemption from the minimum age feature of the amended act. Whether the exemption will be granted on a permanent basis is doubtful, since in cited pupil transportation cases, the courts have not compromised with provisions of the law because of economic factors. Secretary Wirtz indicated that the regulation would be suspended until his Department studies characteristics of the work and dependence of school systems on young drivers.

In pleading their case, the North Carolina officials stressed the fact that the "National Safety Council statistics indicate the average driver has 4.9 accidents per million miles driven. North Carolina's youthful bus drivers have an average of 4.6 accidents per million miles."

The legal questions pertaining to transportation of *parochial school pupils* is quite different from that of transporting *public school pupils*. The former is based primarily upon the constitutionality of legislation designed to expend public funds for sectarian purposes, whereas the latter concerns mainly legislative intent in the degree of discretionary

---

[63] "Federal Wage Law Affects Student Drivers, Increases Budget." *North Carolina Public School Bulletin.* February, 1967. p. 1.

authority delegated to local school boards.

Numerous statutory provisions frequently permit, with judicial sanction, the expenditure of public funds which— even though not construed to benefit sectarian schools—do benefit pupils attending such schools. The extent to which the "child benefit" theory may be applied in the expenditure of public funds for the transportation and other services and costs of children attending parochial schools has been, and still is, a problem with which the courts must struggle.

So far the courts have rendered decisions on at least a score of cases in which the legality of providing transportation to parochial pupils at public expense has been challenged. In the early cases, the courts declared such practices illegal because of constitutional violations. Even in cases where the majority opinions upheld the constitutionality of the statutes authorizing free transportation of parochial pupils, strong dissenting opinions accompanied the decisions.

It was with a background of conflicting opinions of state courts that the United States Supreme Court, in a five-to-four decision, upheld the provisions for free transportation to parochial pupils in the first school bus case to reach it. As is referred to in a preceding chapter of this publication, section 4.4, the court ruled that the New Jersey statute which provided for the transportation of parochial school children at public expense violated neither the "due process" clause of the Fourteenth Amendment nor the First Amendment by giving support to a "religious establishment." [64]

This decision, however, was not to be interpreted as sanctioning the expenditure of public funds for transporting parochial school children without *explicit* provisions in the statute to do so. For example, in the very year the *Everson* case was decided a Pennsylvania court ruled that a school board could not be compelled to furnish free transportation to parochial pupils. The court held that the statute stipulat-

---

[64] *Everson* v. *Board of Education of Ewing Township* (NJ), 330 US 1, 91 LEd 711, 67 SCt 504 (1947).

ing that the board may, out of funds of the school district, provide free transportation for any pupil to and from "public schools" authorized only the transportation of "public school pupils" and not "parochial school pupils."[65]

Similarly, the Supreme Court of Washington interpreted a statute which provided for transportation to "all children" as applicable to "all children in public schools" only and not to "children attending a parochial school." The majority opinion in this case emphasized the fact that transportation of children to parochial schools at public expense constitutes financial aid for a "religious establishment" which is a violation of the state constitution.[66]

More recently, an Alaska court held that a statute providing for the transportation of children to nonpublic schools at public expense is unconstitutional.[67]

Also, in Oklahoma, it was held that a school district could not use its buses for the purpose of transporting students enrolled in a privately-owned Catholic school. In this case the court reasoned that a parent has the right to have his children educated in a parochial school but in so doing, "he is faced with the necessity of assuming the financial burden which that choice entails."[68]

Thenceforth the trend turned in the opposite direction. In only one[69] of six cases reported for 1968 did the court invalidate the legality of transporting nonpublic pupils at public expense. The Supreme Court of Hawaii placed a strict interpretation on the Constitution which states: "Nor shall public funds be appropriated for the support or benefit of any sectarian or private educational institutions."

In the other five cases[70] the courts applied the child bene-

---

[65] *Connell* v. *Board of School Directors*, 356 Pa 585, 52 A(2d) 645 (1947).
[66] *Visser* v. *Noonsack Val. District No. 506*, 33 Wash(2d) 198 (1949).
[67] *Matthews* v. *Quinton* (Alaska), 362 P(2d) 932 (1961).
[68] *Board of Education* v. *Antone* (Okla), 384 P(2d) 911 (1963).
[69] *Spears* v. *Honda* (Hawaii), 449 P(2d) 130 (1968).
[70] *McCanna* v. *Sills*, 103 NJSuper 480, 247 A(2d) 691 (1968); *Board of Education* v. *Gateway Regional High School Dist.*, 104 NJSuper 76, 248 A(2d) 564 (1968); *Honohan* v. *Holt*, 46 OO(2d) 79, 17 OhioMisc 57, 244 NE(2d) 537 (1968); *Cartwright* v. *Sharpe*, 40 Wis(2d) 494, 162 NW(2d) 5 (1968); *Alexander* v. *Bartlett*, 14 MichApp 177, 165 NW(2d) 445 (1968).

fit theory in sustaining the legality of the contested transportation statutes.

The legality of transporting pupils to parochial schools at public expense appears to be a matter for state lawmakers to determine. Since the United States Supreme Court ruled in the *Everson* case that the practice did not violate the Federal Constitution, the individual states apparently have the right to control the matter by constitutional and statutory provisions. This contention is supported by the fact that the constitutional limitation, which formed the basis for the ruling against free transportation to parochial schools in an earlier New York case (*Judd* v. *Board of Education*) was removed by the adoption of a constitutional amendment which now permits the legislature to provide such transportation.[71]

16.10   Secret societies

"Secret societies, such as fraternities, have been considered so detrimental to the high school that at least 25 states have passed anti-fraternity laws. In most of the other 25 states individual school boards have formulated policies and regulations designed to curb the activities and existence of these organizations."[72]

School patrons have questioned the authority of legislatures to enact anti-fraternity statutes, as well as school boards to impose restrictions and penalties on those who affiliate with the secret societies. As evidenced by the number of court cases, the controversy has been so severe as to often lead to litigation. Statutes and school board regulations dealing with the problem have been tested in the courts of record of 17 states in the past century.

1. The first case which was adjudicated in Washington in 1906 grew out of a school board regulation denying fra-

---

[71] *Application of Board of Education,* 199 Misc 631, 106 NYS(2d) 615 (1951).
[72] Edward C. Bolmeier, "The Authority of School Boards to Limit the Attendance of Students Because of Marriage, or Fraternity Membership," *Current Legal Concepts in Education.* University of Pennsylvania Press. Edited by Lee O. Garber, 1966, pp. 148-162.

ternity members the right to participate in the extracurricular activities of the school such as athletics, literary clubs, and music organizations. The student involved protested the board regulation because the fraternity was not a school affair, meetings were held outside of school in homes of students, parents had given their consent, and the board's action was illegal. Nevertheless, the court upheld the school board.[73]

2. A somewhat similar case was decided by an Illinois court in 1908. A school board adopted a rule whereby all students who were members of a secret society would be denied the privilege of representing the school in any literary or athletic contests. Action was brought to enjoin the enforcement of the rule on the ground that it was unreasonable, a Violation of the natural rights of pupils, and discriminatory. The court did not agree and ruled that the board "could control and manage the schools and adopt rules and regulations necessary for that purpose."[74]

3. A legal precedent was reversed in the ruling of a case which arose in Missouri in 1922. Here it was shown that a school board passed a regulation to prohibit fraternity members from representing the school in any capacity or from participating in graduation exercises. The court ruled that the board presented insufficient evidence to prove that secret societies were a detriment to the efficient operation of the school. This was the first and only case in which an antifraternity rule was declared illegal by a court.[75]

4. In 1934, a Massachusetts fraternity case differed from most of the others in that expulsion was resorted to, instead of curtailment of participation in extracurricular activities for violation of an anti-fraternity rule. In upholding the action of the school committee, the court made the following terse statement: "The power to make rules would be vain without the capacity to annex reasonable penalties for their violation."[76]

[73] *Wayland* v. *Board of School Directors*, 43 Wash 441, 86 Pac 642 (1906).
[74] *Wilson* v. *Board of Education of Chicago*, 233 Ill 464, 84 NE 697 (1908).
[75] *Wright* v. *Board of Education of St. Louis*, 295 Mo 466, 246 SW 43 (1922).
[76] *Antell* v. *Stokes*, 287 Mass 103, 191 NE 407 (1934).

5. What is considered to be one of the leading cases on the issue arose in North Carolina in 1944. Here pupils were required to sign pledge cards of nonaffiliation with secret societies. Those who refused to sign the pledges would be denied participation in numerous extracurricular activities, the most effective one being intramural and interscholastic activities or contests. Parents rebelled and brought a test case before the court to determine the legality of the board rule. In rendering a decision in favor of the board the court emphasized that attendance at a public school is not an absolute right and that:

> Schools to be effective and fulfill the purposes for which they are intended must be operated in orderly manner. Machinery to that end must be adopted. The right to attend school and claim the benefits afforded by the public school system is the right to attend subject to all lawful rules and regulations prescribed for the government thereof.[77]

6. Despite the firmness of the North Carolina decision, similar litigation developed in Texas the very next year— 1945. Again the requirement to sign a pledge was challenged as being "discriminatory, unreasonable, and illegal." A class suit brought to enjoin the enforcement of the rule was refused by the court. Plaintiffs were advised that the rule was within legal exercise of power delegated to local trustees by the legislature with one exception—the extension of the rule into vacation periods.[78]

7. The lengthiest case on the fraternity issue was decided in Oregon in 1952. After a year. of controversy over an early Oregon statute forbidding secret societies of any kind, a board resolution was adopted whereby pupils who joined such societies would be subject to suspension or expulsion. Plaintiffs argued that the rule "violated the right of assemblage and was an invasion of parental authority since the

---

[77] *Coggin v. Board of Education of Durham*, 233 NC 765, 28 SE(2d) 527 (1944).

[78] *Wilson* v. *Abilene Independent School District* (TexCivApp), 190 SW(2d) 406 (1945).

clubs met outside of school hours." In disagreeing with this contention, the court followed the reasoning in previous decisions on the issue, by calling attention to the fact that by enrolling in and attending the public schools, the pupils came under the control and discipline of school officials.[79]

8. Ten years later (1962) the issue was litigated again in Ohio. Here the school board of Columbus adopted a regulation prohibiting pupils holding membership in a fraternity or sorority from participating in the usual extracurriculum activities. Plaintiffs objected to the regulations on the ground that if enforced, the school authorities would gain complete control of the pupils' activities and thus deny parents their responsibility to select associates for their children away from school and after school hours. The court was not impressed by such argument, and accordingly upheld the school board action.[80]

In a 1968 Texas case[81] parents unsuccessfully sought to prevent enforcement of a statute which prohibited secret societies in the public schools. They contended that the statute "constitutes an invasion of the right of parental control over their children."

In refuting this contention, the court responded:

> Certainly neither the school system or the church or any other organization however motivated should or could replace parents in the rearing of a child.

> But we believe that our duly constituted independent school districts with appropriate guidance from the Legislature should run our public school system.[82]

Although there have been relatively fewer court cases in-

---

[79] *Burkitt* v. *School District No. 1, Multnomah County,* 195 Ore 471, 246 P(2d) 566 (1952).

[80] *Holroyd* v. *Eibling,* 116 OhioApp 440, 22 OhioOp(2d) 264, 188 NE(2d) 797 (1962).

[81] *Passel* v. *Fort Worth Independent School Dist.* (Tex), 429 SW(2d) 917 (1968).

[82] *Id.,* p. 925.

volving sororities, the courts are no less emphatic in declaring their illegality. For example, a case arose in California[83] where a member of a girl's club, called the "Manana Club" sought to have a rule of the school board invalidated which "prohibited a fraternity, sorority, or club in which the membership was determined secretly."

Even though the court admittedly saw some merits in a secret society, such as those alleged by the club involved, it left it to the judgment of the school board to determine if they were sufficient enough to justify its existence. The court declared:

> High school fraternities, sororities and clubs undoubtedly accomplish good, mostly to those who belong to them, giving them a sense of security, a feeling of being wanted. But the school board has said the harm those societies do outweigh the good, that they are inimical to the government, discipline and morale of the pupils. School boards are professionals in their field, the courts are laymen; the boards are close to the day-to-day affairs of the pupils of secondary schools and the problems which arise in a school community, courts are removed therefrom.[84]

16.11   Marital regulations

As high school marriages increase, school board policies and regulations pertaining to them increase, as does the litigation growing out of the challenged exercise of the board's discretionary authority to regulate marriages. Regarding some aspects of the problem, the courts have spoken with such finality that the legal principles pertaining thereto are firmly established and accepted. In other instances, however, there has been such judicial wavering and vacillation as to leave in doubt what the legal scope of board discretion over the regulation of student marriages may be.

One phase of the problem for which the legal principle

---

[83] *Robinson* v. *Sacramento City Unified School Dist.*, 245 Cal.App(2d) 278, 53 CalRptr 781 (1966).

[84] *Id.*, p. 789.

is well established is that *a school board may not legally
compel attendance of married students.*

1. In the first case[85] involving this question, a 15-year-old
married girl contested the legality of a board regulation and
a juvenile court order to attend a school. In supporting the
girl's complaint, the court ruled that marriage "emanci-
pates" a minor female and accordingly releases her from the
compulsory school attendance laws.

2. The second case[86] dealing with this issue was also adjudicated in Louisiana. Here a 14-year-old married girl denied that absence from school contributed to truancy in her
case and argued that she should not be required to attend
school as ordered by a lower court. On appeal to the state
supreme court, it was again ruled, as in the previous case,
that the girl could not legally be required to attend school,
by virtue   of the fact that she was "irrevocably emanci-
pated."

Another sound legal principle is that *a school board may
not legally prohibit attendance of married students on a
permanent basis.*

1. The facts of an early Mississippi case[87] reveal that a
15-year-old girl was denied admission to a school where the
board contended that "married students are detrimental
to the good government and usefulness of the school . . . and
that the marriage relation brings about views of life which
should not be known by unmarried children." The court
disagreed and accordingly ruled that the board regulations
were arbitrary and unreasonable and therefore void. It upheld the "state of matrimony" as being "honorable."

2. In the second case[88] involving a regulation prohibiting
attendance of a married girl, a school board in Kansas denied readmission of a married girl who had left school tem-
porarily. Apparently the main reason for the board's refusal
to readmit the girl was because of alleged immorality. She

[85] *State* v. *Priest,* 210 La 389, 37 S(2d) 173 (1946).
[86] *In re State in Interest of Goodwin,* 214 La 1062, 39 S(2d) 731 (1949).
[87] *McLeod* v. *State,* 154 Miss 468, 122 So 737 (1929).
[88] *Nutt* v. *Board of Education of Goodland,* 128 Kan 507, 278 Pac 1065
(1929).

had given birth to a child conceived out of wedlock, but was married before the child was born. The court voided the school board action and declared "the mere fact that the girl desired to attend school was of itself an indication of character warranting favorable consideration" and that she should not be prevented "from gaining an education which would better fit her to meet the problems of life."

3. The legal principle that a girl cannot be permanently denied a legal education because of marriage was substantiated by a Texas case[89] in 1966. The case involved a 16-year-old girl who, in her sophomore year in high school, was married and withdrew from school. Subsequently a child was born to the marriage. The girl divorced her husband and sought readmission to the high school. In the meantime the school board formulated a rule designed to permanently exclude such persons from school with the assertion that "A pupil who marries can no longer be considered a youth. By the very act of getting married, he or she becomes an adult and assumes the responsibility of adulthood." In voiding the board's rule, the court stated: "The practical and legal effect is that appellee is deprived of a legal education, except as she might obtain it at her own expense in a private or parochial school."

Although it is established that *a school board may legally prohibit attendance of a student for a limited time immediately following marriage,* there is some question as to the limit of the "limited time."

1. In a Tennessee case[90] it was revealed that a school board resolved that any student marrying during the school term would automatically be suspended for the remainder of the term. The court upheld the board's resolution and indicated its confidence in the professional judgment of school principals who claimed there had been a deterioration of discipline and decorum in the schools due to student mar-

---

[89] *Alvin Independent School Dist.* v. *Cooper* (TexCivApp), 404 SW(2d) 76 (1966).

[90] *State* v. *Marion County Board of Education,* 202 Tenn 29, 302 SW(2d) 57 (1957).

riages and that "confusion and disorder usually occurred immediately after marriage and during the period of readjustment."

2.   In a more recent case [91] the court refused to uphold a regulation of the board that prohibited attendance of a married student for an entire school year. In part, the board's regulation stipulated that: "Any student, either boy or girl, who marries, automatically must withdraw immediately from school and cannot re-enter for one full year. . . ."

In ruling that the board regulation was arbitrary, unreasonable, and void, the court declared that "The fatal vice of the regulation lies in its sweeping, advance determination that every married student regardless of circumstances, must lose at least a year's schooling."

3. A still later case [92] arose in Texas where the Amarillo School Board adopted a policy stating: "Students who marry during the school term must withdraw from school for the remainder of the school year." In accordance with this board policy a sixteen-year-old married girl was denied admission to a junior high school. In reversing a judgment of a trial court, the Court of Civil Appeals of Texas ruled against the board regulation and stated that the rule was "not in conformity with applicable statutes and is unreasonable and arbitrary." Only one of the justices dissented.

According to the only case in point,[93] *a school board may legally suspend a married girl from school during period of pregnancy.* A school board resolution in an Ohio school provided for the temporary withdrawal from school of any student known to be pregnant. The resolution was challenged by a young married pregnant student as being unreasonable, but the court upheld the board resolution which was based on the following alleged factors: the physical

---

[91] *Board of Education* v. *Bentley* (Ky), 383 SW(2d) 677 (1965).

[92] *Anderson* v. *Canyon Independent School District* (TexCivApp), 412 SW (2d) 387 (1967).

[93] *State ex rel. Idle* v. *Chamberlain*, 39 OhioOp(2d) 262, 175 NE(2d) 539 (1961).

well-being of the pregnant student; the possible adverse effect upon the morale of the student body; the possible disruption to the orderly operation of the school's daily activities; and the board's stipulated permission for the student to return to school after the birth of the child.

With the increasing number of pregnancies in high schools, the attendance status of unwed mothers has become a litigious issue. In the first applicable case brought before a federal court,[94] it was revealed that the school board had denied admission to two young unwed mothers.

As a consequence, the girls brought action against the school board with the claim that the exclusion policy of the board violated the due process and equal protection clauses of the Fourteenth Amendment. The court agreed with the girls' complaint, and stated:

> unwed mothers could not be excluded from high schools of the district for sole reason that they were unwed mothers . . . unless on a fair hearing before the school authorities they were found to be so lacking in moral character that their presence in the schools would taint the education of other students.[95]

Apparently the judicial view is that an unwed mother should have the opportunity for rehabilitation and to continue an education for the welfare of the individual as well as society.

The attendance status of an unwed pregnant girl was the subject of litigation in a 1971 Massachusetts case[96] where the high school principal attempted to carry out a board policy which stipulated that: "Whenever an unmarried girl enrolled in Middlesex Regional High School shall be known to be pregnant, her membership in the school shall be immediately terminated."

---

[94] *Perry* v. *Grenada Municipal Separate School Dist.* (Miss), 300 FSupp 748 (1969).

[95] *Id.*, p. 748.

[96] *Ordway* v. *Hargraves* (Mass), 323 FSupp 1155 (1971).

When the pregnancy of the girl was detected she was informed that she could no longer attend *regular* classes, although she could make use of certain school facilities after formal dismissal time, and attend school functions, such as games, dances and plays.

After considering testimony as to the girl's physical and mental condition, and the effect of her presence in the classroom, the court ordered that she be reinstated to her classes. The rationale for the court's decision follows:

> In summary, no danger to petitioner's physical or mental health resultant from her attending classes during regular school hours has been shown; no likelihood that her presence will cause any disruption of or interference with school activities or pose a threat of harm to others has been shown; and no valid educational or other reason to justify her segregation and to require her to receive a type of educational treatment which is not equal of that given to all others in her class has been shown.[97]

Several cases indicate that *a school board may legally prohibit participation of a married student in extracurricular activities.*

1. The first applicable case[98] was tried in the courts of Texas in 1959. The case report indicates that plaintiff, *Kissick*, sought to restrain enforcement of a board resolution which provided that "married students be restricted wholly to classroom work and that they be barred from participating in athletics." Among the contentions made by *Kissick* was that (1) the resolution in question was arbitrary, capricious, discriminatory, and unreasonable, and (2) it was violative of public policy in that it penalized marriage. Nevertheless, the Texas court upheld the board resolution.

2. Just one year later a somewhat similar case was adjudicated in Michigan. The case[99] involved two students who were married several weeks before the school board

---

[97] *Id.*, p. 1158.

[98] *Kissick* v. *Garland Independent School District* (Tex), 330 SW(2d) 708 (1959).

[99] *Cochrane* v. *Board of Education*, 360 Mich 390, 103 NW(2d) 569 (1960).

adopted a rule that "married students attending school.
shall not be eligible to participate in any co-curricular
activities—such as competitive sports." The two students
graduated before the case reached the state supreme court
and therefore the case became moot. Nevertheless, the court
rendered an "advisory opinion." The court was evenly
divided on the issue.

3. Another case [1] resulted from a board ruling which
retroactively prohibited a married boy who was a "star"
basketball player from continuing to participate in the
school's athletic program. In upholding the board regulation, the court was apparently influenced by a statistical
report showing an "alarming" marriage-dropout relationship.

4. The fourth such case [2] reaching a state supreme court
arose in Utah in 1963. The factors involved in the case were
quite similar to those of the other three cases reported in
this category. The court's ruling was also similar to those
in the other jurisdictions in that the board's regulation prohibiting a married boy from participating in the athletic
program was legal. As did other courts, the Utah Supreme
Court placed emphasis upon the fact that school boards, and
not the courts, are endowed with the power to regulate the
schools. Judicial interference would be justified only with
evidence of the board's abuse of discretionary authority.

Another case dealing with the issue arose in Iowa in 1967.
Here the Waterloo Board of Education adopted a policy barring married students from participation in extracurricular
activities. A high school boy who was a regular player on
the basketball team married just before his senior year. In
accordance with the board policy he was denied the right
to play on the team. He sought and obtained an injunction
from the District Court preventing enforcement of the rule.
The board, in collaboration with the Iowa Association of
School Boards, appealed to the Supreme Court. Although

---

[1] *State ex rel. Baker* v. *Stevenson*, 27 OhioOp(2d) 223, 189 NE(2d) 181 (1962).
[2] *Starkey* v. *Board of Education*, 14 Utah(2d) 227, 381 P(2d) 718 (1963).

the boy continued to play on the team and graduated from high school before the Supreme Court rendered its decision, the Supreme Court ultimately did reverse the decision of the District Court, thereby upholding the board rule barring married students from participating in extracurricular activities. It is significant to note, however, that three of the justices dissented.[3]

"The fact that courts have so far upheld the *legality* of board regulations prohibiting married students from participating in extracurricular activities should not be construed as judicial concurrence on the propriety of the regulations." [4]   When courts repeat that they do not rule upon the "wisdom" or "unwisdom" of board regulations, one wonders if the court has reservations regarding the propriety of the rules. Court statements in several of the cases are similar to that made in the 1963 Utah case: "Courts are not concerned with the wisdom or propriety of school boards' rules and regulations prescribing the qualifications for standard participation in extra-curricular activities. . . ." [5]

There is growing doubt in the judiciary and elsewhere as to the legality and propriety of school boards attempting to curtail high school marriages by discriminatory, punitive or other means. Determination of the minimum age limit for marriages is a sociological problem to be dealt with by the legislature and not the school board.

Unless violative of constitutional provisions, the discretionary authority of school boards to regulate pupils appearance and other aspects of behavior, is unlimited. This legal principle is substantiated by a federal district court, in its statement:

---

[3] *Board of Directors of Independent School Dist. of Waterloo v. Green,* 259 Iowa 1260, 147 NW(2d) 854 (1967).

[4] Bolmeier, "The Authority of School Boards to Limit the Attendance of Students Because of Marriage, or Fraternity Membership," p. 160.

[5] Starkey, *op. cit.,* p. 718.

There is no question of the statutory and inherent right of school boards within the State of Utah to promulgate and appropriately enforce reasonable regulations concerning the conduct, deportment, and grooming of students attending public schools placed under their administrative control, providing that such regulations do not offend rights guaranteed by the Constitution of the United States.[6]

16.12 Pupil appearance

It hardly seems necessary that the problem of pupil attire and appearance should go further than the classroom or the principal's office. Nevertheless the control of pupil's appearance is so strongly protested by pupils and parents that school boards have sometimes found it necessary to formulate policy and establish rules and regulations regarding the matter. When these rules and regulations are regarded by parents as an excessive exercise of the board's discretionary authority and an invasion on pupil and parental rights, litigation is possible.

Generally when pupil dress is immodest, offensive to good taste, or for any reason inimical to the best interests of the school, such dress may be forbidden by the school authorities. But the perplexing problem for the courts to decide is when those conditions exist. What may have been considered as a reasonable rule regarding pupil attire several decades ago might not be so regarded today. Consequently board regulations governing pupil dress and styles must conform to the times in which we live in order to be adjudged as reasonable. Certain modes of attire which are considered proper and sensible today might have been outlawed several decades ago as being improper and indecent.

---

6 *Freeman* v. *Flake* (Utah), 320 FSupp 531, 536 (1970).

The seemingly outlandish and ridiculous dress of boys and girls is largely a manifestation of youth's rebellion to conformance and regulation. It seems that when rules and regulations prescribe what must or must not be worn in school, the desire on the part of youth to rebel is kindled. Of course, when the school's prescribed rules are violated it becomes necessary for the school authorities to enforce them; otherwise, disobedience to law would be encouraged in other situations.[7]

For decades the issue of *hairstyles* has been of concern to school authorities, and, since 1965, it has been a constant subject of litigation in the federal courts—almost to the state of boredom.

Despite their reluctance to do so, the federal courts are obligated to deal with the issue when constitutional violations are alleged. As one judge states:

Initially it must be pointed out that it is the Court's responsibility to determine the constitutionality of this School Regulation and not the wisdom of it. I mention this because I feel the issue of hair length is receiving more attention and creating more problems than it deserves. . . . But, in any event, it has become a major problem between school authorities and students, as evidenced by the deluge of court cases in the past three years and is entitled to a constitutional construction.[8]

The same judicial attitude was expressed in a case[9] in which the Fifth Circuit Court of Appeals affirmed a District Court ruling in denying injunctive relief to high school students who were suspended for refusing to shave. The reluctance of the Court to consider the case is indicated by the following statements:

The case is such that the district court felt somewhat put-upon by having to fit a controversy over shaving into

---

[7] Flowers and Bolmeier, *Law and Pupil Control*, p. 6.
[8] *Gere v. Stanley* (Pa), 320 FSupp 852 (1970).
[9] *Stevenson v. Board of Education of Wheeler County, Georgia* (5th Cir), 426 F(2d) 1154 (1970).

an inordinately busy schedule. It was viewed as a problem for school administrators. We share this view. The
entire problem seems miniscule in light of other matters
involving the school system.[10]

But in a recent Idaho case, the judge said:

> Courts will, albeit reluctantly, intervene in conflicts
> which arise in operation of school systems if such con-
> flicts directly and sharply implicate basic constitutional
> values, and such will be done even if disciplinary powers
> of school authorities will be diminished if the regulation
> is not upheld.[11]

In general, suspension of a student for violating a hairstyle regulation is unconstitutional *unless positive proof* is
given to show that it is (1) *disruptive* to the educational
process, (2) *unsanitary*, or (3) *dangerous*. This judicial con-
sensus is provided by three 1971 Federal Court cases, all
reported in the same volume of *Federal Supplement*.

In the first case, originating in Florida, the District Court
found that:

> School board failed to show that long hair had caused
> disruptions in the school, that long hair constituted any
> danger to health and safety of school community; . . .
> any injunctive relief requiring school board to terminate
> students' suspensions for violating long hair provision of
> school dress code would be granted.[12]

In the second case, originating in Iowa, the District Court
ruled that:

> Disruptions arising out of other students' hostile reac-
> tions to a students' appearance is not the type of disrup-
> tion which will render school hair codes constitutional;
> the disruption must flow from condition of the hair itself,
> namely health problems, safety problems, disruption of

---

[10] *Id.*, p. 1156.

[11] *Murphy* v. *Pocatello School Dist.* (Idaho), 480 P(2d) 878 (1971).

[12] *Dawson* v. *Hillsborough County, Florida, School Board* (Fla), 322 FSupp
286 (1971).

other students in their academic pursuits or actual disruption by the long-haired student himself.[13]

In the third case, originating in West Virginia, the District Court held that:

Where school officials failed to show that plaintiffs' long hair style actually created disciplinary problem within school prior to time of his suspension for violation of school dress code forbidding, among other things, long hair or male students, school officials' mere fear that relaxing of ban against long hair would lead to disciplinary problems was insufficient justification for deprivation of constitutional protected rights, and long-haired male student was entitled to readmission.[14]

In a case which summarizes much of the litigation and key court decisions, regarding hair styles, a United States District Court found that: "The great majority of the cases are recent and for the most part stem from the holding of the Supreme Court of the United States in *Tinker*.[15]

The legal principles relating to the school board's discretionary authority governing hairstyles, as judicially decided, are applicable to virtually every phase of pupil appearance, as well as all other aspects of pupil behavior.

16.13 Display of protest insignia

The wearing of insignia such as armbands or buttons has been cause for litigation during a period of student protest and militancy. As was true in the "hairstyle cases," the courts have generally ruled that the practice is legal if done in a manner not disruptive to classroom discipline and decorum. The legal principle is that the display of armbands and buttons constitutes "symbolic expression" which

---

[13] *Turley v. Adel Community School Dist.* (Iowa), 322 FSupp 402, 403 (1971).

[14] *Lambert v. Marushi* (W Va), 322 FSupp 326, 327 (1971).

[15] *Pound v. Holladay*, 322 FSupp 1000, 1002 (1971).

is a right guaranteed to students and others by virtue of the Free Speech Clause of the First Amendment.

For example, in the famous *Tinker* case which received nation-wide publicity, the Supreme Court reasoned that the wearing of the armbands was closely akin to "pure speech" which, we have repeatedly held, is entitled to comprehensive protection under the First Amendment.[16] The court then added: "In our system, students may not be regarded as closed-circuit recipients of only that which the State chooses to communicate."[17]

Unlike *Tinker,* students in a North Carolina high school were *not* permitted to wear armbands (which were black, red, white and blue) to symbolize diverse factions with respect to war and nonwar issues. In this case at least three different antagonistic viewpoints were represented. Moreover, the U. S. District Court found evidence showing that there was:

> . . . advance advertisement of the demonstration, active group participation, marching in the hallways, recruitment of other students to join the several groups, chanting, belligerent and disrespectful attitude towards teachers, incidents of flag disrespect, and threats of violence.[18]

The court concluded:

> In the balancing of First Amendment rights the duty of the state to operate its public school system for the benefit of *all* its children must be protected even if governmental regulations incidentally limit the untrammeled exercise of speech, symbolic or otherwise, by those who would impede the education of those who desire to learn. The interest of the State is superior to the rights of the protestants.[19]

---

[16] *Tinker* v. *Des Moines Independent Community School Dist.* (Iowa), 89 SCt 733, 736 (1969).

[17] *Id.,* p. 739.

[18] *Hill* v. *Lewis* (NC), 323 FSupp 55, 58 (1971).

[19] *Id.,* p. 59.

A United States Court of Appeals, Fifth Circuit explained the circumstances under which a school board could prohibit the wearing of armbands by students in the following statement:

> . . . we believe that the Supreme Court has declared a constitutional right which school authorities must nurture and protect, not extinguish, unless they find the circumstances allow them no practical alternative. As to the existence of such circumstances, they are the judges, and if within the range where reasonable minds may differ, their decisions will govern. But there must be some inquiry, and establishment of substantial fact, to buttress the determination.[20]

Somewhat comparable to the *Tinker* and *Hill* "armband cases," are several "button cases" adjudicated in federal courts. The first such case evolved from a civil rights action for an injunction against high school officials for a regulation prohibiting students from wearing freedom buttons.

The court voided the prohibitory regulation and ruled in favor of the students after it found that "the presence of 'freedom buttons' did not hamper the school in carrying on its regular schedule of activities; nor would it seem likely that the simple wearing of buttons unaccompanied by improper conduct would ever do so."[21]

In a companion case a contrasting decision was rendered, when the court upheld the board and ruled against the protesting students. Here, however, the court found a different situation than the one in *Burnside,* where no disruption of classes or school routine was in evidence; whereas, in *Blackwell,* the court found that "students conducted themselves in a disorderly manner, disrupted classroom procedure, interfered with the proper decorum and discipline of the school and disturbed other students who did not wish to participate in the wearing of the buttons."[22]

---

20 *Butts* v. *Dallas Independent School Dist.,* 436 F(2d) 728, 732 (1971).
21 *Burnside* v. *Byars* (Miss), 363 F(2d) 744, 748 (1966).
22 *Blackwell* v. *Issaquena County Board of Education* (Miss), 363 F(2d) 749, 753 (1966).

In a later case a court of appeals upheld a district court's ruling that a school board had a right to prohibit the wearing of buttons or other insignia as a *precautionary* measure where there was evidence that to permit such wearing could conceivably cause serious disruption and disorder. The rationale of the court's decision is expressed as follows:

> We must be aware in these contentious times that America's classrooms and their environs will lose their usefulness as places in which to educate our young people if pupils come to school wearing the badges of their respective disagreements, and provoke confrontations with their fellows and their teachers. The buttons are claimed to be a form of free speech. Unless they have some relevance to what is being considered or taught, a school classroom is no place for the untrammeled exercise of such right.[23]

Insignia, other than armbands or buttons, may also be prohibited if displayed for unlawful purposes. For example, a district court upheld the suspension of high school students of Mexican descent who, as a means of political expression, wore black berets in disruptive conduct. The court found that: "The evidence is without dispute that the beret was used by the plaintiffs as a symbol of their power to disrupt the conduct of the school and the exercise of control over the student body."[24]

Courts will not condone the display of symbols which could foment racism in the schools. For example, in Louisiana a district court ordered:

> All Confederate flags, banners, signs, expressing the school board's or its employees' desire to maintain segregated schools, and all other symbols or indicia of racism shall be removed from the schools and shall not be officially displayed at school functions of any kind.[25]

23 *Guzick* v. *Drebus* (Ohio), 431 F(2d) 594, 600-601 (1970).

24 *Hernandez* v. *School Dist. Number One, Denver* (Colo), 315 FSupp 289, 291 (1970).

25 *Smith* v. *St. Tammany Parish School Board* (La), 316 FSupp 1174, 1177 (1970).

16.14   Freedom of speech and press

The publication and dissemination of articles and editorials in student newspapers is more specifically related to the "freedom of speech" clause of the Constitution than is the "symbolic expression" of displaying protest insignia. In cases adjudicated thus far, the federal courts have not allowed students as much latitude in "written expression"—particularly when the written material is of a derogatory nature, and which could be injurious to the morale of the school.

In a widely-publicized case a district court upheld a school board's action in the expulsion of high school students for distribution of a student newspaper containing alleged derogatory statements about the school administration. The court concluded that: "It is the opinion of this Court that the interest of the state in maintaining the school system outweighs the protection afforded the speaker by the First Amendment."[26]

On appeal, however, a United States Court of Appeals *reversed* the decision of the District Court with the concluding comment that: "the Board could not have reasonably forecast that the publication and distribution of this paper to the students would substantially disrupt or materially interfere with school procedures."[27]

During the interim between rulings by the district court and court of appeals on *Scoville*, another somewhat similar, but more severe case was adjudicated in a district court. Here a student claimed he was illegally suspended for "exercising his First Amendment right of free speech" when he distributed copies of a newspaper which "contained four-letter words, filthy references, abusive and disgusting language and nihilistic propaganda."[28]

[26] *Scoville* v. *Board of Education of Joliet Township High School Dist. 204* (Ill), 286 FSupp 988, 992 (1968).
[27] *Scoville* v. *Board of Education of Joliet Township High School Dist. 204* (Ill), 425 F(2d) 10, 15 (1970).
[28] *Schwartz* v. *Schuker* (NY), 298 FSupp 238, 240 (1969).

In defense of its ruling, which upheld the school board, the court pointed out that:

> . . . the freedom of speech and association protected by the First and Fourteenth Amendments are not "absolute" and are subject to constitutional restrictions for the protection of the social interest, in government, order and morality . . . the activities of high school students do not always fall within the same category as the conduct of college students, the former being in a much more adolescent and immature stage of life and less able to screen facts from propaganda.[29]

16.15   Searching students' lockers

In attempting to suppress the possession and use of harmful drugs or other incriminating objects of wrongdoing by high school students, school officials frequently resort to searching students' lockers. The legality of such procedure, however, is sometimes challenged because of its alleged conflict with the "searches and seizures" provision of the Fourth Amendment to the United States Constitution.

Generally, court decisions[30] have approved the practice—but with some degree of uncertainty. The right to do so, however, was confirmed by the Kansas State Supreme Court when it described the peculiar legal nature of a student's locker:

> Although a student may have control of his school locker as against fellow students, his possession is not exclusive against the school and its officials. A school does not supply its students with lockers for illicit use in harboring pilfered property or harmful substances. We deem it a proper function of school authorities to inspect the lockers under their control and to prevent their use

---

[29] *Id.*, p. 242.

[30] *In re Donaldson*, 269 CalApp(2d) 509, 75 CalRptr 220 (1969); *People v. Overton*, 20 NY(2d) 360, 229 NE(2d) 596 (1967).

in illicit ways or for illegal purposes. We believe this right of inspection is inherent in the authority vested in school administration and that the same must be retained and exercised in the management of our schools if their educational functions are to be maintained and the welfare of the student bodies preserved.[31]

16.16   Willful misconduct of pupils

The willful misconduct of pupils constitutes one of the most serious and vexing problems of pupil control with which school officials and teachers must cope. To overlook premeditated misbehavior could be detrimental to the future development of the pupil and injurious to the morale and government of the school. To invoke punitive measures is considered by some to be merely a temporary expedient and not a suitable deterrent. Although the latter is the more common practice, it is also the more vulnerable to litigation.[32]

One of the most serious aspects of pupil misconduct has to do with the deliberate destruction or defacement of school property. Under the common law, until recently, the legal principle prevailed that neither a minor child nor his parent is financially responsible for the acts of a child. The growing belief now, however, is that parents should assume legal responsibility (liability) for the damaging acts of their children.

The potential immensity of the liability for this type of pupil misconduct is illustrated by a New Jersey case[33] in which a court rendered a judgment in favor of a school board that sought to recover damages from the parents of a boy who had purposely set fire to a school building. The defendant's son and another boy enrolled in the Palmyra High School, went to the high school on a Sunday night for

[31] *State* v. *Stein*, 203 Kan 638, 456 P(2d) 1 (1969).
[32] Flowers and Bolmeier, *Law and Pupil Control*, p. 7.
[33] *Board of Education of Palmyra* v. *Hansen*, 56 NJ 567, 153 A(2d) 393 (1959).

the alleged purpose of getting some examination papers. The school board charged the boy with setting fire to the school and thus causing damages to the extent of $344,000. The board of education brought its suit under the parent responsibility law in New Jersey which stated:

> Any pupil who shall cut, deface, or otherwise injure any schoolhouse, furniture, fences, outbuildings, or other property of the school district shall be liable to suspension and punishment, and his parents or guardian shall be liable for damages to the amount of the injury to be collected by the board of education in any court having jurisdiction, together with the costs of action.

In answering the counsel's defense claim that the statute applied only during school hours, the court replied: ". . . if the Legislature has the right to confer benefits on the people by way of a free education, it certainly has the right to set up the conditions under which such benefits shall be provided."

The New Jersey court further pointed out that parents who wished to exempt themselves from the provision of statutes applying to public schools could do so by choosing to send their child to a private school.

In a Texas case, parents were successful in an injunction restraining a school board from imposing indefinite suspension of their son, who, with another boy, set fire to a junior high school—causing a damage of $3,800. Although a fine had to be paid, the amount was reduced somewhat by a trial court because of the father's low salary. The appellate court concluded:

> Since it is the policy of the School District to take into account the financial condition of the parents in requiring payments for vandalism, we are of the opinion that the trial court did not abuse its discretion in granting the temporary injunction.[34]

---

[34] *Allen* v. *Chacon* (Tex), 449 SW(2d) 289, 292 (1970).

16.17 Methods employed in enforcing rules against misconduct

Rules and regulations for pupil control are not usually contested in the courts. It is the methods employed in the enforcement of the rules which frequently motivate the actual litigation. Of course school board rules and regulations ordinarily are accompanied by stipulated consequences if they are violated.

The most common methods employed in the enforcement of rules and regulations governing pupil conduct are *corporal punishment, expulsion* and *suspension*.

Corporal punishment, as a means of enforcing pupil control, has been diminishing over the past century. This may be partially due to the fact that legal principles limiting the degree of physical punishment are so firmly established as to make corporal punishment rather ineffective as a deterrent of pupil misconduct. The legal principles derived from court cases indicate that the corporal punishment, if administered, should: (1) be in conformance with statutory enactment; (2) be for the purpose of correction without malice; (3) not be cruel or excessive so as to leave permanent marks or injuries; and (4) be suited to the age and sex of the pupil. Essentially, in order for corporal punishment to be legal, it must be reasonable in the eyes of the judiciary.

There is the possibility that the pendulum is about to swing back toward greater "use of the rod" in the public schools. With the alarming state of juvenile delinquency, some persons attribute the cause to the "luke-warm" discipline measures employed in the public schools. A case[35] adjudicated in 1963 by an Indiana court suggests that the early-established legal principle that a teacher stands *in loco parentis* with respect to the disciplining of the pupils may be predictive of renewed emphasis. In this case, involving the dismissal of a teacher for disciplining a pupil by striking her very lightly, the court made the following comment: "The law is well settled that a teacher stands in loco parentis

---

[35] *Indiana State Personnel Board* v. *Jackson,* 244 Ind 321, 192 NE(2d) 740 (1963).

to this child, and his authority in . . . respect [to administering corporal punishment] is no more subject to question than is the authority of the parent."

The limits of applying the *in loco parentis* principle in the public schools of Pennsylvania were defined by a federal court in the following terms:

> The Supreme Court has cautioned school officials that they do not possess absolute authority over their students. . . . It is clear that the "in loco parentis" section of the Pennsylvania School Code was never intended to invest the school with all the authority of parents over their minor children but only such control as is necessary to prevent infractions of discipline and interference with the educational process.[36]

The legal principle is also firmly established that school authorities may *expel* or *suspend* from school any pupil who disobeys a reasonable rule or regulation. School officials are clothed with considerable discretionary authority in determining whether or not a rule has been violated, and, in the event they conclude that a violation has occurred, they also have discretionary authority in determining the nature of the penalty to be imposed—providing it is not arbitrary or unreasonable. When, however, parents challenge the action of school boards as being beyond the bounds of reasonableness, litigation may develop.

There are a number of cases concerning pupil suspension and expulsion. The terms "suspension" and "expulsion" are sometimes used interchangeably. There is, however, considerable difference in the legal meaning of the two terms. "Suspension" is generally an act of a professional member of the school staff, whereas "expulsion" is a prerogative of the school board. Suspension is usually for a short period of time, or until the pupil conforms to the rule or regulation involved, whereas expulsion is usually permanent or substantially so.

The courts look somewhat askance at acts of suspension,

---

[36] *Axtell* v. *LaPenna* (Pa), 323 FSupp 1077, 1080 (1971).

and particularly at expulsion, as methods for forcing pupils' conformance to rules and regulations. Some incorrigible pupils violate school regulations for the very purpose of being removed from the school environment. It should be realized that when a pupil is denied school attendance he is deprived of education designed for his betterment. Of course when a pupil's misconduct or disobedience is of such a grave nature that his presence is disrupting to the school and detrimental to the morale of the student body, suspension, or even expulsion, is likely to be judicially condoned.

16.18   Procedural due process rights

School board procedures for enforcing rules against alleged misconduct of pupils have become more difficult since the United States Supreme Court indicated applicability of the Fourteenth Amendment and Bill of Rights to all, regardless of age or status.[37]

In essence the *Gault* decision means that before a juvenile can be found guilty and penalized he must be accorded certain procedural due process rights such as: (1) notice of the charges; (2) right to counsel; (3) right to confrontation and cross-examination of the witnesses; (4) privilege against self-incrimination; (5) right to a transcript of the proceedings; (6) right to appellate review.

Strict application of due process rights for pupils of all ages and for all offenses is receiving judicial scrutinization. A Florida case is in point where the issue was "whether the public schools must accord due process of law—charges, notice of hearing, time to prepare for hearing, confrontation of witnesses, appeal, stay pending appeal—in enforcing the school regulations respecting hair length."[38]

The judge in this case pointed out the difficulties which would be encountered by school officials if pupils were

---

[37] *In re Gault*, 387 US 1, 40 OO(2d) 378, 18 LEd(2d) 527, 827 SCt 1428 (1967).

[38] *Conyers v. Pinellas County Board of Public Instruction*, Circuit Court No. 16, 634, 1969, p. 1.

granted due process in all matters of school discipline:

> Consider the chaos in our public schools if we are to permit seven-year-olds and eleven-year-olds and fifteen-year-olds and seventeen-year-olds to demand notice, time to prepare for hearing, confrontation of witnesses, stay of judgment, and appeal each time a school official charges one with violation of a valid regulation and proposed appropriate disciplinary action. . . .

> Our public school authorities have had wished upon them much more than they have asked. This court will not impose upon them the impossible.[39]

Federal courts also frequently minimize the adherence to procedural due process rights for pupils charged with misconduct. In an illustrative case the United States Court of Appeals, Second Circuit, stated:

> . . . we would not regard the procedure for contesting the penalty as of controlling significance. Under all of the circumstances, we do not believe appellant was deprived of due process. . . . Finally, in cases of minor discipline particularly, parent, student, and administrator should remember that substitution of common sense for zealous adherence to legal positions is not absolutely prohibited.[40]

---

[39] *Id.*, p. 8.
[40] *Farrell* v. *Joel* (Conn), 437 F(2d) 160, 163 (1971).

Chapter 17

DISCRETIONARY AUTHORITY OF SCHOOL
BOARDS OVER THE CURRICULUM

Any consideration of the legal aspects of the curriculum is complicated by the diversity of opinion as to what a curriculum really is. On the one extreme, there are those who conceive the curriculum to be only an array of subjects or courses for which credit, in terms of "Carnegie units," is allowed. On the other extreme, some view the curriculum as *all* experiences offered children under the aegis of the school. With this latter interpretation of the curriculum the term, "extracurricular," would obviously be superfluous.

17.1 Allocation of legal authority over the curriculum

Within constitutional limits, the legislature is empowered to determine the types and contents of curricula and the manner of their control.

In rare instances state constitutions provide for specific inclusions in the curriculum, and, to that extent, pre-empt statutory enactments on those items provided for in the constitution. For example, the constitution of Louisiana requires "instruction upon the constitutional system of the state and national government, and the duties of citizenship."[1] The Utah constitution requires "teaching of the metric system."[2] Conversely, several states have in their constitutions certain prohibitive provisions such as those outlawing sectarian instruction.

---

[1] *Louisiana Constitution*, Art. 12, sec. 3.
[2] *Utah Constitution*, Art. 11, sec. 11.

Virtually every state has enacted legislation requiring certain subject matters to be included in the public school curriculum. Illustrative provisions are those that prescribe instruction in the United States Constitution, the state constitution, American history, civics, citizenship, health habits, temperance, evils of narcotics, safety education, and driver education. Conversely, the legislature may tell school authorities what *not* to teach. For example, Michigan has a law which bans instruction in birth control and, until recently, Arkansas and Mississippi had laws prohibiting the teaching of "Darwinism."

Most of the statutes pertaining to the curriculum and its administration are rather general—as they should be—with delegated authority to local boards or professional personnel to determine the specifics. The high degree of local autonomy in this respect should not be construed as a surrender of state authority over the curriculum or other school matters. On the contrary, the supreme authority of the state is evidenced by the very fact that the state may prescribe the scope of control to be exercised by its designated subdivisions.

17.2   Prescribed curricular activities

In reviewing numerous court decisions pertaining to curricular prescriptions, it may be noted that only in a small minority of cases is the legal authority of boards of education challenged in their determination of curriculum matters. (Curriculum content of a sectarian nature is a notable exception.) More frequently, litigation develops from the school board's regulation *requiring* students to pursue certain curriculum activities or *prohibiting* them from engaging in curricular or extracurricular affairs.

As early as 1914 a legal principle denoting the school board's limited scope of authority over the curriculum was established when the Nebraska Supreme Court ruled against a school board which refused a request of a parent to excuse his daughter from studying a specific subject.[3] In sustaining

---

[3] *Kelly* v. *Ferguson*, 95 Neb 63, 144 NW 1039 (1914).

the right of a parent to make a reasonable selection from the course of study the court said:

> The public school is one of the main bulwarks of our nation, and we would not knowingly do anything to undermine it; but we should be careful to avoid permitting our love for this noble institution to cause us to regard it "all in all" and destroy both the God-given and constitutional right of a parent to have some voice in the bringing up and education of his children.

For nearly a century the courts have had to rule on the legality of offering language other than English in the public schools. In virtually all cases the courts have upheld school boards for the inclusion of foreign languages in the curriculum, particularly where there was no conflict with statutory provisions.

The most noteworthy foreign language case was that of *Meyer v. Nebraska*.[4] It was the first and only case on the issue which reached the United States Supreme Court. The factors leading up to the case indicate that, after World War I, a number of states enacted legislation prohibiting the teaching of German to nonpublic and public school pupils. Although the courts of three states (Nebraska, Iowa, and Ohio) had sanctioned the legislation as a legitimate exercise of the police power, the Supreme Court ruled that the legislation was an arbitrary interference with the liberty of parents to control and educate their children, and with the liberty of teachers to pursue their lawful calling, and that it violated the liberty guaranteed by the Fourteenth Amendment to the Constitution of the United States.

Some decades ago there was considerable protest against including anything in the curriculum other than "book-learning." The legality of requiring physical education was frequently challenged. For example, in a California case[5] it was revealed that parents requested their children to be excused from dancing as a part of physical education because

---

[4] *Meyer v. Nebraska*, 262 US 390, 67 LEd 1042, 43 SCt 625 (1923).
[5] *Hardwick v. Board of School Trustees*, 54 CalApp 696, 205 Pac 49 (1921).

of religious grounds. The request was denied and the pupils expelled because of refusal to participate. Although the court held the school authorities had no right to expel the children for their refusal to take part in the dancing, the court upheld the right of the school to include dancing in the curriculum of the school.

Another case[6] concerning participation in physical education was adjudicated more recently. Here a girl refused to engage in the activities of the physical education class because the costumes worn were, in her opinion, "immodest and sinful." Even though the school authorities permitted the girl to wear such costume as she desired and to engage in only such activities as she considered appropriate for the costume chosen, her father objected to the girl's being in the class. He contended that the wearing of different clothes than those prescribed would make the girl stand out as a "speckled bird." The court ruled that the girl was obligated to attend the course in physical education, and maintained that the requirement did not violate her constitutional rights.

In reviewing the court cases dealing with such areas of the curriculum as language, arts, music, mathematics, and science it is significant to note that virtually all of them were adjudicated several decades ago—and in support of the school boards' discretionary actions. It could be concluded from this that by now legal principles have been so firmly established in such matters as to preclude further litigation.

An Illinois case[7] exemplifies how a school board may include elements in a curriculum which were unthinkable several decades ago. A suit was brought for injunction to restrain three high schools from providing driver-training instruction to adults. Suggesting that the common-school curriculum of 1963 is far different from that of 1870, the court upheld the statute which authorized the instruction. With respect to the curriculum content the court reasoned:

---

6 *Mitchell* v. *McCall,* 273 Ala 604, 143 S(2d) 629 (1962).

7 *Acorn Auto Driving School* v. *Board of Education,* 27 Ill(2d) 93, 187 NE(2d) 722 (1963).

The legislature has deemed the public interest to be subserved by the offering of driver education classes in the public schools. Our modern economy and way of life are closely related to the automobile . . . and we do not dispute the need for adult driver education. Public safety and welfare demand it.

17.3   Onset of sex education

A current controversial issue, which is steadily growing in intensity, has to do with the inclusion of sex education in the curriculum. Although parents, school boards, and legislatures are in disagreement on the issue, the courts thus far are consistent in ruling that school boards possess considerable discretionary authority in having sex education incorporated into the curriculum.

An example is afforded by a Kansas case in which the court ruled that "the sex education program conducted by the Topeka Board of Education was a reasonable exercise of its constitutional and statutory authority."[8]

One year later, a case was adjudicated wherein a bylaw of the Maryland State Board of Education was the focus of litigation. It read, in part: "It is the responsibility of the local school system to provide a comprehensive program of family life and sex education in every elementary and secondary school for all students as an integral part of the curriculum including a planned and sequential program of health education."[9] The board adopted the bylaw as an appropriate measure for health education after it studied the problem of pregnant students. Parents, however, alleged the bylaw violated the First Amendment and the Fourteenth Amendment. In its disposition of the case the court "held that the constitutional challenge lacks merit. . . ."[10]

---

[8] *Clemmer* v. *U.S.D. 501,* No. 112,064, District Court of Shawnee County (Kansas, 1969).
[9] *Cornwall* v. *State Board of Education* (Ind), 428 F(2d) 471, 472 (1970).
[10] *Id.,* p. 472.

The issue was litigated in another case when parents of elementary school children challenged the constitutionality of showing film as part of a newly adopted curriculum for family life and sex education. They wanted to know "whether parents are free to educate their offspring in the intimacies of sexual matters according to their own moral and religious beliefs without due interference by the State."[11]

Participation in the program was not compulsory. Nevertheless, parents argued that availability of the "excusable system" was not constitutionally sufficient. The court disagreed.

According to a 1971 court decision, a school board will not be prevented from including sex education in the curriculum, but the courts will not go so far as to always uphold administrative processes in requiring attendance in such courses where the right to free exercise of religion is involved. In this connection, the local board contended that the requirement did not create a *de facto* religion because the course included no "teachings and discussions of sexual intercourse, masturbation, and contraceptions, contrary to religious beliefs of plaintiffs."[12] The court upheld the school board's position and stated:

> . . . This court cannot and does not intend to substitute its judgment in those matters where the State Board of Education and the Commissioner of Education have special expertise. However, in matters of substantial constitutional dimension the Executive and the Legislature are not the determining or final arbiters of what is and what is not constitutional.[13]

The teaching of social studies constitutes a fertile area for litigation, especially in such instances where religious principles are involved. An objective in this phase of the curriculum is to inculcate in pupils attitudes of loyalty and

---

[11] *Medeiros v. Kiyosaki* (Hawaii), 478 P(2d) 314, 315 (1970).

[12] *Valent v. New Jersey State Board of Education*, 114 NJSuper 63, 274 A(2d) 832, 834 (1971).

[13] *Id.*, p. 836.

patriotism.

17.4   Authority to teach theory of evolution

After nearly a half century of controversy and litigation, it appears that the issue of teaching the theory of evolution in the public schools has finally been resolved—at least as far as the courts are concerned. The issue received much publicity when, in 1927, a Tennessee law was tested in the famous *Scopes* case. As is generally known, Scopes was convicted for violating the Tennessee law for teaching in the public schools "a certain theory that denied the story of the divine creation of man, as taught in the Bible, and did teach instead thereof that man descended from a lower order of animals."[14]

The Supreme Court of Tennessee emphasized that while it was within one's right to oppose anti-evolution law elsewhere, that right did not extend to public school teachers while in the classroom.

Statutory and judicial vacillation on the issue continued for several decades, until 1968, when the United States Supreme Court, in reversing the judgment of the Supreme Court of Arkansas, held that the anti-evolution statute was unconstitutional.

In explaining the court's rationale for its decision, Justice Fortas remarked:

> The State's undoubted right to prescribe the curriculum for its public schools does not carry with it the right to prohibit, on pain of criminal penalty, the teaching of a scientific theory or doctrine where the prohibition is based upon reasons that violate the First Amendment. It is much too late to argue that the State may impose upon the teachers in its school any conditions that it chooses, however restrictive they may be of constitutional guarantees. . . .[15]

---

[14] *Scopes* v. *Tennessee*, 154 Tenn 105, 289 SW 363 (1917).

[15] *Epperson* v. *Arkansas*, 393 US 97, 21 LEd(2d) 228, 89 SCt 266, 272 (1968).

Mississippi was one of the last states to retain an anti-evolution provision in its statutes. In 1970, however, the statute. was invalidated in the case of *Smith* v. *State*. In this case a prospective teacher challenged the statute on the grounds that she was being deprived of the opportunity "to gain a basic educational foundation from which she can receive the necessary technical, scientific training required to engage in the profession or business which depends upon scientific knowledge of anthropology and related subjects."[16]

The Mississippi court followed the precedent established in *Epperson* that the anti-evolution statutes "are in contravention of the First Amendment to the Constitution of the United States."

17.5   Requirements to salute the flag

As early as 1937, cases involving the authority of schools to require, as part of the school program, pupils to salute the flag of the United States and take the oath of allegiance, confronted the state courts. In virtually all instances the state courts upheld the legality of the requirements.

Since the issue involved provisions of the United States Constitution it was not long before the cases were appealed to the United States Supreme Court. There were two important cases initiated by the Jehovah's Witnesses which gained world-wide recognition. In the first of these two cases, *Minersville* v. *Gobitis*, 1940,[17] the Supreme Court upheld a lower court ruling that it was within the rights of a school board to require the flag salute as a means of achieving a feeling of national unity.

Just three years later the Supreme Court was called upon again to consider the issue in *West Virginia State Board of Education* v. *Barnette*, 1943.[18] This time the court ruled in favor of Barnette, a Jehovah's Witness, thereby reversing the

---

[16] *Smith* v. *State* (Miss), 242 S(2d) 692, 694 (1970).

[17] *Minersville School Dist.* v. *Gobitis* (Pa), 310 US 586, 84 LEd 1375, 60 SCt 1010 (1940).

[18] *West Virginia State Board of Education* v. *Barnette*, 319 US 624, 87 LEd 1628, 63 SCt 1178 (1943).

decision of the *Gobitis* case. In substance, the Supreme
Court held that a school board, in compelling pupils to
salute and pledge allegiance to the American flag transcends
constitutional limitations on its powers and "invades the
sphere of intellect and spirit which it is the purpose of the
First Amendment to our Constitution to reserve from all
official control."

The flag salute issue has been adjudicated in state courts
several times since the *Barnette* decision. In general, the
state courts have followed the legal precedent established in
the last previous United States Supreme Court ruling.

For example, in 1966, the Supreme Court of New Jersey
ordered a school board to reinstate children who had been
excluded from school because of their refusal to salute the
flag of the United States.[19] Their refusal was based upon
their religion (Black Muslims) where they were taught that
"their sole allegiance was to Almighty God Allah and that
the flag was but a symbol, it would be contrary to their
teachings to pledge allegiance to any flag. . . ."

The court expressed regret that the teachings were such
as "to cause children not to participate in a common ceremony of respect to the Flag, which is itself the emblem of
those freedoms which all Americans are privileged to enjoy,"
but nevertheless recognized that "those freedoms, as contemplated by Federal and State Constitutions and by State
Law, are broad enough to encompass the beliefs of those
who, like the petitioner, claim conscientious scruples."

Slight deviations in the circumstances do not seem to alter
the ruling in *Barnette*. For example, a federal court held
that a student could not be excluded from the classroom
during the pledge of allegiance merely "for reasons of conscience to participate in Pledge in any different way from
those who participate." The court stated: "The student is
free to select his form of expression, so long as it does not
materially infringe the rights of other students or disrupt

---

[19] *Holden* v. *Board of Education, Elizabeth,* 46 NJ 279, 216 A(2d) 387
(1966).

school activities."[20]

Similarly, in a Florida case a United States District Court ruled in favor of a student who was suspended from school as a result of his refusal to stand during the pledge of allegiance. The court stated:

> The right to differ and express one's opinions, to fully vent his First Amendment rights, even to the extent of exhibiting disrespect for our flag and country by refusing to stand and participate in the pledge of allegiance, cannot be suppressed by the imposition of suspensions.[21]

Teachers, as well as students, need not obey a statutory flag salute requirement "that all students and teachers, except those who object for 'religious reasons' must stand, salute the flag and recite in unison the pledge of allegiance." The case in point[22] reveals that a social science teacher "claimed that he would refuse to engage in a mandatory flag salute ceremony, not for religious reasons, but because he could not 'in good conscience' force patriotism upon his classes."[23] The teacher added "I love my country, I respect my flag and other symbols of my country, but I am repulsed by the idea that this should be forced on anyone. I cannot in good conscience do it."[24] After consideration of the issues raised in this case and preceding cases, in which provisions of the First and Fourteenth Amendments were involved, the Court of Appeals of Maryland concluded that the salute requirement and punishment provision of the Maryland law "are unconstitutional and void."

17.6 Requirements for Bible and prayer exercises

The flag salute and the pledge of allegiance constitute very minute elements in the school curriculum. Moreover,

---

20 *Frain* v. *Baron*, 307 FSupp 27, 32 (1969).

21 *Banks* v. *Board of Public Instruction of Dade County*, 314 FSupp 285, 296 (1970).

22 *State* v. *Lundquist* (Md), 278 A(2d) 263 (1971).

23 *Id.*, p. 266.

24 *Id.*, p. 274.

they are objected to by only a small minority of the citizenry
—namely, the Jehovah's Witnesses. Using the Bible and
reciting prayers, however, are of much more import in the
public school curriculum. In such matters, curricular activities are generally regarded to be sectarian in nature, and
since there are several hundred different religious sects in
America, it is understandable that there is great variance in
public opinion as to the manner and extent the reading of
scriptures from the Bible and the recitation of prayers should
be emphasized in the public school curriculum.

For over a century the state courts have been confronted
with the issues, and, in recent years, the United States Supreme Court has had to rule upon them. A review of the
court cases dealing with Bible reading and recitation of
prayers reveals different stages of judicial development. At
first, the courts generally upheld the practice, contending
that such matters were for state legislatures and boards of
education to decide. Later, the courts still upheld the reading of the Bible and the recitation of prayers as legal elements of the curriculum—but with the reservation that
pupils would not have to participate in the exercises, nor
could they be penalized for not participating.

Most recently, however, prescribed Bible reading and
the recitation of *mandated* prayers have been declared by the
United States Supreme Court to be violative of the First
Amendment and the Fourteenth Amendment of the United
States Constitution, regardless of whether or not pupils are
required to participate. It may be concluded, therefore, that
state statutes and school board policies prescribing Bible
reading and recitation of prayers as elements of the public
school curriculum are unconstitutional and illegal.

Despite the rulings of the United States Supreme Court
in *Engel* and *Schempp, supra* Section 4.4, some schools still
attempt to conduct religious exercises in various manners
and degrees. In general, however, the courts do not veer
away from declaring them unconstitutional. For example,
the United States Court of Appeals Seventh Circuit reversed
a federal district court's ruling which had upheld the recita-

tion of a brief verse (prayer) by children in a kindergarten class before their morning snack.

In explaining the ruling, the court stated:

> We are of the view that the verse is a prayer and that its compulsory recitation by kindergarten students in a public school comes within the proscription of the first amendment, as interpreted by the Supreme Court in the "school prayers" cases.[25]

Also, in a New Jersey case a court ruled that:

> Program of local board of education establishing "period for the free exercise of religion" which was implemented by providing for period in school gymnasium prior to formal opening of school, in which students who wished to join in the exercise would listen to "remarks" of the chaplain read from the Congressional Record, with period for meditation and conclusion of the reading, was unconstitutional establishment of religion, and not essential to free exercise of religion.[26]

17.7   Extracurricular activities

On the basis of court cases referred to in a publication[27] dealing with the legal aspects of extracurricular activities it is evident that extracurricular activities, and particularly competitive athletics, are in a state of confusion and dubiety. A number of the activities which are permitted and conducted in the public schools fall in the "twilight zone" as far as their legal place in the public school program is concerned.

The courts should not be blamed for the uncertainty of the legal place of extracurricular activities in a public school

---

[25] *De Spain* v. *De Kalb Community School Dist.* (Ill), 384 F(2d) 836, 837 (1968).

[26] *State Board of Education* v. *Board of Education of Netcong*, 108 NJSuper 564, 262 A(2d) 21, 22 (1970).

[27] J. David Mohler and Edward C. Bolmeier, *Law Governing Extracurricular Activities*. Cincinnati: The W. H. Anderson Company. 1968. 185 pp.

program. It is not for the courts to decide what shall constitute a school program and how it shall be administered. That is the responsibility of the legislature and the legally constituted public school officials (school board) to whom authority is delegated. The judiciary is reluctant to interfere with their prerogatives. The primary function of the courts in cases involving extracurricular activities is whether their inclusion, administration, and support are in harmony with state constitutional provisions. Within constitutional and statutory limits, the school board has the authority and responsibility to decide what shall be included in the entire school program, including extracurricular activities.

There has been controversy and litigation concerning the authority of athletic associations over a member school's athletic affairs.

> It is an established legal principle that the board of education has the authority to control the entire school program, curricular and extracurricular. But school boards also have the authority to permit their schools to join high school associations, thereby relinquishing a portion of their control over the extracurricular program by agreeing to abide by the constitution and by-laws of the association.[28]

The school board is not likely to interfere with disputes between a school and the association with which it is affiliated. Moreover, the courts will not interfere, as is indicated by a judicial statement:

> The Louisiana High School Athletic Association purports to be, and has been considered by our courts a voluntary association. The general rule in Louisiana is that courts will not interfere in the internal affairs of a voluntary association so long as its affairs and proceedings are conducted fairly and honestly, and after the due notice to all parties involved.[29]

---

[28] J. David Mohler and Edward C. Bolmeier, *Law Governing Extracurricular Activities*. Cincinnati: The W. H. Anderson Company, 1968, p. 72.
[29] *David* v. *Louisiana High School Athletic Assn.*, 244 S(2d) 292, 293-294 (1971).

Even though state statutes are not likely to prescribe the extracurricular activities for a public school program, some do stipulate the manner of their control. The law of North Carolina is illustrative:

> County and City boards of education shall make all rules and regulations necessary for the conducting of extra curricular activities in the schools under their supervision, including a program of athletics, where desired, without assuming liability therefor; provided, that all interscholastic athletic activities shall be conducted in accordance with rules and regulations prescribed by the State Board of Education. [30]

The uncertainties of the legal place of extracurricular activities in a public school program would be removed by the simple process of "curricularizing the extracurricular."

It is highly possible that eventually this will be accomplished. Because of the over-emphasis on the athletic program, there is a growing pressure from many quarters for a review and refinement of the total school program. The pressure stems partially from the assumption that the exclusive purpose of a public school is to *educate all children.* If this assumption is correct it would follow that activities which are not educational in purpose would not have a place in the public school program.

Finally, it has been suggested that application of the following steps would add legality and propriety to the "extracurricular" program of a school: (1) Determine and then admit the activities that are educational in character. (2) Recognize the activities as a legitimate part of the total curriculum. (3) Support the activities by public funds. (4) Make the activities available to all children who could profit therefrom. (5) Do not prohibit participation as a punitive device. [31]

---

[30] *Public School Laws of North Carolina,* 1965, Chap. 115, sec. 35(d).

[31] Evelyn Fulbright and Edward C. Bolmeier, *Courts and the Curriculum.* Cincinnati: The W. H. Anderson Comany, 1964, pp. 164-167.

TABLE OF CASES

References are to section numbers

297

State ex rel. Smith v. St. Paul, City of, 128 Minn 82, 150 NW 389 (1914): **12.7**

Stephens v. Bongart, 15 NJMisc 80, 189 Atl 131 (1937): **16.6**

Stevenson v. Board of Education of Wheeler County, Georgia, 426 F(2d) 1154 (1970): **16.12**

Streich v. Board of Education of Aberdeen, 34 SD 169, 147 NW 779 (1914): **16.3**

Swann v. Charlotte-Mecklenburg Board of Education (NC), 91 SCt 1267 (1971): **3.2, 4.6, 16.8**

Szilagyi v. State, 249 Ind 400, 231 NE(2d) 221 (1967): **12.10**

Taggart v. Board of Directors of Canon-McMillan J. Sch. Sys., 409 Pa 33, 185 A(2d) 332 (1962): **15.6**

Teachers Association, Central High School Dist. No. 3 v. Board of Education, Nassau County (NY), 312 NYS(2d) 252 (1970): **15.6**

Tibbals, People ex rel. v. Board of Education of Port Huron, 39 Mich 635 (1878): **12.7**

Tinker v. Des Moines Independent Community School Dist., (Iowa), 393 US 503, 21 LEd(2d) 731, 89 SCt 733 (1969): **4.6, 16.13**

Todd Coronway v. Landsdowne School Dist. No. 785, in the Court of Common Pleas of Delaware County, Pennsylvania, June Term, (1951): **15.6**

Township 143 North Range 55 Cass County In re (ND), 183 NW(2d) 520 (1971): **10.5**

Toyah Independent School Dist. v. Pecos-Barstow Independent School (Tex), 466 SW(2d) 377 (1971): **12.10**

Tripp v. Board of Examiners of City of New York, 44 Misc(2d) 1026, 255 NYS(2d) 526 (1964): **15.2**

Tudor v. Board of Education (NJ), 348 US 815, 75 SCt 25 (1954): **4.4**

Turley v. Adel Community School Dist. (Iowa), 322 FSupp 402 (1971): **16.12**

United States v. Butler, 56 SCt 312 (1936): **1.3**

United States v. Montgomery County Board of Education (Ala), 395 US 225, 23 LEd(2d) 263, 89 SCt 1670 (1970): **4.6**

Valent v. New Jersey State Board of Education, 114 NJSuper 63, 274 A(2d) 832 (1971): **17.3**

Village of Blaine v. Independent School Dist. No. 12 (Minn), 138 NW(2d) 32 (1965): **13.4**

Visotcky v. City Council of Garfield, 113 NJSuper 263, 273 A(2d) 597 (1971): **12.7**

Visser v. Noonsack Valley Dist. No. 506, 33 Wash(2d) 198 (1949): **16.9**

Ward v. San Diego School Dist., 203 Cal 712, 265 Pac 821 (1928): **12.7**

Watts v. Seward School Board (Alaska), 395 P(2d) 372 (1964): **15.4, 15.9**

Wayland v. Board of School Directors, 43 Wash 441, 86 Pac 642 (1906): **16.10**

Wayman v. Board of Education, 5 OhioSt(2d) 248, 34 OhioOps 473, 215 NE(2d) 394 (1966): **12.1**

Wesley v. Board of Education of Nicholas County (Ky), 403 SW(2d) 28 (1966): **12.9**

RESOURCE PUBLICATIONS FOR STUDY OF THE SCHOOL IN THE LEGAL STRUCTURE

BOOKS

Abraham, Henry J. FREEDOM AND THE COURT. New York: Oxford University Press, 1967. 335 pp. (Attempts to analyze and evaluate the basic problem differentiating individual and community rights in those spheres that constitute such basic rights and liberties as freedom of religion, freedom of expression, due process of law, and political and racial equality.)

Abraham, Henry J. The Judiciary: THE SUPREME COURT IN THE GOVERNMENTAL PROCESS. Boston: Allyn and Bacon, 1969. 122 pp. (Designed for use by the general public as well as students of government and politics at all levels, the book explains and evaluates: (1) American courts in practice, (2) the Supreme Court and basic freedoms, and (3) courts and public policy.)

Alexander, Corns, and McCann. PUBLIC SCHOOL LAW: CASES AND MATERIALS. St. Paul, Minn.: West Publishing Company, 1967. 734 pp. (The book represents an effort to provide a logical arrangement of case material which will provide an in-depth examination of the problems concerning the law and public education. All cases referred to, regardless of age, are intended to provide the legal basis for public school operation in the United States today.)

Allen, Hollis P. THE FEDERAL GOVERNMENT AND EDUCATION. New York: McGraw-Hill Book Co., 1950. 330 pp. (Original and complete study of Education for the Hoover Commission Task Force on Public Welfare. Considerable emphasis on federal aid to education.)

American Association of School Administrators. FEDERAL POLICY AND THE PUBLIC SCHOOLS. Washington: The Association, 1967. — pp. (A series of nine essays dealing with aspects of federal government and public education. Available in bound single volume after June 1967. The series begins with the essay, "The Search for a New Role for the Federal Government in Education" and ends with "Principles to Govern the Emerging Federal, State, and Local Partnership.")

——. THE FEDERAL GOVERNMENT AND PUBLIC SCHOOLS. Washington: The Association, 1965. 71 pp. (Provides a basis for study and understanding of the problems and issues inherent in the changing relationships among various levels of government. Calls for thoughtful consideration of crucial issues and opportunities facing Americans.)

———. RELIGION IN THE PUBLIC SCHOOLS. Washington: The Association, 1964. 67 pp. (Examines the effect of recent decisions of the Supreme Court on the issues of Bible reading and prayer in the public schools, and suggests constructive means by which public school administrators could guide the development of local policies and practices in keeping with Supreme Court decisions.)

Antieau, Chester James, Phillip Mark Carroll, and Thomas Carroll Burke. RELIGION UNDER THE STATE CONSTITUTIONS. Brooklyn, N. Y.: Central Book Company, Inc., 1965. 277 pp. (A survey of religious questions that have arisen under the state constitutions. Chapter Two: Constitutional Bans upon Aid to Church-Related Educational Institutions. Chapter Three: Religion in the Public Schools.)

Appenzeller, Herb. FROM THE GYM TO THE JURY. Charlottesville, Virginia: The Michie Company, 1970. 225 pp. (The author cites numerous court cases and personal experiences to indicate liability of school officers, administrators and teachers for pupil injuries relating to supervision, instruction, facilities and equipment, player injuries and spectator injuries. Emphasis is placed upon the avoidance of injuries and resultant litigation.)

Barker, Lucius J. and Twiley W. Barker, Jr. (Editors) CIVIL LIBERTIES AND THE CONSTITUTION. Englewood Cliffs, N. J.: Prentice-Hall, Inc., 1970, 471 pp. (A compilation of commentaries and cases focused on timely issues such as: (1) free exercise of religion and church-state relations; (2) freedom of expression and association; (3) rights of persons accused of crime; and (4) problems related to racial justice. Most of the judicial decisions on civil-liberties issues referred to are those of the United States Supreme Court.)

Beem, Harlan D. AN INTRODUCTION TO LEGAL BIBLIOGRAPHY FOR THE NON-PROFESSIONAL STUDENT. Carbondale, Illinois: Educational Research Bureau, Southern Illinois University, 1960. 110 pp. (Designed as an introductory manual for students not preparing for a career in law.)

Benedetti, Eugene. SCHOOL LAW MATERIALS: CASES AND PROBLEMS. Dubuque, Iowa: Wm. C. Brown Company, 1964. 200 pp. (Designed for use as a textbook in school law. At the conclusion of each chapter are questions and problems dealing with that treated topic.)

Blackwell, Thomas Edward. COLLEGE LAW: A GUIDE FOR ADMINISTRATORS. Washington: American Council on Education, 1961. 347 pp. (Written to assist the college administrator in planning procedures to avoid the possibility of litigation.)

Blaustein, Albert P. and Clarence Clyde Ferguson, Jr. DESEGREGATION AND THE LAW. Second edition revised. New York: Vintage Books, 1962. 359 pp. (The story of BROWN v. BOARD OF EDUCATION, the school segregation case.)

Blum, Virgil C. FREEDOM IN EDUCATION: FEDERAL AID FOR ALL CHILDREN. Garden City, New York: Doubleday & Company, 1965. 235 pp. (Focus on the freedom of the individual pupil. Presents the church's argument for federal aid to education—public and private.)

Boles, Donald E. THE BIBLE, RELIGION, AND THE PUBLIC SCHOOLS. Second edition. Ames, Iowa: Iowa State University Press, 1963. 341 pp. (Examines the constitutionality of sectarian instruction in the public schools in light of various state constitutions, statutes, court decisions, and the historic past.)

Bolmeier, E. C. (editor) LEGAL ISSUES IN EDUCATION—ABRIDGED. Charlottesville, Virginia: The Michie Company, 1970. 363 pp. (Abridged treatment of thirty-eight doctoral dissertations in the field of school law at Duke University. The book is divided into eight parts: I, Pupil Personnel; II, Teacher Personnel; III, Segregation of the Races; IV, Tort Liability; V, Higher Education; VI, The School Program; VII, School Board Membership and Authority; VIII, Legal Studies not Involving Case Law.)

Bolmeier, Edward C. LEGAL LIMITS OF AUTHORITY OVER THE PUPIL. Charlottesville, Virginia: The Michie Company, 1970. 150 pp. (Deals essentially with "state versus parental authority over the pupil" as revealed by court cases. Issues treated fall into three main categories: (1) Compulsory and Prohibitory School Attendance; (2) Curriculum Activities; (3) Control Over Student Behavior.)

Bolmeier, Edward C. TEACHER'S LEGAL RIGHTS, RESTRAINTS AND LIABILITIES. ASLaw Series. Cincinnati: The W. H. Anderson Company, 1971. 149 pp. (This contribution to the ASLaw Series, is a case report dealing with such controversial issues as: (1) right of tenure; (2) teachers dismissal; (3) leaves of absence; (4) right of association; (5) teaching controversial issues; (6) right to strike; and (7) liability for pupil injuries.)

Breckenridge, Adam Carlyle. CONGRESS AGAINST THE COURT. Lincoln, Nebraska: The University of Nebraska Press, 1970. 160 pp. (The author analyzes factors which influenced the Congress to pass a law based largely on opposition to a few Supreme Court decisions, which, it was claimed, upset the balance between the rights of the individual and the needs of society. The cited cases indicate the attempt of Congress to overrule the objectionable decisions through legislation.)

Brubacher, John S. THE COURTS AND HIGHER EDUCATION. San Francisco: Jossey-Bass, Inc., Publishers, 1971. 150 pp. (The author attempts to: (1) acquaint academic policy makers with the attitude of the courts; (2) demonstrate in which areas of policy, administrators and governing boards have firm authority; (3) provide a catalogue of pertinent cases in readable language; (4) specify limits of authority; and (5) offer authoritative guidelines.)

Bryson, Joseph E. LEGALITY OF LOYALTY OATH AND NON-OATH RE-
QUIREMENTS FOR PUBLIC SCHOOL TEACHERS. Asheville: Miller Printing Co., 1963. 105 pp. (Determines the legality of loyalty oath and
non-oath laws with respect to public school teachers through
analysis of constitutional and statutory provisions, court decisions
and legal theory. Adapted from a doctoral dissertation.)

Bryson, Joseph E. (editor) UPSURGE AND UPHEAVAL IN SCHOOL LAW.
Topeka, Kansas: Nolpe, 1970. 210 pp. (Essentially the proceedings of the Nolpe Convention held in Cleveland, 1969. Subjects
included in the publication are: (1) The Principal's Role in
Collective Negotiations; (2) Tributes to Lloyd E. McCann, Robert
L. Drury, and Newton Edwards; (3) The Legality of Shared Time;
(4) The Legal Rights of Untenured Teachers; (5) The Warren
Court and the Public Schools; (6) Racial Integration; (7) A Look
at City Administration; (8) Constitutional Protection of Protest;
and (9) Reflections of "Upsurge and Upheaval—Thirty Years of
School Law" in a dialogue by Lee O. Garber and Edward C.
Bolmeier.)

Chambers, M. M. THE COLLEGES AND THE COURTS SINCE 1950. Danville,
Illinois: The Interstate Printers and Publishers, Inc., 1964. 415
pp. (Examines nearly 500 cases decided by the higher state and
federal courts pertaining to higher education.)

Chambers, M. M. HIGHER EDUCATION IN THE 50 STATES. Danville,
Illinois: The Interstate Printers & Publishers, Inc., 1970. 453 pp.
(Presents detailed tables and graphs in answering the questions
pertaining to state investments, traditions, and practices and their
probable effect on the future of tax support for higher education.)

CONSTITUTIONS OF THE UNITED STATES: NATIONAL AND STATE. Prepared
by Columbia University Legislative Drafting Research Fund. Dobbs
Ferry, N. Y.: Oceana Publications, Inc., 1962. (Contains the Constitution of the Federal government and of the fifty states with
amendments to date. Each state constitution contains an article
usually captioned, "Education.")

Corwin, Edward S. THE CONSTITUTION AND WHAT IT MEANS TODAY.
New York: Atheneum, 1963. 342 pp. (Utilizes principally the decisions of the United States Supreme Court down to 1958 to determine the meaning of the Constitution. Frequently quoted in
other publications.)

de Camp, L. Sprague. THE GREAT MONKEY TRIAL. Garden City, N. Y.:
Doubleday and Company, 1968. 538 pp. (A narrative and well-
documented account of the famous *Scopes* evolution trial of 1925,
at Dayton, Tennessee. Much space is devoted to the forensic
battle waged between William Jennings Bryan (the fundamentalist)
and Clarence Seward Darrow (the agnostic).)

Dolbeare, Kenneth M. and Phillip E. Hammond. THE SCHOOL PRAYER DECISIONS. Chicago: The University of Chicago Press, 1971. 164 pp. (An interview study reveals that, in several communities, extensive religious observances are continued in the public schools despite the Supreme Court rulings of *Vitale* in 1962 and *Schempp* in 1963. Consideration is given to the question: "How can decisions be rendered at the national level and be without effect at the local board?")

Douglas, William O. THE BIBLE AND THE SCHOOLS. Boston: Little, Brown & Company, 1966. 65 pp. (An expansion of a lecture the author was to have delivered on November 22, 1963. Gives a history of the "religion" cases that have come before the Supreme Court and the court's reasoning in arriving at decisions.)

Drury, Robert L. Editor. LAW AND THE SCHOOL SUPERINTENDENT. Vol. 1 of NOLPE Series. Cincinnati: The W. H. Anderson Company, .1958. 339 pp. (Designed to acquaint the school superintendent with the legal aspects of his position, together with an understanding of the law as it relates to tenure, qualifications, compensation, duties, etc.)

——— and Kenneth C. Ray. ESSENTIALS OF SCHOOL LAW. New York: Appleton-Century-Crofts, 1967. 215 pp. (Striking duplication of content and organization with authors 1965 publication, PRINCIPLES OF SCHOOL LAW. Intended purpose is to present minimum essentials of school law for both general and specific understanding and information.)

——— and Kenneth C. Ray. PRINCIPLES OF SCHOOL LAW. New York: Appleton-Century-Crofts. 1965. 356 pp. (Written by a practicing attorney in the field of school law and a professor of school law and administration. It is a combination of "textual-court case methods as a technique that could be adopted in the field of school law, to the teaching and learning process.)

Duker, Sam. THE PUBLIC SCHOOLS AND RELIGION: THE LEGAL CONTEXT. New York: Harper & Row, 1966. 238 pp. (Presents a selection of the language used by the Justices of the Supreme Court in deciding issues relating to religion and the schools.)

Edwards, Newton. THE COURTS AND THE PUBLIC SCHOOLS. Third edition. Chicago: The University of Chicago Press, 1971. 710 pp. (The original and popular text is updated with a preface and an additional chapter by former student, Lee O. Garber. The major contribution of this new edition is to identify (1) cases which have departed from former precedents and established new ones, and (2) cases which deal with new issues, raised by changing social conditions, for which there were no precedents.)

Eidenberg, Eugene and Roy D. Morey. AN ACT OF CONGRESS. New York: W. W. Norton & Co., 1969. 256 pp. (The scope of the book covers the relevant major events preceding the passage of the

Elementary and Secondary Education Act of 1965, and its subsequent modifications. A major purpose of the authors is "to offer a working description of the American policy process by focusing on the issue of federal aid to education.")

Erickson, Donald A. PUBLIC CONTROLS FOR NONPUBLIC SCHOOLS. Chicago: The University of Chicago Press, 1969. 242 pp. (A comprehensive treatise on legal educational, social, and ethical issues in state regulations of nonpublic schools. Among subjects treated are: (1) the Old Order Amish, (2) church-related systems, and (3) schools devoted to circumventing edicts of the Supreme Court.)

Fellman, David. THE CONSTITUTIONAL RIGHT OF ASSOCIATION. Chicago: The University of Chicago Press, 1963. 110 pp. (Spells out, in a preliminary way, the meaning of the constitutional guaranty of the right of association.)

———. RELIGION IN AMERICAN PUBLIC LAW. Boston: Boston University Press, 1965. 113 pp. (The Gaspar G. Bacon Lectureship on the Constitution of the United States for 1963-64 with respect to the concepts of religious freedom and of the separation of church and state.)

Findlay and Findlay. YOUR RUGGED CONSTITUTION. Stanford, Calif.: Stanford University Press, 1969. 290 pp. (The authors portray an accurate picture of our Federal Constitution by referring, in a logical manner, to each of its Articles and Amendments. Clever illustrations add comprehensiveness to the book.)

Flowers, Anne and Edward C. Bolmeier. LAW AND PUPIL CONTROL. Vol. 1 of ASLaw Series. Cincinnati: The W. H. Anderson Company, 1964. 194 pp. (An exhaustive study of court decisions governing a selected number of important aspects of pupil control.)

The Foundation of the Federal Bar Association. EQUAL JUSTICE UNDER LAW: THE SUPREME COURT IN AMERICAN LIFE. Washington: The Association, 1965. 143 pp. (Designed to tell the story of the Supreme Court of the United States and to explain the unique power it holds in the American system of government.)

Francis, Samuel N. PENNSYLVANIA SCHOOL LAW. Cleveland: Banks-Baldwin Law Publishing Co., 1971. (A comprehensive encyclopedic treatise published in three large volumes "covering every phase of Pennsylvania School Law and Administration." Volume I assembles information concerning regulations and directives of the State Department of Education; Volume II contains the Pennsylvania Public School Codes; Volume III contains additional miscellaneous law relating to schools and education.)

Fulbright, Evelyn R. and Edward C. Bolmeier. COURTS AND THE CURRICULUM. Vol. 2 of ASLaw Series. Cincinnati: The W. H. Anderson Company, 1964. 197 pp. (Undertakes to make clear and practical, from court decisions, the body of fundamental legal principles governing the curriculum.)

Fuller, Edgar and Jim B. Pearson (editors). EDUCATION IN THE STATES: NATIONWIDE DEVELOPMENT SINCE 1900. Washington, D. C.: NEA, 1969. 772 pp. (Second volume of a research project on a nationwide basis, with 16 areas of concern to all states. Designed as a university text and research reference. Chapters with legal implication bear such titles as: (1) Constitutional and Legal Basis for State Action; (2) State Departments of Education Within State Governments; (3) State Organization for Service and Leadership to Local Schools; and (4) Impacts of Federal Programs of State Departments of Education.)

Fuller, Edgar and Jim B. Pearson (editors). EDUCATION IN THE STATES: HISTORICAL DEVELOPMENT AND OUTLOOK. Washington, D. C.: NEA, 1969. 1475 pp. (First volume of a monumental and intensive research project with special emphasis on state departments of education of each state and five outlying areas. Ranges from descriptions of the relatively simple activities of the early superintendents to complex current staff organizational charts. Identifies weaknesses and strengths and directions for future development.)

Gaddy, Dale. THE SCOPE OF ORGANIZED STUDENT PROTEST IN JUNIOR COLLEGES. Washington, D. C.: American Association of Junior Colleges, 1970. 26 pp. (Based upon the findings of a research project, answers are given for such questions as: (1) To what extent are junior colleges experiencing protest? (2) In what region of the country do protests occur most often? (3) Have junior colleges developed "riot plans" for implementation when disturbances occur? (4) What are the issues of protest?)

Garber, Lee O. Editor. CURRENT LEGAL CONCEPTS IN EDUCATION. Philadelphia: University of Pennsylvania Press, 1966. 325 pp. (A symposium on School Law commemorating the 50th anniversary of the Graduate School of Education of the University of Pennsylvania. Examines aspects of the increasing involvement of government and law in school affairs of local communities.)

——. EDUCATION AS A FUNCTION OF THE STATE. Minneapolis: Educational Test Bureau, 1934. 99 pp. (Shows proper relationship of state educational system to organized society and to the individual by analysis of debates of constitutional conventions; clarifies relation of state to education as defined by courts; court application of concept to practical problems of administration.)

——. HANDBOOK OF SCHOOL LAW. New London, Conn.: Arthur C. Croft Publications, 1954. 165 pp. (Deals with principles gleaned from court decisions with respect to recurring questions of school law and acquaints school personnel with some of their rights, duties, and responsibilities.)

——. Editor. LAW AND THE SCHOOL BUSINESS MANAGER. Danville, Illinois: The Interstate Printers and Publishers, Inc., 1957, 331 pp. (Attempts to bring together those legal principles which are of particular significance to those interested in the procurement and allocation of school funds.)

——. THE YEARBOOK OF SCHOOL LAW. Annual since 1950. Danville, Illinois: The Interstate Printers and Publishers, Inc. (Treats those decisions dealing with "schools" and "school districts," decided by the higher state and federal courts during a one-year period. Contains bibliography and special articles of current interest.)

—— and Newton Edwards. SCHOOL LAW CASEBOOK SERIES. Nos. 1-8. Danville, Illinois: The Interstate Printers and Publishers, Inc. (Series gives a brief statement of legal principles supported by excerpts from leading court cases. No. 1. The Public School in our Governmental Structure, 1962. 106 pp.; No. 2. The Law Relating to the Creation, Alteration, and Dissolution of School Districts, 1962. 95 pp.; No. 3. The Law Governing Teaching Personnel, 1962. 117 pp.; No. 4. The Law Governing Pupils, 1962. 124 pp.; No. 5. The Law Governing School Board Members and School Board Meetings, 1963. 96 pp.; No. 6. Tort Liability of School Districts and School Boards, 1963. 105 pp.; No. 7. The Law Governing School Property and School-Building Construction, 1964. 116 pp.; No. 8. The Law Governing the Financing of Public Education, 1964. 104 pp.)

Gauerke, Warren E. LEGAL AND ETHICAL RESPONSIBILITIES OF SCHOOL PERSONNEL. Englewood Cliffs, N. J.: Prentice-Hall, Inc., 1959. 302 pp. (Designed to acquaint one with some minimum legal obligations and rights, and leads to deeper understanding of ethical choices.)

——. SCHOOL LAW. New York: The Center for Applied Research in Education, Inc., 1965. 116 pp. (Gives a summary of the sources and scope of school law. Chapters are devoted to school law as it affects teachers, pupils, and board members.)

Giannella, Donald A. Editor. RELIGION AND THE PUBLIC ORDER. Chicago: The University of Chicago Press, 1964. 280 pp. (A review of aspects of church and state and of religion, law, and society.)

Griffiths, William E. RELIGION, THE COURTS, AND THE PUBLIC SCHOOLS. Vol. 3 of the ASLaw Series. Cincinnati: The W. H. Anderson Company, 1966. 244 pp. (Deals primarily with court decisions that have been rendered in cases involving religion and the public schools. Identifies trends in judicial thinking, isolates legal principles, and summarizes their implications.)

Hachten, William A. THE SUPREME COURT ON FREEDOM OF THE PRESS. Ames, Iowa: The Iowa State University Press, 1968. 316 pp. (Essentially a collection of decisions of the Supreme Court that relate to freedom of expression. Concludes that a press that uses its freedom with courage, restraint, and responsibility need not fear curtailment by the Supreme Court of the United States.)

Hamilton, Robert R. and Paul R. Mort. THE LAW AND PUBLIC EDUCA-
TION. Brooklyn: The Foundation Press, Inc., 1959. Second edition.
641 pp. (Presents cases in which the courts have influenced the
"direction of education through their decisions." Topics covered
include: employment and discharge of teachers, school board elections, and district re-organization.)

—— and E. Edmund Reutter, Jr. LEGAL ASPECTS OF SCHOOL BOARD
OPERATION. New York: Columbia University, 1958. 199 pp. (Presents
the minimum essentials of the legal aspects of local school operation—the basic legal rights, duties, privileges, and responsibilities
entailed in the public school enterprise.)

Hazard, William R. EDUCATION AND THE LAW. New York: The Free
Press, 1971. 480 pp. (Contains narrations, cases from state and
federal courts, and journal articles pertaining to the following
main areas: (1) Public Schooling and the Law; (2) Church, State,
and Schools; (3) Civil Rights and Education; (4) Pupils, Parents,
and School Policies; (5) Teacher-Board Relations; (6) School
Funds, School Property, and the Law; (7) Tort Liability of Teachers and Schools.)

Hill, Roscoe and Malcolm Feeley. AFFIRMATIVE SCHOOL INTEGRATION.
Beverly Hills, California: Sage Publications, 1968. 172 pp. (Depicts
efforts to overcome de facto segregation in urban schools as found
in case studies of Evanston, Berkeley, New Haven, Pasadena, St.
Louis, Albany, San Francisco, and Chicago. Viewpoints on the
problems are expressed respectively by an educator, a lawyer, a
sociologist, and a political scientist.)

Holmes, Grace W. (editor) LAW AND DISCIPLINE ON CAMPUS. Ann
Arbor, Michigan: The Institute of Continuing Legal Education,
1971. 381 pp. (A compilation of issues treated in four parts: Part
I—Campus Tensions: Challenge and Responsibility; Part II—Administrative Discipline; Part III—Law Enforcement in Crisis; Part
IV—The Aftermath of Crisis. In addition to the main text, thirteen appendixes provide pertinent information relative to the
issues discussed.)

Holmes, Grace W. (editor) STUDENT PROTEST AND THE LAW. Ann Arbor,
Michigan: The Institute of Continuing Education, 1969. 403 pp.
(Suggestions for educators, lawyers and others for understanding
the law's role in matters of student protest. Consists of an edited
transcript of a national conference proceedings (May 1969). Special emphasis is given to overall problems categorized as: (1) student rights, (2) questions of violence and coercion; and (3) civil
liberties aspects of both.)

Howard, Charles G. and Robert S. Summers. LAW: ITS NATURE, FUNC-
TIONS AND LIMITS. Englewood Cliffs, N. J.: Prentice-Hall, Inc.,
1965. 466 pp. (Designed to illustrate how the legal system operates
and its main functions.)

Howe, Mark DeWolfe. CASES ON CHURCH AND STATE IN THE UNITED STATES. Cambridge, Mass.: Harvard University Press, 1952. 393 pp. (Collection of important cases that have arisen in the United States pertaining to the exercise of religious freedom. Chapter five deals with religion and education.)

Hudgins, H. C., Jr. THE WARREN COURT AND THE PUBLIC SCHOOLS. Danville, Virginia: The Interstate Printers and Publishers, 1970. 178 pp. (An analysis of landmark Supreme Court decisions during the Warren administration, 1953-1969, which have a bearing on the public schools. Subject areas fall under the headings of (1) religion, (2) segregation, and (3) academic freedom. Other pertinent decisions prior to 1953 are also treated briefly.)

Johnson, George M. EDUCATION LAW. East Lansing, Michigan: Michigan State University Press, 1969. 258 pp. (Stated purpose is to examine the laws—federal, state, and local—that regulate some important relationships in elementary, secondary, and higher education. Topical treatment of legal issues in seven chapters, each of which is concluded with "notes" which, in the main, are citations of pertinent court cases.)

Kempin, Frederick G., Jr. LEGAL HISTORY: LAW AND SOCIAL CHANGE. Englewood Cliffs, N. J.: Prentice-Hall, Inc., 1963. 117 pp. (Narrates the development of the institutions of law—its courts, juries, judges, and lawyers—and traces the beginnings and development of selected legal concepts.)

Kigin, Denis J. TEACHER LIABILITY IN SCHOOL-SHOP ACCIDENTS. Ann Arbor, Michigan: Prakken Publications, Inc., 1963. 128 pp. (Contains information that "will be of assistance to everyone with responsibility in the field of vocational education where the use of machines is required.")

Kramer, Robert. Editor. "School Pupils and the Law." LAW AND CONTEMPORARY PROBLEMS. Vol. 20, No. 1. School of Law. Duke University. Winter 1955. 195 pp. (A symposium concentrating upon certain key aspects of the relationship in a democratic society between the pupils, their parents, and the public school.)

Lamorte, Michael, Harold W. Gentry, and D. Parker Young. STUDENTS' LEGAL RIGHTS AND RESPONSIBILITIES. ASLaw Series. Cincinnati: The W. H. Anderson Company, 1971. — pp. (Deals with such litigious issues as (1) personal appearance; (2) freedom of expression; (3) rights of married students; (4) secret organizations; (5) search of students' lockers; and (6) procedural due process.)

Leibee, Howard C. TORT LIABILITY FOR INJURIES TO PUPILS. Ann Arbor, Michigan: University of Michigan, 1965. 97 pp. (Explores on a state-by-state basis the statutes as they apply to responsibility and liability of school districts and school personnel in various accident situations. Gives court cases at the conclusion of each section to substantiate the liability of the district and personnel involved.)

Legislative Reference Service, Library of Congress. THE CONSTITUTION OF THE UNITED STATES OF AMERICA: ANALYSIS AND INTERPRETATION. Washington: U. S. Government Printing Office, 1964. 1693 pp. (Gives annotations of cases decided by the Supreme Court of the United States to June 22, 1964.)

Linn, John Phillip (editor). CRITICAL ISSUES IN SCHOOL LAW. Topeka, Kansas: Nolpe, 1971. 199 pp. (As stated in the foreword of the publication "This volume contains the proceedings of the 1970 Nolpe Annual Meeting. It makes available to all a wealth of material on the most challenging problems of our time—the use of the strike in school employer-employee relations, desegregation through busing; disparities in educational resources; decentralization; student dissent; and church-state relations, among others.")

Manwaring, David R. RENDER UNTO CAESAR: THE FLAG-SALUTE CONTROVERSY. Chicago: The University of Chicago Press, 1962. 321 pp. (Presents in detail the legal controversy over the compulsory flag salute in public schools.)

Marnell, William H. THE FIRST AMENDMENT: THE HISTORY OF RELIGIOUS FREEDOM IN AMERICA. Garden City, N. Y.: Doubleday and Company, Inc., 1964. 247 pp. (A history of world events that preceded the writing of the first amendment. Analyzes reasons behind his belief that "a wall of separation which would bar that spirit from making itself felt in secular concerns can never be built, because it would have to bisect the human heart.")

McCann, Lloyd E. LEGAL PROBLEMS IN THE ADMINISTRATION OF EDUCATION BY EDUCATIONAL AND NON-EDUCATIONAL GOVERNMENT AGENCIES. Tucson: University of Arizona, 1964. 170 pp. (Analyzes the intergovernmental controls through which public education is administered in the United States.)

McCord, John H. (editor) WITH ALL DELIBERATE SPEED: CIVIL RIGHTS THEORY AND REALITY. Urbana, Ill.: University of Illinois Press, 1969. 205 pp. (This book contains six articles emerging from a symposium in which the history of the Civil Rights Movement is traced since its origin in 1776. Contributors were·selected on the basis of their reputation as crusaders and public teachers for civil rights.)

McDaniel, Jesse L. and Edward C. Bolmeier. LAW GOVERNING ACQUISITION OF SCHOOL PROPERTY. Vol. 4 of ASLaw Series. Cincinnati: The W. H. Anderson Company, 1966. 185 pp. (Concerned with all court decisions of higher state courts involving all aspects of acquisition of property for public school use.)

McGhehey, M. A. THE SCHOOL ATTORNEY. 1835 K. Street, N. W., Washington, D. C.: Educational Service Bureau, Inc., 1969. 45 pp. (Discusses the role of the school board attorney as related to duties, functions, selection, compensations, and control of the school attorney.)

Michaelsen, Robert. PIETY IN THE PUBLIC SCHOOLS. New York: The Macmillan Company, 1970. 274 pp. (An examination of the high points in the history of the relationship between religion and the public schools. The three main types of sources are: (1) selected materials relating to American religious history; (2) the work and thought of major educational leaders; and (3) significant court cases.)

Michen, Charles M. THE LAW OF THE STUDENT: A MANUAL OF STUDENT RIGHTS. West Chester, Penn.: West Chester State College, 1966. 74 pp. (A legal reference book which presents the rights of public school students. Information taken from records of court decisions.)

Mohler, J. David and Edward C. Bolmeier. LAW GOVERNING EXTRA-CURRICULAR ACTIVITIES. Vol. 5 in the ASLaw Series. Cincinnati: The W. H. Anderson Company, 1968. (Presents legal principles derived from court cases dealing with (1) use of public funds for extracurricular activities (2) regulation for pupil participation (3) authority of athletic associations to control and (4) tort liability of those involved.)

National Education Association. LOCAL, STATE, FEDERAL PARTNERSHIP IN SCHOOL FINANCE. Washington: The Association, 1966. 165 pp. (Report comprises the papers presented at the Ninth Annual Conference on School Finance by the Committee on Educational Finance of the N. E. A.)

——, Research Division. THE PUPIL'S DAY IN COURT: REVIEW OF 1966. School Law Series, Research Report 1967-R7. Washington: The Association, 1967. 61 pp. (Presents digests of 83 judicial decisions in cases of direct concern to pupils in the public schools. The material was compiled from court decisions published in the NATIONAL REPORTER SYSTEM during the calendar year 1966. An annual publication.)

——, Research Division. THE TEACHER'S DAY IN COURT: REVIEW OF 1966. School Law Series, Research Report 1967-R6. Washington: The Association, 1967. 60 pp. (Contains digests of 69 judicial decisions which were published in the NATIONAL REPORTER SYSTEM during the calendar year 1966. With rare exceptions, the litigants in these court cases were teachers or other professional school personnel in the public elementary and secondary schools. An annual publication.)

——, Research Division. WHO IS LIABLE FOR PUPIL INJURIES? Washington: National Commission on Safety Education of the N. E. A., 1963. 72 pp. (Explores what can be done to prevent school accidents, and what the legal liabilities of the school districts and school personnel are when pupils are injured.)

Nolte, M. Chester. GUIDE TO SCHOOL LAW. West Nyack, N. Y.: Parker Publishing Company, 1969. 238 pp. (An authoritative handbook designed to guide school administrators in such timely issues as:

(1) political and personal rights of school employees; (2) authority to discipline and control pupils; (3) employee welfare rights; (4) liability for pupil injury; (5) responsibility for school facilities; (6) powers of the local board of education; (7) collective bargaining.)

Nolte, M. Chester (editor). LAW AND THE SCHOOL SUPERINTENDENT. Vol. I (second edition) of the Nolpe Series. Cincinnati: The W. H. Anderson Company, 1971. 295 pp. (This edition resembles the first in title only. Otherwise there are numerous changes, such as editor, contributors, and issues. The book is divided into four parts: I, General overview of the legal status of the superintendent; II, Desegregation issues; III, Church-state relations; and IV, Collective bargaining and free speech.)

Nolte, M. Chester and John Phillip Linn. SCHOOL LAW FOR TEACHERS. Danville, Illinois: Interstate Printers and Publishers, Inc., 1963. 343 pp. (Aids school personnel in understanding and exercising their rights and responsibilities before the law and heightens their appreciation of law as it regulates the conduct of individuals.)

Nordin, Virginia Davis (editor). GAULT: WHAT NOW FOR THE JUVENILE COURT? Ann Arbor, Mich.: Institute of Continuing Legal Education, 1968. 218 pp. (A treatise growing out of the Supreme Court's decision, *In re Gault*, which revolutionized thinking regarding treatment of juvenile offenders by law enforcement officials and others, by granting procedural rights to minors in a manner comparable to cases involving adults. Special emphasis is given to substantive discussions of rights to counsel, judicial review, notice, and fair procedure.)

THE OBSCENITY REPORT. New York: Stein and Day, Publishers, 1970. 130 pp. (Contributors are anonymous. Because of the controversial nature of the Report to the Task Force on Pornography and Obscenity, it was not intended originally to be released for public consumption, but was done so "because of the American people's constitutional right to a free press and to the circulation of ideas." Contains a brief concluding section on educational implications.)

Office of Education, U. S. Department of Health, Education, and Welfare. DUAL ENROLLMENT IN PUBLIC AND NONPUBLIC SCHOOLS. Washington: U. S. Government Printing Office, 1965. 93 pp. (Focuses on the development and operation of dual enrollment programs in nine communities in the United States.)

——. EDUCATION '65: A REPORT TO THE PROFESSION. Washington: U. S. Government Printing Office, 1966. 100 pp. (Catalogues federal programs designed to help American educators carry on the work of education.)

——. STATE EDUCATION: STRUCTURE AND ORGANIZATION. Washington: U. S. Government Printing Office, 1964. 156 pp. (A state-by-state examination of the state education agencies responsible for elementary and secondary education programs.)

Peterson, Rossmiller, and Volz. THE LAW AND PUBLIC SCHOOL OPERA-
TION. New York. Harper and Row, Publishers, 1969. (A voluminous publication, with a comprehensive outlook, designed to
serve as a textbook in school law. Useful as a source book of
classified court decisions and judicial interpretations on virtually
all major educational topics.)

Phay, Robert E. and Jasper E. Cummings, Jr. STUDENT SUSPENSIONS AND
EXPULSIONS. Chapel Hill, North Carolina: Institute of Government, University of North Carolina, 1970. 51 pp. (Proposes school
board code which is divided into three parts: I, contains eight
rules that proscribe certain types of student conduct that may
result in long-term suspension or expulsion; II, sets out a procedural code of twenty sections for trying alleged violation of the
rules; III, contains provisions for removing dangerous students.)

Phay, Robert E. (editor) TRUSTEE RESPONSIBILITY FOR THE CAMPUS IN
CRISIS. Chapel Hill, North Carolina: Institute of Government,
University of North Carolina, 1970. 71 pp. (A compilation of
thirteen presentations made at a conference for university trustees,
where trustees and administrators sought answers to the question
of law to prevent and deal with crisis situations. Consideration
was given to the role of the law in the institutional setting as it
affects the rights and responsibilities of students, faculty, administrators, and trustees.)

Powell, Theodore. THE SCHOOL BUS LAW: A CASE STUDY IN EDUCATION,
RELIGION, AND POLITICS. Middletown, Conn.: Wesleyan University
Press, 1960. 334 pp. (A study of the role of religious groups as a
political force.)

Punke, Harold H. THE TEACHER AND THE COURTS. Danville, Illinois:
The Interstate Printers and Publishers, Inc., 1970. (Designed as a
text in courses which prepare teachers for service. Discusses licens-
ing, contracts, assignment, pay, tenure and retirement benefits.)

Remmlein, Madaline Kinter. THE LAW OF LOCAL PUBLIC SCHOOL
ADMINISTRATION. New York: McGraw-Hill Book Company, 1954.
271 pp. (Presents general treatment of local school administration
from legal point of view. Differs from usual text in that it does
not describe and evaluate practices or enunciate policy. Principles
of law are stated and their application described in terms of legal
theory only.)

—— and Martha L. Ware. Editors. AN EVALUATION OF EXISTING FORMS
OF SCHOOL LAWS. Vol. 2 of NOLPE Series. Cincinnati: The W. H.
Anderson Company, 1959. 253 pp. (Uses a survey approach to
give an authoritative evaluation of existing attitudes toward various types of school legislation. Attention is given to statutory
interpretation and statute drafting.)

Remmlein, Madaline Kinter and Martha L. Ware. SCHOOL LAW. Third edition. Danville, Virginia: The Interstate Printers and Publishers, 1970. 388 pp. (Topics deal with: (1) contracts of employment and tenure; (2) collective negotiations; (3) salaries; (4) leaves of absence; (5) defamation; (6) transportation; (7) textbooks; (8) control of pupil conduct; (9) retirement; and (10) rights and restrictions of teachers.)

Reutter, E. Edmund, Jr. THE SCHOOL ADMINISTRATOR AND SUBVERSIVE ACTIVITIES. Teachers College, Columbia University: Bureau of Publications, 1951. 136 pp. (Examines the prevalence of loyalty oaths in the United States. Includes sections of both state and local action in this area.)

Reutter, E. Edmund, Jr. SCHOOLS AND THE LAW. Dobbs Ferry, N. Y.: Oceana Publications, Inc., 1970. 121 pp. (This readable treatise for the layman is in its third edition. It is slightly lengthier but otherwise quite similar to earlier editions. It presents succinctly and without documentation, information dealing with course selection, personnel hiring, control of pupils, and financing education.)

Reutter, E. Edmund, Jr., and Robert R. Hamilton. THE LAW OF PUBLIC EDUCATION. Mineola, New York: The Foundation Press, Inc., 1970. 654 pp. (The unique feature of this book as related to other works in the field is that it is a combination textbook and casebook. The concluding section of the publication deals with "highlights" of the law of public education.)

Rezny, Arthur A. Editor-in-chief. LEGAL PROBLEMS OF SCHOOL BOARDS. Vol. 5 of the NOLPE Series. Cincinnati: The W. H. Anderson Company, 1966. 163 pp. (Explores the legal principles pertaining to some of the involvements of a school board in current educational issues.)

— and Madaline Kinter Remmlein. A SCHOOLMAN IN THE LAW LIBRARY. Danville, Illinois: Interstate Printers and Publishers, Inc., 1962. 64 pp. (Describes law books and how they are to be used by schoolmen, primarily graduate students of school law.)

Rice, Charles E. THE SUPREME COURT AND PUBLIC PRAYER. New York: Fordham University Press, 1964. 202 pp. (A critique on the public school prayer decisions.)

Schwab, Joseph J. COLLEGE CURRICULUM AND STUDENT PROTEST. Chicago: The University of Chicago Press, 1969. 303 pp. (Designed for *all* students—not protestors alone. The emphasis is more medical than legal. A brief section, however, deals with the law and legal reasoning pertaining to a "practical prescription.")

Seitz, Reynolds C. Editor. LAW AND THE SCHOOL PRINCIPAL. Vol. 3 of NOLPE Series. Cincinnati: The W. H. Anderson Company, 1961. 266 pp. (Contains 15 chapters, contributed by school-law authorities, dealing with significant legal problems confronting the principal and other school personnel.)

Sims, O. Suthern, Jr. (editor). NEW DIRECTIONS IN CAMPUS LAW EN-
FORCEMENT: A HANDBOOK FOR ADMINISTRATORS. Athens, Georgia:
The University of Georgia for Continuing Education, 1971. 79 pp.
(A discussion on such topics as: (1) alternative to chaos; (2) campus law enforcement; (3) the officer as educator; (4) campus
emergency planning; (5) the police and student demonstrators;
and (6) professional campus law enforcement.)

Singer, H. Halleck and Charles M. Micken. THE LAW OF PURCHASING.
Danville, Illinois: Interstate Printers and Publishers, Inc., 1964.
136 pp. (An attempt "to isolate and classify those legal principles
that govern in the administration of the financial program of the
public schools.")

Sizer, Theodore R. Editor. RELIGION AND PUBLIC EDUCATION. Atlanta:
Houghton Mifflin Company, 1967. 361 pp. (Attempts to resolve
issue of religion in public schooling by bringing into an integrated
focus the traditional lines of inquiry—legal or constitutional, philo-
sophical, theological, historical, psychological and social.)

Spurlock, Clark. EDUCATION AND THE SUPREME COURT. Urbana, Illinois: University of Illinois Press, 1955. 252 pp. (Provides selected
Supreme Court opinions bearing on education in a form useful to
teachers and laymen.)

Steinhilber, August W. and Carl J. Sokolowski. STATE LAW ON COM-
PULSORY ATTENDANCE. U. S. Department of Health, Education, and
Welfare. Washington: U. S. Government Printing Office, 1966.
103 pp. (Provides summaries of the current law on compulsory
attendance, contained in statutes, regulations, and opinions of attorneys general, and courts of law, together with the citations to
the sources of law.)

——. STATE LAW RELATING TO TRANSPORTATION AND TEXTBOOKS FOR
PAROCHIAL SCHOOL STUDENTS AND CONSTITUTIONAL PROTECTION OF
RELIGIOUS FREEDOM. U. S. Department of Health, Education, and
Welfare. Washington: U. S. Government Printing Office, 1966.
45 pp. (A review of constitutional and statutory provisions, with
judicial interpretations, pertaining to transportation and textbook
provisions for parochial pupils.)

Stinnett, T. M., Jack H. Kleinmann, and Martha L. Ware. PROFESSION-
AL NEGOTIATIONS IN PUBLIC EDUCATION. New York: The Macmillan
Company, 1966. 309 pp. (Attempts "to provide basic information
on all aspects of the professional negotiation process.")

Strahan, Richard Dobbs. LEGAL BRIEFS FOR SCHOOL ADMINISTRATORS.
Houston: Gulf School Research Development Association, 1967.
(Compilation of briefs published periodically dealing with familiar
topics in the area of pupil discipline and management. Most cases
referred to were adjudicated in Texas Courts.)

Swalls, Fred. LEGAL ASPECTS OF STUDENT TEACHING. Danville, Illinois: Interstate Printers and Publishers, Inc., 1966. 37 pp. (Cites excerpts of statutes authorizing student teaching in 12 states.)

TEACHER CONTRACT DEMANDS. Albany, N. Y.: Thealan Associates, Inc., 90 State Street, 1970. 48 pp. (A technical handbook designed for school board negotiators and other school officials. Some of the twenty-six articles deal with negotiation procedures, teaching hours, loads, facilities, leaves, academic freedom, fringe benefits, and compensation.)

Tiedt, Sidney W. THE ROLE OF THE FEDERAL GOVERNMENT IN EDUCATION. New York: Oxford University Press, 1966. 243 pp. (Presents in "one volume a concise analysis of the historical background of the role of the federal government in education, representative arguments for and against the government's greater involvement in educational concerns, a presentation of the questions revolving around aid to private schools, and a discussion of the present and future aspects of this complex problem.")

Tussman, Joseph. THE SUPREME COURT ON CHURCH AND STATE. New York: Oxford University Press, 1962. 305 pp. (Brings together in one volume the important cases dealing with religion and education decided by the Supreme Court prior to 1954.)

United States Commission on Civil Rights. CIVIL RIGHTS U.S.A.: PUBLIC SCHOOLS, SOUTHERN STATES, 1962. Washington: U. S. Government Printing Office, 1962. 217 pp. (Presents an overview of administrative, legislative, and judicial developments since 1954 in all the Southern states where schools were organized and operated on a racially segregated basis.)

—— . RACIAL ISOLATION IN THE PUBLIC SCHOOLS. Washington: U. S. Government Printing Office, 1967. Vol. I, 276 pp; Vol. II, (Appendices) 293 pp. (Substantiates belief that racial isolation in the schools serves as a deterrent to the full development of the country's human resources. Presents evidence of the harmful effects of such isolation on young people and on our society.)

United States Department of Health, Education, and Welfare. EQUALITY OF EDUCATIONAL OPPORTUNITY. Washington: U. S. Government Printing Office, 1966. Vol. I, 737 pp. Vol. II, 548 pp. (Volume I is the report mandated by Section 402 of the Civil Rights Act of 1964, concerning the lack of availability of equal educational opportunities in public educational institutions. Volume II constitutes the Supplemental Appendix to the Survey on EQUALITY OF EDUCATIONAL OPPORTUNITY: Correlation tables.)

Ware, Martha L. Editor. LAW OF GUIDANCE AND COUNSELING. Vol. 4 of NOLPE Series. Cincinnati: The W. H. Anderson Company, 1964. 178 pp. (Explains areas of liability that may confront the school counselor in the use and dissemination of information contained in school records.)

Wise, Arthur E. RICH SCHOOLS, POOR SCHOOLS. Chicago: The University of Chicago Press, 1968. 228 pp. (Author proposes that differences in educational opportunity in the United States deny the citizens of a state the equal protection of the laws in violation of the Fourteenth Amendment. The three sets of cases which form the basis of the work are: (1) school desegregation cases, (2) reapportionment cases, and (3) indigent dependent cases.)

Young, D. Parker. THE LEGAL ASPECTS OF STUDENT DISSENT AND DISCIPLINE IN HIGHER EDUCATION. Athens, Georgia: Institute of Higher Education, University of Georgia, 1970. 65 pp. (A monograph covering such topics as: (1) Nature of Discipline; (2) Relationship Between Student and the School; (3) Relationship Between Courts and the School; (4) Due Process in Student Dissent; (5) Equal Protection; (6) Judicial Intervention in Scholastic Affairs.)

Young, D. Parker and Donald D. Gehring. BRIEFS OF SELECTED COURT CASES AFFECTING STUDENT DISSENT AND DISCIPLINE IN HIGHER EDUCATION. Athens, Georgia: Institute of Higher Education, University of Georgia, 1970. 49 pp. (Treats: (1) Relationship Between Students and the Institution; (2) Relationship Between Courts and Education; (3) State Actions; (4) Scholastic Affairs; (5) Due Process; (6) Speaker Bans; (7) Search and Seizure; (8) Interim Suspension and Equal Protection.)

ARTICLES

Due to the innumerable articles dealing with school law published in educational and law journals, no attempt is made to list them here. Many of them may be found by the use of EDUCATION INDEX and INDEX TO LEGAL PERIODICALS.

Articles referring to school legislation and litigation frequently appear in such journals as: AMERICAN EDUCATION, PHI DELTA KAPPAN, NATION'S SCHOOLS, SCHOOL MANAGEMENT, and SOCIAL EDUCATION. (The March 1971 issue of NATION'S SCHOOLS contains a special series of six articles—"School Law: The Trends and the Trials"—devoted to current legal problems in education, the most important cases and trends in judicial interpretation.)

Also many articles involving the public schools are written by law professors and other legal experts and published in law journals. Virtually every law school publishes a monthly LAW REVIEW.

YEARBOOKS OF SCHOOL LAW

The first series of the Yearbooks was published during the period 1933-42. They were suspended in 1942 due to diverted services, for the cause of World War II, by the editor, M. M. Chambers, and other regular contributors.

After the interim (1942-50), publication of a yearbook of school law was resumed in 1950 under the sponsorship and editorship of Lee O. Garber. Since that time the organizational pattern of the publication has become noticeably standardized. However, the size of the yearbook has grown from year to year, due to added features, as well as to the increasing number of court cases reported in the NATIONAL REPORTER SYSTEM.

Beginning with the 1967 issue, Professor E. Edmund Reutter, Jr., joined Garber as collaborator for three successive years. Professor Reynolds Seitz co-authored the 1971 volume. In the introduction of the 1971 YEARBOOK, Professor Garber announces: "I have relinquished my interest in all future issues of this publication to the National Organization on Legal Problems in Education (NOLPE)."

"The 1971 issue, like its predecessors considers cases dealing with schools and school districts that were decided in a particular year. The cases reported in this volume (420) are those decided by federal courts and state appellate courts. . . ."

NOLPE PUBLICATIONS

One of the purposes of the National Organization on Legal Problems of Education has been to disseminate school-law information to its members. This purpose has been notably achieved by a steady and rapid increase of contributions to school-law literature in its various publications.

Noteworthy of the various publications is the NOLPE SCHOOL LAW REPORTER. Since 1961 it has been edited by Reynolds Seitz. It is issued monthly and contains digests of important school-law cases reported to the editor by eight regional reporters. Since many persons interested in court decisions do not have access to law libraries, this service has a widespread utilization. Also a companion publication, NOLPE NOTES, considerably smaller in size, is issued each month under the editorship of Don Moran. It reports special recent court cases and annotates recent publications.

NOLPE also sponsors the publication of books on school-law subjects. The first five of these books are entitled: LAW AND THE SCHOOL SUPERINTENDENT (1958, and revised 1971); EVALUATION OF EXISTING FORMS OF SCHOOL LAWS (1959); LAW AND THE SCHOOL PRINCIPAL (1961); THE LAW OF GUIDANCE AND COUNSELING (1964) and LEGAL PROBLEMS OF SCHOOL BOARDS (1966).

NOLPE CONVENTION PROCEEDINGS are published and circulated to members. The title of 1969 Proceedings is "Upsurge and Upheaval in School Law" and for 1970 it is "Critical Issues in School Law."

A NOLPE MONOGRAPH SERIES of five volumes was published during 1971: "Legal Aspects of Control of Student Activities by Public School Authorities," by E. Edmund Reutter, Jr.; "Rights and Freedoms of Public School Students," by Dale Gaddy; "Suspension and Expulsion of Public School Students," by Robert Phay; "Crime Investigation and Prevention in the Public Schools," by William G. Buss; "Student Records," by Henry E. Butler. (Each volume is priced at $3.50.)

Beginning with the Fall, 1970 issue, NOLPE publishes NOLPE SCHOOL LAW JOURNAL. It is published semi-annually and circulated to each member of the organization. The first issue contains seven articles on current and significant issues contributed by well-recognized authorities. (Single copy rate is $2.50.)

In 1966, Madaline Remmlein, who was the main pioneer in the establishment of NOLPE, as well as its first president, prepared a booklet which was published under the title of NOLPE: THE FIRST TEN YEARS. The evolution of the organization and its accomplishments are treated under the headings of "Conception," "Birth," "Infancy" and "Growing Up."

The growth of NOLPE is evidenced by the 1970 NOLPE DIRECTORY, which lists the names and addresses of its 1398 members, as of July 1, 1970. The DIRECTORY, like other NOLPE publications, may be ordered from the Secretariat: 825 Western, Topeka, Kansas 66606.

NEA PUBLICATIONS

Numerous reports on legal phases of the schools are published by the National Education Association, some of which are made available free or at nominal costs for members and others who order them. These reports are prepared by members of the staff who are experienced in legal research and who also have the necessary up-to-date data at their disposal.

Some of the reports are included in the NEA RESEARCH BULLETIN. Others are published annually in special publications—exemplified by "The Pupil's Day in Court" and "The Teacher's Day in Court." Still others are published in pamphlet form from time to time as legal problems of school personnel arise.

Also affiliated organizations of NEA—especially the American Association of School Administrators—publish materials on legal matters pertaining to the schools. Several are listed in the bibliography of this publication. Many of them are sent, as a service, to members of the Association and are available at reasonable cost to others who order them.

GOVERNMENT PUBLICATIONS

As the federal involvement in education increases, the published materials by governmental agencies increase accordingly. The innumerable governmental publications dealing with school matters range from leaflets and pamphlets to voluminous books.

The United States Office of Education collects and disseminates information pertaining to the schools. The availability of informative material is evidenced by its PUBLICATIONS OF THE OFFICE OF EDUCATION, 1970, in which it states: "This catalog identifies all OE publications currently available. The annotated list contains approximately 550 titles, including revised editions of surveys which the OE has been conducting annually since 1869. . . . Through these publications the Office seeks to fulfill an important part of its responsibilities for describing the condition and needs of education throughout the United States."

Of the various publications of the USOE, educators are most familiar with AMERICAN EDUCATION (official organ of the Office). It is "dedicated to keeping educators, school and college administrators, parents, and businessmen up-to-date on current issues and programs throughout the country, detailing Federal, State, and local use of tax dollars in education." The subscription rate of the magazine is $7.00, and may be ordered from the Superintendent of Documents, Government Printing Office, Washington, D. C. 20402.

SERVICE PUBLICATIONS

The Harvard Center for Law and Education, a non-profit organization, publishes a series of booklets dealing with legislation and court decisions pertaining to education. The publications contain articles, notes and commentary, and digests of important and current court cases.

Educational Service Bureau publishes a variety of materials on the topic of public school negotiations, foremost of which is EDUCATORS NEGOTIATING SERVICE. It is designed to keep educators "abreast of the latest developments in all matters related to collective bargaining in public education." Subscription rate is $78.00 per year. ENS is a division of Educational Service Bureau, Inc., 1835 K. Street, N. W., Washington, D. C. 20006.

Some state institutions publish materials designed to inform those within the state who are interested in school law developments. A notable example is SCHOOL LAW BULLETIN, published at the Institute of Government University of North Carolina at Chapel Hill, and edited by Robert E. Phay. As stated in the first issue, October, 1970: "The SCHOOL LAW BULLETIN is a new service from the Institute of Government to North Carolina attorneys and school administrators who have an interest in the field of school law. The Bulletin will be published quarterly. It will summarize recent court decisions and opinions of the North Carolina Attorney General and report on pending or enacted legislation during legislative years. Most issues also will consider a specific school law problem in some detail. The topic discussed in this issue is school regulation of student appearance."

DOCTORAL DISSERTATIONS

Doctoral dissertations constitute a growing source of objective information pertaining to legal features of the school. Some of the institutions of higher learning, offering graduate courses in school law, produce a significant number of applicable theses and dissertations. For example, the institution with which the writer is associated has had approximately 50 doctoral dissertations in the area of school law completed since 1950.

In 1965, M. Chester Nolte compiled for NOLPE a list of "289 doctoral dissertations on subjects related to school law listed in either the DISSERTATION ABSTRACTS or in the Phi Delta Kappa listings of dissertations completed." Then again, in 1969, in cooperation with The ERIC Clearinghouse on Educational Administration, Professor Nolte compiled a bibliography of 503 school law dissertations (1952-1968). In most instances, the references in the listings give the author's name, title of dissertation, type of degree for which the dissertation was submitted, number of pages, and the year completed.

NATiONAL REPORTER SYSTEM

In most law libraries may be found a National Reporter System which includes all cases from all courts of record in all states and gives the actual opinion of the court in each. The system is divided into geographical sections as indicated by the following:

THE ATLANTIC REPORTER. "Atl" or "A(2d)" (Connecticut, Delaware, Maine, Maryland, New Hampshire, New Jersey, Pennsylvania, and Vermont.)

THE CALIFORNIA REPORTER. "Cal" (Contains complete reports of all cases decided by the Supreme Court and district courts of appeal of California since 1960.)

THE NEW YORK SUPPLEMENT. "NYS" or "NYS(2d)" (Contains complete reports of cases decided by the Supreme Court and lower courts of record in the state of New York.)

THE NORTHWESTERN REPORTER. "NW" or "NW(2d)" (Iowa, Michigan, Minnesota, Nebraska, North Dakota, South Dakota, and Wisconsin.)

THE NORTHEASTERN REPORTER. "NE" or "NE(2d)" (Illinois, Indiana, Massachusetts, New York, Ohio, and Rhode Island.)

THE PACIFIC REPORTER. "Pac" or "P(2d)" (Alaska, Arizona, California, Colorado, Hawaii, Idaho, Kansas, Montana, Nevada, New Mexico, Oklahoma, Oregon, Utah, Washington, and Wyoming.)

THE SOUTHEASTERN REPORTER. "SE" or "SE(2d)" (Georgia, North Carolina, South Carolina, Virginia, and West Virginia.)

THE SOUTHERN REPORTER. "So" or "S(2d)" (Alabama, Florida, Louisiana, and Mississippi.)

THE SOUTHWESTERN REPORTER. "SW" or "SW(2d)" (Arkansas, Kentucky, Missouri, Tennessee, and Texas.)

THE SUPREME COURT REPORTER. Contains complete reports of cases decided by the United States Supreme Court. THE FEDERAL REPORTER reports cases decided in the Federal Circuit Courts of Appeals, and the FEDERAL SUPPLEMENT reports cases decided in the lower federal courts.

THE AMERICAN DIGEST SYSTEM. Constitutes a series of digests of cases from 1658 to date. It is useful for quickly locating, in certain Reporter Systems, the complete cases and court opinion reports.

CORPUS JURIS SECUNDUM. A series of many volumes containing legal principles reported in encyclopedic form. Volumes 78 and 79 include the area of "Schools and School Districts." Somewhat similar to AMERICAN JURISPRUDENCE, it is helpful in the identification and organization of a research project.

AMERICAN LAW REPORTS (ALR). Useful in school-law research. Annotations contained in ALR review the substance of what has been decided in various cases on the same point.

GLOSSARY

SELECTED LEGAL TERMS

Abrogation—the act of abolishing or repealing, as by later enactment.

Action—a suit or a lawsuit.

Ad litem—prosecution or defense of a suit on behalf of a pupil incapacitated by infancy.

Allegation—statement in pleadings, reciting what the pleader expects to prove.

Amicus curiae—friend of the court, not a party to the action directly involved.

Annotation—explanatory or supplementary note to, or commentary on, a principal text such as a constitution, statute, or court decision.

Appellant—the party who takes an appeal from one court to another.

Appellee—the party against whom an appeal is taken.

Arbiter—a chosen or appointed umpire or judge.

Assault—an attempt to beat another, without actually touching him.

Battery—an unlawful beating or other wrongful physical violence inflicted on another.

Caveat emptor—let the buyer beware.

Certiorari—a writ issued by a superior court directing an inferior court to send up for review the records and proceedings in a case.

Code—a compilation of statutes, scientifically arranged.

Common law—legal principles derived from usage and custom or from court decisions affirming such usages and customs, as distinguished from law created by constitutions and statutes and court interpretations thereof.

Contract—an agreement for sufficient consideration to do or not to do a particular thing.

Criminal liability—liability to fine or imprisonment or both, as distinguished from civil liability to compensate by paying damages.

Damages—pecuniary compensation or indemnity which may be recovered in court in a civil action.

De facto—in fact, actually.

De jure—legally, as a matter of law.

Declaratory relief—a judgment which declares the rights of the parties or expresses the opinion of the court on a question of law, without ordering anything to be done.

Decree—order of court of equity announcing the legal consequences of the facts found.

Defendant—the party against whom relief or recovery is sought in a court action.

Demurrer—allegation by one party that other party's allegations may be true but, even so, are not of such consequences as to justify pro-

333

ceeding with the case.

Dictum—statement of legal principle in a court decision which is not necessitated by the facts or the law of the case.

Dissenting opinion—the opinion in which a judge announces his dissent from the conclusions held by the majority of the court.

Due process—the exercise of the powers of government in such a way as to protect individual rights.

Enjoin—to require a person, by writ of injunction from a court of equity, to perform, or to abstain or desist from, some act.

Estoppel—a bar raised by the law which prevents one from alleging or denying a certain fact because of his previous statements or conduct.

Ex officio—by virtue of his office.

Ex post facto law—passed after an occurrence, and which retrospectively changes the legal consequences of that act.

Ex rel.—legal proceeding instituted in the name and on behalf of the state but on the information and at the instigation of an individual who has a private interest in the matter.

Injunction—a judicial order requiring a party to take or refrain from some specified action.

In loco parentis—in place of the parent.

In re—concerning.

Inter alia—among other things.

Invalid—not binding; lacking in authority.

Ipso facto—by the fact itself.

Laches—omission to assert a right for an unreasonable and unexplained length of time.

Majority opinion—the statement of reasons for the views of the majority of the members of the bench in a decision in which some of them disagree.

Malfeasance—commission of an unlawful act.

Mandamus—a writ to compel a public body or its officers to perform a duty.

Misfeasance—improper performance of a lawful act.

Nolens volens—with or without consent.

Nonfeasance—omission to perform a required duty.

Nuisance—a continuous condition not authorized by law which causes hurt, inconvenience, or damage.

Plaintiff—one who brings an action.

Plenary—full, conclusive.

Police power—legislative prerogative to enact laws for the comfort, health, and prosperity of the state and people.

Power of parens patriae — inherent authority of a lawmaking body to provide protection for legally incapable persons such as minors.

Precedent—a decision considered as furnishing an example or authority for an identical or similar case afterward arising on a similar question of law.

Prima facie—at first view.

Quantum meruit—an implication that the defendant had promised to pay plaintiff as much as he reasonably deserved for his services.

Quasi—as if, or almost as if it were.

Quo warranto—method of trying title to a public office which was never lawfully held.

Referendum—the practice of referring to the voters measures passed by the legislative body for their approval or rejection.

Remand—to send back a cause to the same court out of which it came, for trial or some further action on it there.

Res adjudicata—a matter judicially decided.

Rescission of contract—cancellation or abrogation by the parties, or one of them.

Respondent—defendant in certain kinds of cases.

Respondeat superior—responsibility of a master for acts of his servants.

Restrain—to prohibit from action; to enjoin.

Scienter—allegation that the defendant knew the circumstances leading to his injury.

Slander—the malicious defamation of a person in his reputation, profession, or business, by words.

Stare decisis—principle that when a court has made a declaration of a legal principle it is the law until changed by competent authority.

Subpoena—writ commanding attendance in a court under a penalty.

Tort—a civil wrong not arising out of contract.

Ultra vires—acts beyond the scope of authority.

Void—having no legal force or binding effect.

Waive—to renounce or abandon a right.

INDEX

References are to section numbers

"ANTI-GUIDELINES BILL," 3.2

ATTORNEY GENERAL, 2.8,

CERTIFICATION OF TEACHERS, 15.2

CHIEF STATE SCHOOL OFFICER
Dismissal, 9.3
Qualifications, 9.2
Relationship to State Board, 9.5
Removal authority over local board members, 12.5
Salary, 9.4
Selection, 9.1
Term, 9.3

CHILD-BENEFIT THEORY, 16.9

COMMISSIONER OF EDUCATION
City, 12.3
New York, 15.13
United States, 2.9, 3.1, 3.4

COMPULSORY ATTENDANCE
General principles governing, 16.6

CONSTITUTIONALITY
Property Tax, use for financing public schools, 14.4

CONSTITUTIONS, STATE, 5.1 et seq.

CONSTITUTION, UNITED STATES
Article I, legislative branch, 1.5
Article II, executive branch, 1.5
Article III, judicial branch, 1.5, 4.1
Fifth Amendment, 1.4, 15.10
First Amendment, 1.4
Fourteenth Amendment, 1.4, 16.9, 16.18, 17.2, 17.4

CORPORAL PUNISHMENT, 16.17

CORWIN, EDWIN C., 1.2, 1.4

COURTS, FEDERAL SYSTEM OF
Circuit Court of Appeals, 4.1
District Court, 4.1
Supreme Court, 4.1
Jurisdiction of, 4.2